Guidelines,
Informal Controls, and the
Market Place

THE GRADUATE SCHOOL OF BUSINESS
UNIVERSITY OF CHICAGO

FIRST SERIES (1916–1938)
Materials for the Study of Business
Edited by DEAN LEON CARROLL MARSHALL and
DEAN WILLIAM HOMER SPENCER

SECOND SERIES (1938–1956)
Business and Economic Publications
Edited by DEAN WILLIAM HOMER SPENCER

THIRD SERIES (1959–   )
Studies in Business
Edited by DEAN W. ALLEN WALLIS
and DEAN GEORGE P. SHULTZ

Guidelines, Informal Controls, and the Market Place

Policy Choices in a Full Employment Economy

Edited and with an Introduction by

GEORGE P. SHULTZ

and

ROBERT Z. ALIBER

The University of Chicago Press · Chicago · London

Library of Congress Catalog Card Number: 66-23699

THE UNIVERSITY OF CHICAGO PRESS, CHICAGO & LONDON

THE UNIVERSITY OF TORONTO PRESS, TORONTO 5, CANADA

Printed in the United States of America

Foreword

The creation of new knowledge is one of the high purposes of a university, and it is usually the product of long and painstaking thought and inquiry, which universities are uniquely equipped to support. Such discoveries are as vital to business as to all of our other institutions; and research about problems related to business operations is a major function of the Graduate School of Business of the University of Chicago.

At the School, scholars drawn from many different disciplines bring their varied talents and methods to bear on special problems and methods of business. Research has both a basic and an applied character; the truth is sought assiduously, wherever the search may lead; and results are available to all who have the capacity and the need to employ them.

Beyond the *discovery of knowledge* lies its *dissemination*. To be effective, knowledge and ideas must move outward from the University to the business community. Results of work at the School must be published and made available.

Half a century ago the School inaugurated a significant publications program, and the present volume is its most recent expression.

The series, Materials for the Study of Business, was initiated in 1916, under the editorship of Dean Leon Carroll Marshall, and was continued by Dean William Homer Spencer. Fifty titles were published, and many became classics in their fields. In 1938 the series was renamed Business and Economic Publications, under the editorship of Dean Spencer, and thirteen titles were published. Additionally, in the two decades prior to 1948, the School published some seventy monographs under the general title, Studies in Business Administration. The current Studies in Business series was initiated under Dean W. Allen Wallis, who edited the first six volumes.

This volume, twelfth in the current series, contains the proceedings of a conference held at the University of Chicago in late April, 1966, to discuss guidelines and informal controls by which the federal Executive seeks to affect the behavior of individual businesses, banks, and labor unions. The growth and extension of guidelines constitute a major policy development of recent years, yet there had been little careful, systematic investigation and discussion of their origins and legal bases, their intended and observed effects, and possible alternative courses of action. The Chicago conference, made possible through the generosity of the Charles R. Walgreen Foundation, brought together leaders of thought and action—businessmen, government officials, bankers, legal scholars, labor leaders, journalists, and economists. Eight papers prepared for the conference, together with discussions and summations, make up this volume.

The distinguished roster of conference participants, the importance of the matters that engaged their attention, and the quality of their contributed papers and comments make this volume a significant contribution to the discussion of public policy. We trust that the contents of this volume will stimulate further research into a most important area of governmental-business relationships, broaden and enlighten debate, and give policymakers—in private as well as public life—facts and perspectives leading to sound decisions.

GEORGE P. SHULTZ, *Dean*
Graduate School of Business
University of Chicago

Acknowledgments

The short period between the date of the conference in late April and the scheduled date of the appearance of this book testifies to the intense cooperation of many. We want especially to thank Harry Dreiser, who coordinated the details involved in a rapid process of publication; Elizabeth Rey, who exercised a skillful editorial hand in developing material from the discussion sessions of the conference; Mary Hamilton, who put together the appendixes; and Judith Gartung and Barbara Otis, who worked out the details of the conference, managing a wide variety of tasks with good sense and good humor.

We also wish to thank George J. Stigler, Executive Director of the sponsoring Walgreen Foundation, for his ideas about and participation in the conference, for his wit, and for his money—in that order.

GEORGE P. SHULTZ
ROBERT Z. ALIBER

Contents

GEORGE P. SHULTZ AND ROBERT Z. ALIBER

Introduction

GUIDELINES: THEIR DEVELOPMENT AND THE ISSUES RAISED

The spread of informal guides designed by the executive branch of the federal government to affect the behavior of individual businesses and labor unions has been a major policy development of recent years. The United States now has guidelines for prices and wages, for the extension of United States bank credits abroad, for direct investment abroad by United States companies, and for some commodity imports. These guidelines have been increasing in variety and have also become more explicit in content.

The United States is not alone in adopting such measures. Somewhat similar efforts have been made in Great Britain and Continental Western Europe to restrain inflationary pressures. There the approach is commonly known as "incomes policy." The rationale for this policy, both here and abroad, is that informal controls make it possible to achieve higher levels of employment and avoid either rising prices or the need for formal price and wage ceilings.

Despite their growth in importance, guidelines policies have received remarkably little careful, systematic discussion. How guidelines emerged, what they have achieved, where they are going, and where they should be going—these are matters of grave importance. It is the minimum of prudence to examine these informal controls—and the alternative policies which could be adopted—and to examine them promptly, thoroughly, and dispassionately.

This volume reflects such an effort—an examination of the rationale for guidelines and of experience with them. It contains the papers prepared for and the discussions during a conference held at The University of Chicago in late April, 1966. The participants included men in positions of leadership in the institutions dealing with the problems involved: government, banks, industrial firms, labor unions, the press, and the academic community.

This introduction reviews the development of guidelines policies in the United States and identifies some of the principal issues. In reading this and other parts of the book, the reader is urged to keep in mind not only the issues posed by the guidelines themselves, but the problems to which those guidelines are addressed. Whether or not one agrees with the present public policies, the problems involved are genuine and serious. They deserve constructive evaluation and an effort to develop workable private as well as public policies.

THE GUIDEPOST DEVELOPMENT: HISTORY AND VARIETY[1]

Although guideposts for wages and prices have only recently become conspicuous as operating policies of the government, the ideas involved are not new. The analytical basis of these policies goes back at least to the mid-1930's. At that time the view emerged that private decision makers in many sectors of the American economy have wide and continuing discretion in their choices of private policies. According to this analysis, prices can be "administered" by large firms, and through collective bargaining with trade unions, wages too can be set at a point determined by an administrative process as distinct from a competitive market process. Regardless of whether the discretion is as great as it appears or whether the pressures of the market place really control private decision makers, the belief is widespread that substantial discretion exists. Gardner Ackley, Robert M. Solow, and E. H. Phelps Brown all point up that belief in their papers, just as Milton Friedman in his paper and comments argues that it is an essential—and essentially wrong—centerpiece in the guidepost policy. The presumed discretion in

---

[1] A note on terminology: We have used *guidelines* in its general sense to include voluntary controls without regard to their objectives. When discussing particular programs, however, we have followed official terminology. The 1962 Economic Report of the President refers to *guideposts* for wages and prices, and later programs refer to *guidelines* for business investment and the extension of bank credit abroad.

effect defines a band of possible wage and price levels and this band is the target of the guideposts.

WAGE-PRICE GUIDEPOSTS

The economic relationships involved in the guideposts for wages and prices were given early expression in the labor agreement signed in 1948 by the General Motors Corporation and the UAW-CIO. This agreement provided that changes in real wages, through an "annual improvement factor," should be based on the productivity trend for the economy as a whole.[2]

On the side of public policy, appeals for private restraint in wage and price increases appeared in President Eisenhower's Economic Reports for 1957 and subsequent years, and the idea of a productivity guideline was advanced in general terms. The 1962 Economic Report of President Kennedy, however, developed the guidepost idea in far greater detail, and the present guidepost policies derive from that report.

The reasoning behind this detailed statement was somewhat as follows: The price increases in the 1955–58 period, which continued in moderated form during the period of relatively high unemployment in 1958–61, gave rise to widespread concern that, if unemployment began to decline, prices might again increase substantially even though unemployment and excess capacity were substantial. Higher prices would greatly worsen the already large United States balance-of-payments deficit. Thus rising prices might lead to the adoption of restrictive policies long before the unemployment rate declined substantially. The guideposts were presented in the belief that, if they were effective, the United States economy could operate at somewhat higher levels of employment without engendering price increases.

While the 1962 guideposts were put forward explicitly as a contribution to discussion, they shortly became entwined with governmental policies and presidential actions in the celebrated steel dispute of 1962. Especially since early 1965, government officials have—some would say have inevitably—pronounced on an increasing number of wage and price decisions. If many decisions

---

[2] Excerpts from this agreement and from the Economic Reports of Presidents Eisenhower, Kennedy, and Johnson appear in the appendixes.

went unnoticed and others were praised, some were found to be "inflationary." As this process continued, successive statements of guideposts became more explicit. The 1965 and 1966 reports contained an estimate of 3.2 per cent as the average productivity gain to which wage settlements should be related.

Procedurally, the wage-price guideposts were enunciated by the government after little formal consultation with labor or management. Indeed, as Robert M. Solow brings out, there was considerable skepticism of the potential contribution that affected parties can make to the development of appropriate guideposts. E. H. Phelps Brown and Arthur M. Ross, on the other hand, indicate the sharply different approach followed in Great Britain and in various Western European countries. At any rate, in the United States those most directly affected were not involved in the formulation of guideposts either as general propositions or explicit standards for behavior.

There have been striking developments, too, in the administration of the wage-price guideposts. The process of persuasion and education took on in some instances the form of a dramatic confrontation in which a variety of governmental powers as well as words become involved. And in more recent months, as Gardner Ackley brings out, the drama of public confrontations has given way to a quiet process of consultation, but conducted behind closed doors.

GUIDELINES FOR FOREIGN TRADE AND INVESTMENT

The programs announced by the Federal Reserve Board and the Department of Commerce in March, 1965, represent the major use of informal controls on international transactions of United States firms. As described in the appendixes and in the papers by Harry G. Johnson and Allan H. Meltzer, these programs set standards for private activity abroad and established an explicit reporting mechanism. The Federal Reserve Board requested United States commercial banks and other United States financial institutions to limit increases in their credits abroad in 1965 to 5 per cent over the December, 1964, levels. At the same time, the Department of Commerce requested the five hundred largest United States industrial firms to limit the expansion of their net foreign payments in 1965 to 80 per cent of the 1964 expansion. These programs were extended and somewhat modified in 1966. About four hundred additional companies were brought under the investment program and the bases for calculating individual company and bank guidelines were adjusted.

These measures followed a series of steps taken by the United States government, at times in cooperation with foreign governments, to help achieve a more satisfactory balance of international payments. Despite measures taken before 1965, the United States payments deficit declined slowly; in 1958, the deficit was $3.5 billion; in 1964, $2.8 billion. As some United States payments abroad declined, others, especially for investment abroad, increased. In June, 1963, the administration proposed an Interest Equalization Tax to curtail offerings of foreign securities in the United States capital market, including those issued by the foreign subsidiaries of United States firms. Such offerings declined sharply. As a consequence, however, United States bank credits to foreigners and United States direct investment abroad increased. In both cases, a substantial part of the foreign investment consisted of transfers of liquid funds from United States firms to their foreign subsidiaries. Thus the 1965 guidelines are part of a continuing series of measures to deal with the United States problem in its balance of payments.

Procedurally, these guideline programs stand in sharp contrast to the wage-price guideposts. Informal consultations were held with representatives of the major organizations involved while the guidelines were being formulated, and their announcement followed full-scale meetings with these parties. In the case of commercial banks, the number initially involved in major programs abroad was small, and they were long accustomed to close relationships with the Federal Reserve Board. In the case of business firms, the Department of Commerce invited consultation on individual company plans in an effort to take special needs into account and to work out specific accommodations between private plans and public policies.

Informal controls have also been used to an increasing extent on United States foreign trade. When existing tariffs have proven ineffective in limiting competition from abroad, imports in the United States market have been limited by quota arrangements developed on an informal basis. In August, 1957, for example, importers of crude petroleum were asked "voluntarily" to restrict imports to slightly over one million barrels a day or face mandatory controls. The quotas were revised downward in 1958, and the Pentagon stopped buying petroleum from companies that did not abide by them. Since the voluntary program included only imports of crude petroleum, companies reacted by increasing their imports of petroleum products from sixty thousand barrels a day in 1957 to three hundred thousand barrels a day in late 1958. In March, 1959, mandatory quotas were placed on imports of crude petroleum and petroleum products.

In the mid-1950's informal controls, sometimes called voluntary export quotas, were applied to sales of Japanese cotton textiles in the United States. Imports of textiles from Japan had increased rapidly and United States producers sought relief through escape clauses of tariff legislation. The President was apparently about to raise tariffs when the Japanese offered to restrict their sales in the United States market. After the offer was accepted, other countries greatly increased their exports of similar products in the United States market. The Japanese were understandably upset and United States producers also reacted negatively to continued growth of imports. A multilateral cotton textile arrangement was then negotiated, under which the exporting countries limit sales of each of a wide variety of products to certain agreed amounts, with provisions for annual increases in the quotas.

We conclude this review of the evolution of guidelines policy by noting the development of conflict among the individual programs. In the spring of 1966, for example, the possibility of an increase in the price of shoes was related to a sharp rise in the price of hides. Export quotas were adopted to keep the price of hides down in the United States, and there followed negotiations between shoe manufacturers and the government. Thus an effort was made to achieve stability in the price level, but at the cost of weakening the United States balance-of-payments position.

In general, then, although the concept of guidelines has evolved over a considerable period, it has been implemented rapidly, once given explicit content. Procedurally the programs have varied, although the general tendency has been to develop increased consultation among government officials and key union, corporate, and financial officials on the relationship between private decisions and public policy. This new relationship, hailed in some quarters and damned in others, emerges as a key element of government-by-guidelines and a central issue for further consideration.

The Issues

The wide variety of questions that can be raised about the development and use of guidelines policy may be divided into four groups. First are the issues of workability, involving assessment of whether private decisions are altered in any meaningful way by these policies. Second are the issues of impact, involving analysis of the implications of changes in private decisions, if such changes do indeed occur. Third are issues of procedure, involving the examination of ways in which guidepost policies are developed and administered. Finally, there is the search for alternatives, with the implication that the problems are serious and must somehow be addressed by public policy.

WORKABILTY

The means to achieve workability cover a spectrum of possible efforts by government: pronouncements about wage-price-productivity relationships designed to educate the country in general and key decision makers in particular; persuasion in an individual case directed at a union, a company, or both; and the use of powers now available to the President and others in the executive branch of the government, with the powers sometimes directly and sometimes only remotely related to the wage and price-setting process.

What is the method by which general education or even individual persuasion becomes effective? Can this method produce an impact over an extended period of time? Gardner Ackley points to the importance of hammering home the basic arithmetic. Certainly there can be no doubt that the volume of discussion about wage-price-productivity relationships has increased markedly during the 1960's, although it sometimes seems difficult to move this discussion beyond the calculation of 3.2 per cent into the economics of the matter. If there is to be an impact, however, rank and file union members, for example, must be persuaded that their interests are served by taking less money than they can get. Or alternatively, their leaders must be persuaded to sell them on the idea that their union is acting responsibly by keeping their wage increases to a moderate level. Here, of course, is the point where involvement of those leaders in the formulation of the guideposts becomes of critical importance.

In terms of results to date, the testimony of bargainers at the conference and elsewhere is clear, although Robert M. Solow cites more general evidence that at least leaves the case open. If the guideposts are meaningful at the bargaining table, according to negotiators, they are so mainly in raising sights in a few areas rather than bringing them down generally. As Frederick Livingston points up in his comments, it is important to distinguish between a ploy and a genuine factor in bargaining. At any rate, the effort to make guideposts work through the process of education and persuasion necessarily faces the issues posed by the methods involved, and suggests the need to seek ways of formulating guideposts that at the same time will be educational and persuasive.

As the implementation of guidelines and guideposts moves toward the use of the powers of government and toward relationships involving regulatory possibilities, their impact becomes more identifiable. If it is difficult to show a result on the general level of wages and prices, the real target, it is possible to point to particular prices that have been affected by the combination of guideposts plus power. At the same time, there have apparently been some direct results in limiting the increase of business investment and the extension of bank credits abroad.

In general, then, the guideposts and guidelines have clearly had some identifiable impact on private decisions, with the clearest examples associated with the use of governmental powers and with settings involving regulatory relationships.

THE BROADER IMPACT

Another set of issues involves the relationship between apparent workability and real success. Practitioners of guidelines and analysts of their use must watch carefully for areas of slippage by which an impact achieved in one area is canceled out by indirect effects in another and related area. The earlier discussion of import quotas illustrates this problem in part, as does Allan H. Meltzer's discussion of the program to restrict the increase of bank credits extended abroad. The decline in deposits held by foreigners in United States banks, possibly related to the imposition of guidelines, was of such magnitude as to cancel out the direct results achieved in reducing the flow of new bank credits during 1965.

Aside from the problem of slippage is a set of issues derived from the fact that guideline policies tend to be quite uneven in their application. Gardner Ackley concedes that this is a weakness in the program. To illustrate its consequences, one need only observe the reaction of a worker or union which has exercised restraint to the widely publicized and large increases obtained in the construction trades. Here unevenness affects ultimate workability of the program.

The economist, on the other hand, raises a different type of issue. Uneven application results in a change in relative prices and thereby weakens the incentives inherent in the price system to bring about corrections of various imbalances. Thus, is it an achievement to maintain lower than market prices of copper and thereby weaken incentives to substitute other materials for this relatively scarce resource? Or, as Meltzer brings out, the encouragement of corporate borrowing abroad serves to raise interest rates abroad relative to those in the United States, thus aggravating a basic cause of the imbalance in our international payments.

Still another type of issue to which the economist is most sensitive has to do with the structure of guidelines. The programs for bank credits and business investment both relate a firm's allowable activity in the future to the activity of that firm in recent years. Those banks and industrial companies which have been active on the international front in the past are allowed greater activity in the future. Competition from new or recent entrants to international business is therefore restricted, with consequences that are undesirable, especially in the long run.

Thus, success in the use of guidelines has broad implications, particularly when the impact of their use is uneven. On the one hand, there is the problem of slippage and the frustration of the programs in achieving general objectives, and on the other hand, there is interference with incentives to bring about a desirable reassignment of resources.

ISSUES OF PROCEDURE

Issues of procedure arise whether the method of application is mainly educational or mainly oriented to the use of presidential or regulatory power; however, they are most dramatic and insistent in the latter types of cases. In part the issues are legal, and these are discussed in part II of this volume. In part as well, though, they are general issues about the governmental process.

On the strictly constitutional side, Philip Kurland's analysis suggests that whatever issues may be involved are related to the legislative base for executive action rather than to the exercise of government influence and power. But many other issues of a legal nature remain, as is suggested by the frequency with which they were discussed during the conference.

In one form or another, these issues involve the right to "due process." Are affected parties entitled to be heard as part of the method through which standards are formulated? Which private decisions will be singled out for the pressure of persuasion or power? Should there be a formal method for presentation of points of view, data, and analysis that differs from that of government officials? What range of sanctions can be legitimately exercised to achieve a private decision in line with the stated public interest?

On the other hand, as Gardner Ackley points out, preoccupation with formal procedures may do more harm and create more bureaucracy and interference with private decisions than even an enthusiastic lawyer would want, let alone a harassed businessman or union leader. Nevertheless, if more and more effort is to be applied to securing adherence to guidelines, more attention will have to be directed to the procedures involved and the fairness of those procedures.

Other issues of procedure lead back to the problems of workability and of the implementation of any general guide to private behavior. Acceptance of guidelines is likely to be facilitated if there is provision for a consultative process in their formulation. Yet, the views of those consulted may differ sharply from the views of those responsible for public policy. Should a broad bargaining process involving private parties be the means of setting public policy? This is truly a dilemma, as both Gardner Ackley and Robert M. Solow point out. The resolution of this issue in Great Britain and Continental Western Europe has clearly been in the direction of broad consultation, reflecting in part that patterns of collaboration among private sectors of the economy and government are more highly developed in those areas. Should the United States move in this direction? If it does not, it seems likely that guideposts for wages and prices will have fewer and fewer friends among union leaders and businessmen.

It was noted earlier that guidelines for business investment and bank credits abroad were developed through an informal consultative process. It was also noted that in the implementation of wage-price guideposts private discussions, or perhaps negotiations, between company and government officials have developed on a widening scale. Although this growing net of relationships is commended in some quarters it is sharply questioned in others. What arrangements are being worked out behind closed doors? What anticompetitive tendencies are implicitly condoned if not encouraged? And, as Harry G. Johnson says, the procedure itself has the characteristics of movement toward a corporate state. This important issue is better posed early than late in the game.

THE SEARCH FOR ALTERNATIVES

Gardner Ackley in his address to the conference called upon those opposed to guidelines to suggest alternatives that are "constructive and superior." With these issues in particular, it is much easier to be critical than constructive, let alone superior. The view is widely held that the combination of relative price stability and relatively high unemployment characteristic of the late 1950's and early 1960's is not satisfactory. An economy in high gear not only uses resources more fully and yields higher output, but is also a most effective way to deal with such pressing social problems as poverty, discrimination, and teen-age frustration in the labor market.

What can be done to maintain reasonable stability in the general price level at these higher levels of economic performance? Of course, monetary and fiscal measures are the prime tools of economic policy but, within a framework established through such general measures, guidelines and incomes policies represent the answer given most attention throughout the free world. But it is yet to be demonstrated that the performance of these policies equals the promise. In addition, the policies themselves raise a host of subsidiary issues which cannot be ignored. The search for alternatives, then, is of urgent importance.

It is frequently remarked that the alternative to guideposts is formal controls. Coverage would be wider, at least in theory, and procedural arrangements would provide for hearings in any individual case. Administration would probably be by a tripartite process, so consultation would be built-in. Clearly, formal controls have some advantages, but the United States experience with wage and price stabilization during the Korean conflict was hardly reassuring. The workability of the controls and the furor and procedural entanglements entailed bring no happy memories. And, it must be noted, formal controls are subject to the same economic questions as the informal ones. This may be *an* alternative, but experience suggests it is not a particularly good one, especially in the absence of a national crisis.

Many alternatives were suggested during the conference and are discussed in the papers to follow. None has the "magic wand" quality that makes guidelines so appealing in concept, and they all force into the open difficult issues of political economy. The suggestions fall into three broad groups, in many ways reinforcing each other and certainly not mutually exclusive—or, for that matter, not incompatible with continued use of some forms of guidelines.

1. *Formal efforts to identify bottlenecks in product and labor markets and to alleviate the bottlenecks by intensive efforts to affect supply, demand, or both.* In this proposal, advanced particularly by John T. Dunlop, the emphasis is moved away from exhortation or persuasion toward underlying forces. In this approach the government would use its market and program powers to keep the general wage level from rising rapidly and the general price level in reasonable stability. It would do this by, for example: (a) vigorously undertaking training and mobility programs to build up the supply of labor in areas and occupations where shortages are acute and wages are being bid and bargained up at a rapid rate; (b) altering the timing of government contracts to relieve demand pressures where these are great—for example, in the present construction boom along the Gulf Coast; and (c) maintaining readiness to change plans for government buying and selling, including stockpiling, where necessary to support price stability.

2. *Basic reform in the international monetary system.* Measures to control many aspects of international trade and finance have been piled one on top of another in an effort to balance United States international payments. These regulatory efforts have been continuously frustrated. Reflecting that frustration, Harry G. Johnson, Allan H. Meltzer, and Milton Friedman all suggest a more general reform involving more flexible exchange rates and a removal of the United States commitment to maintain a fixed relationship between gold and the dollar. Shifts in the relative value of the dollar in comparison with other currencies would then bring about a balance of payments. No one cited a cross of gold speech but the idea is very much alive.

3. *Measures to make labor and product markets more competitive and more flexible.* Individually, such measures may not seem like an "alternative" to guideposts, but together they could work powerfully in the direction of lowering the unemployment rate at which inflation becomes a serious issue. Among the measures mentioned in this category are these: (*a*) vigorous efforts in the areas of education and retraining, combined with an improved system of information in labor markets and an improved employment service; (*b*) repeal or modification of the Davis-Bacon and Walsh-Healy Acts; (*c*) establishment of a lower minimum wage for teen-agers, where unemployment is a particularly serious problem; (*d*) reduction of barriers to international trade, including elimination of import quotas; and (*e*) vigorous efforts to enforce the antitrust laws.

A review of these alternatives shows that guidelines are not the only possible policy. It also shows that all the alternatives are genuinely controversial.

GUIDE TO THE BOOK

The remaining sections of this book incorporate the papers prepared for the conference, discussions in plenary sessions, and summaries of discussions in the workshops.

Part I presents policy perspectives on wage-price guideposts. It contains the papers by Friedman and Solow, and discussion between them at the conference on each other's paper and position. Gardner Ackley's comments at the conclusion of the conference are in this section.

Part II covers experience with guideposts and guidelines here and abroad. Dunlop examines the United States experience and suggests governmental measures to ease price-raising pressures in "bottleneck" areas. E. H. Phelps Brown describes the British experience, especially the administrative aspect of guideposts, and assesses its meaning for the United States. Both Johnson and Meltzer evaluate the success of guidelines intended to reduce the United States payments deficit and gold losses and the growth of foreign-owned dollars.

Part III centers on the legal processes involved in guideposts. The commentators speak to issues raised in Kurland's paper as well as the somewhat broader political administrative issues.

Part IV presents the reports by Fleming, Brown, Schultz, and Stigler of the discussions in the workshops which they chaired.

Two appendixes present selections from documents through which the development of guideposts and guidelines may be traced.

The editors hope that the entire volume captures the spirit of the conference, "to clarify the central issues and enlarge the range of information and ideas available in the formation of both private and public policy."

PART I

Guidelines in Perspective

MILTON FRIEDMAN

What Price Guideposts?

MILTON FRIEDMAN is Paul Snowden Russell Distinguished Service Professor in the Department of Economics at the University of Chicago and is president-elect of the American Economics Association. He argues against the guideposts on theoretical and practical grounds and for tackling the problem of inflation in terms of what he sees as the basic causal factor, a rapidly rising money supply.

The student of inflation is tempted to rejoin, "I've heard that one before," to exhortations now emanating from Washington. Since the time of Diocletian, and very probably long before, the sovereign has repeatedly responded to generally rising prices in precisely the same way: by berating the "profiteers," calling on private persons to show social responsibility by holding down the prices at which they sell their products or their services, and trying, through legal prohibitions or other devices, to prevent individual prices from rising.[1] The result of such measures has always been

The author has drawn at various points in this paper on his book, *Inflation: Causes and Consequences* (New York: Asia Publishing House, 1963), which contains two lectures that he gave in Bombay, India, in 1963.

[1] In a market economy, prices of particular goods and services, including labor services, are always changing relatively to one another, some rising, others falling, some rising rapidly, others slowly, and so on. When rises predominate, in some sense which allows for the relative importance of the items whose prices are considered, there is inflation; when declines predominate, there is deflation. This definition is purposely vague because there is no unique way to measure the "average" behavior of prices; different indexes

17

the same: complete failure. Inflation has been stopped when and only when the quantity of money has been kept from rising too fast, and that cure has been effective whether or not the other measures were taken.

The first section of this paper explains why the attempts to hold down individual wages and prices have failed to stop inflation. Direct control of prices and wages does not eliminate inflationary pressure. It simply shifts the pressure elsewhere and suppresses some of its manifestations.

Inflation is always and everywhere a monetary phenomenon, resulting from and accompanied by a rise in the quantity of money relative to output. This generalization is not an arithmetical proposition or a truism, and it does not require a rigid relation between the rates of rise in prices and in the quantity of money. The precise rate at which prices rise for a given rate of rise in the quantity of money depends on such factors as past price behavior, current changes in the structure of labor and product markets, and fiscal policy. The monetary character of inflation, as the second section points out, is an empirical generalization backed by a wide range of evidence which suggests that substantial changes in the demand for money seldom occur except as a reaction to a sequence of events set in train by changes in the quantity of money. It follows that the only effective way to stop inflation is to restrain the rate of growth of the quantity of money.[2]

Given inflationary pressure, rises in recorded or quoted prices

often give different answers not only about the size of any price change, but even about its direction. These differences are sometimes very large and are important for many purposes. In the context of this paper, however, they are not. We shall restrict attention to cases in which the general tendency for prices to rise is so clear and widespread that it would be reflected in just about every broadly based index number.

[2] As Robert Solow pointed out in his comments on this paper at the conference, the argument of the other sections of this paper (sections I, III, and IV) is almost entirely independent of my generalization about the central role of the quantity of money in the inflationary process. The words inflationary pressure can be interpreted to mean an aggregate nominal demand in excess of the value of prior (or potential) output at prior prices. Whether this excess nominal demand reflects a change in the quantity of money, as I believe it generally does, or a change in velocity produced, for example, by changes in fiscal policy or investment demand, as others may believe, the analysis of the effects of price and wage guidelines or controls is precisely the same.

I am indebted to Mr. Solow for making this point explicit at the conference.

and wages can be suppressed to some extent. The less severe the inflationary pressure, and the more vigorous and effective the enforcement of price controls, the greater the extent to which the manifestations of inflation can be suppressed. As the third section points out, such suppressed inflation is far more harmful, both to efficiency and freedom, than open inflation, and the more effective the suppression, the greater the harm. It is highly desirable to avoid inflation but if, for whatever reason, that is not feasible, it is far better that inflation be open than that it be suppressed.

The final section of the paper asks what harm, if any, will be done by the guideposts. Even granted that compulsory price and wage controls cannot stop inflation and can do great harm, may not some measure of voluntary compliance by businessmen and union leaders ease the tasks of other instruments of policy and enable businessmen and union leaders to display their sense of social responsibility? In my opinion, the answer is clearly in the negative. Compliance with the guideposts is harmful because it encourages delay in taking effective measures to stem inflation, distorts production and distribution, and encourages restrictions on personal freedom.

Entirely aside from their strictly economic effects, guidelines threaten the consensus of shared values that is the moral basis of a free society. Compliance with them is urged in the name of social responsibility; yet, those who comply hurt both themselves and the community. Morally questionable behavior—the evading of requests from the highest officials, let alone the violation of legally imposed price and wage controls—is both privately and socially beneficial. That way lies disrespect for the law on the part of the public and pressure to use extralegal powers on the part of officials. The price of guideposts is far too high for the return, which, at most, is the appearance of doing something about a real problem.

I. WHY DIRECT CONTROL OF PRICES AND WAGES DOES NOT ELIMINATE INFLATIONARY PRESSURE

An analogy is often drawn between direct control of wages and prices as a reaction to inflation and the breaking of a thermometer as a reaction to, say, an overheated room. This analogy has an element of validity. Prices are partly like thermometers in that they register heat but do not produce it; in both cases, preventing a measuring instrument from recording what is occurring does not prevent the occurrence. But the analogy is also misleading. Breaking the thermometer need have no further effect on the phenomenon being recorded; it simply adds to our ignorance. Controlling prices, insofar as it is successful, has very important effects. Prices are not only measuring instruments, they also play a vital role in the economic process itself.

A much closer analogy is a steam-heating furnace running full blast. Controlling the heat in one room by closing the radiators in that room simply makes other rooms still more overheated. Closing all radiators lets the pressure build up in the boiler and increases the danger that it will explode. Closing or opening individual radiators is a good way to adjust the relative amount of heat in different rooms; it is not a good way to correct for overfueling the furnace. Similarly, changes in individual prices are a good way to adjust to changes in the supply or demand of individual products; preventing individual prices from rising is not a good way to correct for a general tendency of prices to rise.

Suppose that there is such a general tendency, and suppose that some specific price (or set of prices), say, the price of steel, is prevented from rising. Holding down the price of steel does not make more steel available; on the contrary, given that other prices and costs are rising, it reduces the amount that producers can afford to spend in producing steel and is therefore likely to reduce the amount available from current production. Holding down the price of steel does not discourage buyers; on the contrary, it encourages consumption. If the suppressed price is effectively enforced and not evaded by any of the many channels that are available to ingenious sellers and buyers some potential buyers of steel must be frustrated —there is a rationing problem. Chance, favoritism, or bribery will have to decide which buyers succeed in getting the steel. Those who succeed pay less than they are willing to pay. They, instead of the steel producers, have the remainder to spend elsewhere. Those who fail will try to substitute other metals or products and so will divert their demand elsewhere; the excess pressure is shifted, not eliminated.

The situation is precisely the same on the labor market. If wages are tending to rise, suppressing a specific wage rise will mean that fewer workers are available for that type of employment and more are demanded. Again rationing is necessary. The workers employed have less income to spend, but this is just balanced by their employers having larger incomes. And the unsatisfied excess demand for labor is diverted to other workers.

But, it will be said, I have begged the question by *starting* with a general tendency for prices to rise. Can it not be that this general tendency is itself produced by rises in a limited number of prices and wages which in turn produce sympathetic rises in other prices and wages? In such a case, may not preventing the initial price and wage rises nip a wage-price or price-price spiral in the bud?

Despite its popularity, this cost-push theory of inflation has very limited applicability. Unless the cost-push produces a monetary expansion that would otherwise not have occurred, its effect will be limited to at most a temporary general price rise, accompanied by unemployment, and followed by a tendency toward declining prices elsewhere.

Suppose, for example, a strong (or stronger) cartel were formed in steel, and that it decided to raise the price well above the level that otherwise would have prevailed. The price rise would reduce the amount of steel people want to buy. Potential purchasers of steel would shift to substitute products, and no doubt the prices of such substitutes would tend to rise in sympathy. But there is now another effect. Steel producers would hire fewer workers and other resources. These would seek employment elsewhere, tending to drive down wages and prices in other industries. True, wages and prices might be sticky and decline only slowly, but that would only delay the downward adjustments and only at the expense of unemployment.[3]

A textbook example is provided by John L. Lewis and the United Mine Workers. Coal mining hourly earnings rose by "163 per cent from 1945 to 1960. Bituminous coal mining employment dropped from 284,000 to 168,000. By way of comparison, in the same period, manufacturing production hourly earnings rose . . .

---

[3] Note that even for such a temporary effect, it is not enough that there exist monopolies of business and labor; it is necessary that monopoly power increase; otherwise, relative prices will already have become adjusted.

122 per cent and manufacturing employment rose."[4] High coal prices undoubtedly put upward pressure on the prices of oil and gas; but the high unemployment put downward pressure on other prices.

The only example I know of in United States history when such a cost-push was important even temporarily for any substantial part of the economy was from 1933 to 1937, when the NIRA, AAA, Wagner Labor Act, and associated growth of union strength unquestionably led to *increasing* market power of both industry and labor and thereby produced upward pressure on a wide range of wages and prices. This cost-push did not account for the concomitant rapid growth in nominal income at the average rate of 14 per cent a year from 1933 to 1937. That reflected rather a rise in the quantity of money at the rate of 11 per cent a year. And the wage and cost-push had nothing to do with the rapid rise in the quantity of money. That reflected rather the flood of gold, initiated by the change in the United States price of gold in 1933 and 1934 and sustained by the reaction to Hitler's assumption of power in Germany.

The cost-push does explain why so large a part of the growth in nominal income was absorbed by prices. Despite unprecedented levels of unemployed resources, wholesale prices rose nearly 50 per cent from 1933 to 1937, and the cost of living rose by 13 per cent. Similarly, the wage cost-push helps to explain why unemployment was still so high in 1937, when monetary restriction was followed by another severe contraction.

The popularity of the cost-push theory of inflation, despite its limited applicability, stems I believe from two sources: first, the deceptiveness of appearances; second, the desire of governmental authorities to shift the blame for inflation.

One of the fascinating features of economic relations is the frequent contrast between what is true for the individual and what is true for the community. Time and again the one is precisely the opposite of the other. Each individual takes for granted the prices of the things he buys and regards himself as having no effect on them; yet, consumers as a whole greatly affect those prices by the

---

[4] Yale Brozen, "Guide Lines and Wage Laws: How Should Wage Changes Be Determined?" unpublished paper, p. 8.

combined effects of their separate actions. Each individual can determine the amount of currency he carries around in his pocket; yet, all individuals together may have nothing to say about the total amount of currency to be carried around; that may be determined by monetary authorities, the individuals being free only to shuffle it around and transfer it from one to the other. Indeed, it is precisely this contrast between what is true for the individual and for the community that underlies many, perhaps most, common economic fallacies. They arise from invalid generalization from the individual to the community.

The widespread belief in the cost-push theory of inflation is a striking example. To each businessman separately, inflation tends to come in the form of increasing costs, and, typically, he correctly regards himself as having to raise the price at which he sells because his costs have risen. Yet, those cost rises may themselves reflect an increase in demand elsewhere and simply be part of the process whereby the demand increase is transmitted; and his ability to raise his price without a drastic decline in sales reflects the existence of excess demand. The monetary expansion and the associated increase in money demand take place through mysterious, widely dispersed, and largely invisible channels. The cost and price increases are their visible tracks.

In a recent elementary economics textbook, Alchian and Allen have given a vivid illustration of how a price rise produced by a demand increase can make itself felt to almost all the participants in the process as a cost-push:

> Pretend that for some reason people's desire for meat increases. . . . Housewives reveal an increased demand by buying more meat than formerly at the current prices in the meat markets. . . . [T]he increased demand takes its toll of inventories. . . . [The] butcher will buy more meat than usual the next day in order to restore his inventory from its abnormally low level. . . . Just as butchers use inventories, so packers . . . also rely on inventories. . . . [A]ssume that the first day's change in demand was within that inventory limit and therefore was met without a price increase.
>
> Packers restore inventories by instructing their cattle buyers . . . to buy more cattle than usual. But with all the packers restoring their inventories in this manner, the number of cattle available for sale each day are inadequate to meet the increased total demand *at the old price*. . . .

> [T]he buyers will begin to raise their offers . . . until the price rises to the point where the packers will not want to buy more meat . . . than is available from the cattlemen. . . .
>
> [T]he packers experience *a rise in costs* . . . [so] the packers must charge a higher price to butchers if they are to continue as profitable meat packers. . . . The butchers, in turn, post higher prices to the housewives. When housewives complain about the higher price, the butcher in all innocence, honesty, and correctness says that it isn't his fault. The cost of meat has gone up. . . . And the packers can honestly say the same thing.[5]

To almost all participants, therefore, a rise in price produced by excess demand appears to take the form of a rise in costs that enforces a higher price.

The interpretation of inflation as a reflection of cost-push is greatly fostered by governmental authorities. In modern times, the government has direct responsibility for the creation and destruction of money; it determines what happens to the quantity of money. Since inflation results from unduly rapid monetary expansion, the government is responsible for any inflation that occurs.[6] Yet, governmental authorities, like the rest of us, while only too eager to take credit for the good things that occur, are most reluctant to take the blame for the bad things—and inflation generally is regarded as a bad thing. Their natural tendency is to blame others for the inflation that governmental policies produce—to castigate the rapacious businessman and power-hungry labor leader rather than point to the government printing press as the culprit.

The 1966 *Annual Report* of the Council of Economic Advisers is an amusing and distressing example. It has a 31-page chapter on "Prospects for Cost-Price Stability" that so far as I have been able to determine has only two passing references to "monetary policy" and does not even contain the word "money"—a treatment of money strictly comparable to the way a rigid Puritan writing a book about love might have handled "sex." In the page and a half section on "Determination of the Price Level," there is no mention

---

[5] Armen A. Alchian and William R. Allen, *University Economics* (Belmont, Calif.: Wadsworth Publishing Co., 1964), pp. 105–7.

[6] To repeat in a specific context the point made earlier, note that precisely the same argument would hold if, as many believe, it is fiscal policy rather than monetary policy that accounts for the excess demand.

of the government's role until the last of eight paragraphs where the main emphasis is on the government's role as a customer and on governmental measures that directly affect costs. The one sentence in this section on the government's role in affecting aggregate demand is simply: "Fiscal policies help determine the over-all size of markets" (p. 65). Similarly, in the Council's explicit discussion of monetary policy elsewhere in the report (pp. 44–52), there is no reference at all to inflation or price level, although there is a passing reference to "spending." The careful reader of this 186-page report will have to wait until page 176, in a historical chapter on experience under the Employment Act, to find the first explicit recognition that there is any relation between monetary policy and inflation!

II. INFLATION IS A MONETARY PHENOMENON

Yet, the central fact is that inflation is always and everywhere a monetary phenomenon.[7] Historically, substantial changes in prices have always occurred together with substantial changes in the quantity of money relative to output. I know of no exception to this generalization, no occasion in the United States or elsewhere when prices have risen substantially without a substantial rise in the quantity of money relative to output or when the quantity of money has risen substantially relative to output without a substantial rise in prices. And there are numerous confirming examples. Indeed, I doubt that there is any other empirical generalization in economics for which there is as much organized evidence covering so wide a range of space and time.

[7] The word money is used in at least three different senses: (1) as in "money balances" when the reference is to the pieces of paper we carry in our pocket or the credits to our account on the books of banks—this is the sense in which I shall use it; (2) as in "making money" when the reference is not to a counterfeiter but to a recipient of income; and (3) as in "money markets" when the reference is to "loans" or "credit," paper claims that cover a vastly broader range of instruments than those we designate "money" in the first sense. Confusion among these meanings underlies much misunderstanding about the role of money in economic affairs. In particular, confusion between the first and third has led to great overemphasis on the "credit" effects of governmental monetary policy rather than the effects on the quantity of money. Hence, the statement that inflation is a monetary phenomenon is sometimes interpreted not as I do in the text but as indicating that inflation reflects changes in credit markets.

Some confirming examples are extremely dramatic and illustrate
vividly how important the quantity of money is by comparison
with everything else. After the Russian Revolution of 1917, there
was a hyperinflation in Russia when a new currency was introduced and printed in large quantities. Ultimately, it became almost
valueless. All the time, some currency was circulating which had
been issued by the prerevolutionary Czarist government. The
Czarist government was out of power. Nobody expected it to
return to power. Yet, the value of the Czarist currency remained
roughly constant in terms of goods and rose sharply in terms of
the Bolshevik currency. Why? Because there was nobody to print
any more of it. It was fixed in quantity and therefore it retained
its value. Another story has to do with the United States Civil
War. Toward the end of the war, the Union troops overran the
place where the Confederates had been printing paper money to
finance the war. In the course of moving to a new location, there
was a temporary cessation of the printing of money. As a result,
there was also a temporary interruption in the price rise that had
been proceeding merrily.

The fact that inflation results from changes in the quantity of
money relative to output does not mean that there is a precise,
rigid, mechanical relationship between the quantity of money and
prices, which is why the weasel-word "substantial" was sprinkled
in my initial statement of the proposition. First, over short periods,
the rate of change in the quantity of money can differ and sometimes by appreciable amounts from the rate of change in nominal
income or prices because of other factors, including fiscal policy.
Second, and more important, changes in the quantity of money do
not make their effects felt immediately. It may be six months or
a year or a year and a half before a change in the quantity of
money appreciably affects nominal income or prices. Failure to
allow for this difference in timing is a major reason for the misin-
terpretation of monetary experience. Third, and most important of
all, there is a systematic and regular difference between changes
in money and in prices in the course of an inflationary episode
that is itself part of the very process by which monetary changes
produce changes in prices.

The typical life history of an inflation is that the quantity of
money per unit of output initially increases more rapidly than

prices. During this period, the public does not anticipate price rises, interprets any price rise that occurs as temporary, and hence is willing to hold money balances of increased "real" value (i.e., corresponding to a larger volume of goods and services) in the belief that prices will be lower in the future. If the quantity of money continues to increase faster than output, however, prices will continue to rise, and sooner or later the public will come to anticipate further price rises. It then wishes to reduce its money balances not only to their former real value but to an even smaller level. Cash has now become a costly way to hold assets, since its purchasing power is decreasing. People therefore try to reduce their cash balances. They cannot, as a whole, do so in nominal terms (i.e., in terms of dollars), because someone or other must hold the amount in existence. But the *attempt* to do so bids up prices, wages, and nominal incomes. The result is to reduce "real" balances. During this stage, therefore, prices rise more rapidly than the quantity of money, and sometimes much more rapidly. If the rate of rise of the quantity of money stablizes, no matter at how high a level, the rate of price rise will ultimately settle down also. The total price rise may bear very different relations to the rise in the quantity of money per unit of output depending on the size of the monetary expansion. In moderate inflations, as for example the rise in prices in the United States by a third from 1896 to 1913, prices and money may rise by about the same percentage. In really substantial inflations, such as have occurred in recent decades in many South American countries, the price rise will generally be several times the monetary rise; in hyperinflations, the price rise will be many times the monetary rise.

The United States today is in the early stages of such an episode. From 1961 to 1965, the quantity of money per unit of output rose more rapidly than prices—the typical initial reaction. From early 1965 to early this year, the monetary rise has been accelerated, and the price rise has accelerated even more rapidly as anticipations of inflation have become widespread. As of now, if the rate of monetary growth were stabilized at the high level attained in 1965, the rate of price rise would continue to accelerate for a time. Even if the rate of monetary growth were sharply reduced, prices would continue to rise for a time under the combined influence of earlier monetary growth and changing anticipations.

Why should money be so critical a factor in price level behavior? Why should it occupy such a central role in the process? The key to an answer is the difference, already referred to, between the *nominal* quantity of money, the quantity of money expressed in terms of dollars, and the *real* quantity of money, the quantity of money expressed in terms of the goods and services it will buy or the number of weeks of income it is equal to.

People seem to be extraordinarily stubborn about the real amount of money that they want to hold and are unwilling to hold a different amount, unless there is a strong incentive to do so. This is true over both time and space.

Let me illustrate with currency in circulation alone, which is more comparable among countries and over time than a broader definition of money, including deposits. In the United States, the amount of currency held by the non-banking public amounts to roughly four weeks' income. I know that this result seems surprising. When I ask people separately whether they have as much as four weeks' income in the form of currency, I have rarely had anyone say yes. Part of the explanation is that about one-fifth of the currency is held by businesses such as retail stores. The main explanation, I am sure, is that there are a small number of people who hold very large sums in this form while the rest of us hold more moderate amounts. In any event, that is what the figures show. The fascinating thing is that the corresponding number was not very different a century ago. In 1867 people on the average held about five weeks' income in the form of currency, compared to today's four weeks' income. In the interim this number has gone as low as 2¼ weeks' income in 1929, as high as 8½ weeks' in 1946. That is a substantial range, it is true, but those are long periods spanning major changes in circumstance.

This range, moreover, contains the figures for most countries in the world. In Israel, the amount held is about the same as in the United States, a little over four weeks' income; in Japan and Turkey, about five weeks' income; in Greece and Yugoslavia, about six weeks' income; in India, about seven weeks' income. Again, these are not negligible differences; yet, they are small compared to the differences among the countries in wealth, economic structure, political forms, and cultural characteristics.

Even these relatively small differences over time and space can be largely explained by a few major factors, of which the prevalence of deposit banking is perhaps the single most important.

Given that people are so stubborn about the amount they hold in the form of money, let us suppose that, for whatever reasons, the amount of money in a community is higher than people want to hold at the level of prices then prevailing. It does not for our purposes matter why, whether because the government has printed money to finance expenditures or because somebody has discovered a new gold mine or because banks have discovered how to create deposits. For whatever reason, people find that although on the average they would like to hold, let us say, the four weeks' income that they hold in the United States, they are actually holding, say, five weeks' income. What will happen? Here again it is essential to distinguish between the individual and the community. Each individual separately thinks he can get rid of his money and he is right. He can go out and spend it and thereby reduce his cash balances. But for the community as a whole the belief that cash balances can be reduced is an optical illusion. The only way I can reduce my cash balances in nominal terms is to induce somebody else to increase his. One man's expenditures are another man's receipts. People as a whole cannot spend more than they as a whole receive. In consequence, if everybody in the community tries to reduce the nominal amount of his cash balances, on the average nobody will do so. The amount of nominal balances is fixed by the nominal quantity of money in existence and no game of musical chairs can change it.

But people can and will try to reduce their cash balances and the process of trying has important effects. In the process of trying to spend more than they are receiving, people bid up the prices of all sorts of goods and services. Nominal incomes rise and real cash balances are indeed reduced, even though nominal balances, the number of dollars, are not affected. The rise in prices and incomes will bring cash balances from five weeks' income to four weeks' income. People will succeed in achieving their objective, but by raising prices and incomes rather than by reducing nominal balances. In the process, prices will have risen by about a fifth. This in a nutshell and somewhat oversimplified is the process whereby changes in the stock of money exert their influence on the price level. It is oversimplified because there is a tendency to overshoot, followed by successive readjustments converging on the final position, but this complication does not affect the essence of the adjustment process.

Emphasis on the key role of the quantity of money leaves open the question of what produced the changes in the quantity of money. Hence, if an analysis of inflation is to deal not only with the change in the quantity of money but with what brought it about, it will be a very pluralistic theory. Historically, the actual sources of monetary expansion have been very different at different times and in different places.

In United States history, the most dramatic inflations have been wartime inflations—those associated with the Revolution, when prices skyrocketed and the declining value of the money produced the phrase "not worth a continental," and with the War of 1812, the Civil War, and the two world wars, in all of which prices roughly doubled. In these episodes, the increase in the quantity of money was produced mainly by the printing of money to pay for governmental wartime expenses.

But even these episodes are not wholly to be explained in that fashion. In the final year of the World War I inflation (1919–20), when prices rose at their most rapid pace, the government budget was in surplus, and the rapid increase in the quantity of money was being produced for private, not governmental, purposes.

The two main periods of peacetime inflation in the United States were in the 1850's and from 1896 to 1913. Both were parts of worldwide movements. The first resulted from the gold discoveries in California, the second from the development of a commercially feasible cyanide process for extracting gold from low-grade ore plus gold discoveries.

There is a widespread belief that inflation is somehow related to government deficits. This belief has a sound basis. The existence of deficits tempts governments to finance them by printing money (or the equivalent, creating deposits), hence deficits have often been the source of monetary expansion. But deficits per se are not necessarily a source of inflation. As already noted, the federal budget ran a surplus during 1919–20 when prices rose rapidly; similarly, there were extremely large surpluses immediately after World War II, when prices also rose rapidly. On the other side, the budget was in deficit during 1931–33, when prices fell sharply.

Deficits can contribute to inflation by raising interest rates and so velocity; for the rest they are a source of inflation if and only if they are financed by printing money.

The same considerations apply to other alleged sources of inflation. Increasingly strong trade unions can be a source of inflation if by their actions they produce unemployment and if a government committed to full employment expands the quantity of money as part of a policy of eliminating unemployment. This particular chain of events has often been alleged but, as already noted, seldom observed in the United States. More generally, a full employment policy can be a source of inflation if it produces undue monetary expansion.

III. Suppressed Inflation Is Worse than Open Inflation

The distinction between inflation and deflation, important as it is, is less important than the distinction between open inflation, one in which prices are free to rise without governmental price controls, and suppressed inflation, one in which the government attempts to suppress the manifestations of the inflationary pressure by controlling prices, including prices not only of products but also of factor services (i.e., wage rates, rents, interest rates) and of foreign currencies (i.e., exchange rates).

Open inflation is harmful. It generally produces undesirable transfers of income and wealth, weakens the social fabric, and may distort the pattern of output. But if moderate, and especially if steady, it tends to become anticipated and its worst effects on the distribution of income are offset. It still does harm, but, *so long as prices are free to move,* the extremely flexible private enterprise system will adapt to it, take it in stride, and continue to operate efficiently. The main dangers from open inflation are twofold: first, the temptation to step up the rate of inflation as the economy adapts itself; second, and even more serious, the temptation to attempt cures, especially suppression, that are worse than the disease.

Suppressed inflation is a very different thing. Even a moderate inflation, if effectively suppressed over a wide range, can do untold damage to the economic system, require widespread government intervention into the details of economic activity, destroy a free enterprise system, and along with it, political freedom. The reason is that suppression prevents the price system from working. The government is driven to try to provide a substitute that is extremely inefficient. The usual outcome, pending a complete monetary reform, is an uneasy compromise between official tolerance of evasion of price controls and a collectivist economy. The greater the ingenuity of private individuals in evading the price controls and the greater the tolerance of officials in blinking at such evasions, the less the harm that is done; the more law-abiding the citizens, and the more rigid and effective the governmental enforcement machinery, the greater the harm.✓

A dramatic illustration of the difference between open and suppressed inflation is the contrast between the experience of Germany after World War I and after World War II. This happens to be one of those beautiful examples that history turns up for us from time to time in which experience is almost in the nature of a controlled experiment, because the difference in the character of the monetary phenomena is so great compared to differences in other relevant respects. After World War I, Germany had an open inflation of extremely large magnitude. It is difficult for us to contemplate the kind of inflation Germany experienced at that time because it is so extreme. A student of mine, Phillip Cagan, wrote a doctoral dissertation on hyperinflation in different countries, which has become something of a classic. He had the problem of how to define hyperinflation. He defined it as beginning when prices started to rise at the rate of more than 50 per cent a month. In the German hyperinflation after World War I, there were periods when prices rose not 50 per cent a month but doubled every week and some occasions on which they were doubling every day. Indeed, it got to the point that firms started to pay their employees their wages three times a day—after breakfast, lunch, and dinner, so that they could go out and spend them before they lost their value. That was really a whopping inflation, yet it went on for something like three years.

The inflation did untold harm to Germany. The impoverishment of the middle classes, the arbitrary redistribution of income, and the frantic instability unquestionably helped to lay the groundwork for Hitler's emergence later. Looked at, however, from the purely technical point of view of its effect on production, the astounding thing is that until the last six months of the inflation, total output in Germany never declined. Indeed, Germany was one of the few countries in the world that did not experience a great depression in 1920–21, when prices in the gold standard part of the world dropped by 50 per cent. Total output remained up. Why? Because the inflation was open. Prices were allowed to rise freely and hence the price system could still be used to allocate resources. Of course, after a time people started to use all sorts of escalation devices to link their contracts to the value of the mark in the foreign exchange market, which was also a free market price, and so on. The price system, however, could work even under those handicaps.

After World War II, Germany was under inflationary pressure as a result of an increase in the quantity of money during the war and the fixation of prices. By our usual standards, the pressure was substantial. If prices had been allowed to rise freely immediately after the war, the price level would probably have quadrupled. That is a large price rise. But it is negligible by comparison with the price rise after World War I which has to be described in terms of factors like 10^{10}. The price rise after World War II, however, was suppressed. Ordinarily, it is extremely difficult to suppress a price rise of that magnitude, to enforce price control when the market price would be four times the controlled price. But there were certain especially favorable circumstances from the point of view of enforcing price control in Germany at that time. Germany was occupied by the armed forces of Britain, France, and the United States, and the occupation forces enforced price control.

The result of suppressing inflation was that output in Germany was cut in half. The price system was not allowed to function. People were forced to revert to barter. Walter Eucken in an article describing this period tells the story of people who worked in a factory making pots and pans. They would work there for two or three days and then they would be given their pay in the form of aluminum saucepans. They would take the saucepans and spend the rest of the week scouring the countryside trying to find some farmer who would be willing to trade a few potatoes or other produce for the saucepans. That is not a very efficient way to organize resources. It was so inefficient that something had to be done and something was done. People developed their own forms of money. Cigarettes came into use as money for small transactions and cognac for large transactions—the most liquid money I have ever come across. But even with these expedients, suppressed inflation cut output in half from the level at the immediate end of the war. ✓

In 1948 as you know, the so-called German miracle began. It was not a very complicated thing. It amounted to introducing a monetary reform, eliminating price control, and allowing the price system to function. The extraordinary rise in German output in the few years following this reform was not owing to any miracle of German ingenuity or ability or anything like that. It was the simple, natural result of allowing the most efficient technique people have ever found for organizing resources to work instead of preventing it from working by trying to fix prices here, there, and everywhere.

Although this is the most dramatic example, numerous other examples can be cited of a less extreme kind. In the immediate postwar period, I visited Europe and spent some time in Britain and France. Both countries at that time had widespread price controls. But there was an important difference. The people of Britain were relatively law-abiding, the people of France were not. The result was that Britain was being strangled by the law obedience of her people and France was being saved by the black market.

The reason suppressed inflation is so disastrous, as these examples suggest, is that the price system is the only technique that has so far been discovered or invented for efficiently allocating resources. If that is prevented from operating, something else must be substituted. What do we substitute? It is always some kind of clumsy physical control.

A striking current example is provided by India with its system of exchange control and import licenses. In the past decade, India has experienced a price rise of something between 25 and 50 per cent. In the main, this price rise has been open, although there have been some price controls. There has been, however, one important glaring exception—the price of foreign exchange. The official price of the dollar or the pound sterling in terms of the rupee is precisely the same today as it was ten years ago. If the price of the rupee was anywhere close to being right then, it cannot be right now. And of course it is not right. The effect has been to encourage people to try to import goods because they are artificially cheap and to discourage them from trying to export goods because the amount of rupees they can get for the foreign exchange proceeds of exports will buy less at home than before. Imports and exports are highly sensitive areas. Even moderate changes can have very large effects. The result has been a serious foreign exchange crisis. India at first allowed her foreign exchange reserves to run down until today reserves are very small. In addition, direct controls over imports have been increasingly tightened and all sorts of special measures have been taken to subsidize and encourage exports. Certain categories of imports have been banned entirely. For other categories, import licenses have been given on a more and more limited scale. And even so, the exchange rate has been able to be maintained only because of very large additional grants of foreign aid.

The result has been incredible waste and inefficiency, proliferating bureaucracy, and widespread corruption and bribery. In my opinion, the pegging of the exchange rate is the key to India's economic failure. Setting it free, along with the wiping away of the mountains of regulations exchange control has engendered, is the most important single step that India could take to unleash its very real potentialities.

The experience of India could be duplicated manyfold. I cite it only because it happens to be the case with which I am most intimately familiar.

India is a far-off land. But the same process has been getting under way in the United States. As in India, the pegging of exchange rates is the most conspicuous example of the suppression of inflation in the United States, and it has been having the same effects. The changes in tourist allowances; the "voluntary" quotas imposed on the exports of foreign countries to us; the establishment of a cartel agreement among banks to limit foreign loans, an agreement that would be clearly illegal if privately entered into but that is urged in the name of patriotism and is policed by the Federal Reserve System; the so-called voluntary foreign exchange program for business enterprises, administered by the Department of Commerce and constituting an extralegal exchange control arrangement—these are but a sample and a foretaste of what suppressed inflation implies.

A perhaps even more illuminating foretaste is furnished by the recent developments in connection with copper, which combine internal price restraint with control of exchange rates. The posted

American producer price of blister copper is being kept, by pressure from Washington, at about 36 cents a pound, well below the world price. The result, of course, is that it is profitable to export copper. Accordingly, the export of copper without a license has been prohibited and full-fledged governmental export control of copper has been introduced. Needless to say, not even the government can live with such a price discrepancy when the United States must import copper. The United States government has therefore made a deal with Chile involving Chile's selling us copper at 36 cents a pound in return for our giving them a development loan of $10 million at highly favorable terms.[8] A bit of quick arithmetic yields a gross price of copper, including the value to Chile of the soft loan, of between 40.6 and 41.6 cents a pound, or almost precisely Chile's current export price of 42 cents a pound.[9] Such shenanigans to conceal the United States government's evasions of its own guidelines would be as humorous as they are ludicrous if the episode were not such a disheartening harbinger of what currently looks like the wave of the future. Again, in a futile effort to hold down the price of copper, the United States government sold 200 million tons of copper from its stockpile at the price of 36 cents a pound it has been trying to peg. Since the market price of scrap plus the cost of converting it was at the time about 50 cents a pound, this amounted to splitting the melon of $56 million with the users of copper lucky enough to buy from the government at the fixed price.

The United States had widespread experience with the results of price and wage controls during World War II, and New York City's housing difficulties are a current reminder of their long-reaching effects, since New York is the only city in the land that still has rent controls as a heritage of the war. The memory of this experience leads government officials to disavow any intention of imposing explicit price and wage controls. But voluntary controls are no improvement, except as they are more readily evaded. Let them be abided by, and the consequences will be the same.

---

[8] See *Wall Street Journal*, January 31, 1966.

[9] I am indebted to David Kleinman for calling this episode to my attention and for the calculations referred to. Since this was written, Chile has raised her export price sharply.

IV. WHAT HARM WILL BE DONE BY THE GUIDEPOSTS?

Even granted that legally imposed and vigorously enforced wage and price ceilings covering a wide range of the economy would do enormous harm, some may argue that the enunciation of guideposts, their approval by businessmen and labor leaders, and voluntary compliance with them, or even lip service to them, is a palliative that can do no harm and can temporarily help until more effective measures are taken. At the very least, it may be said, it will enable businessmen and labor leaders to display their sense of social responsibility.

This view seems to me mistaken. The guideposts do harm even when only lip service is paid to them, and the more extensive the compliance, the greater the harm.

In the first place, the guideposts confuse the issue and make correct policy less likely. If there is inflation or inflationary pressure, the governmental monetary (or, some would say, fiscal) authorities are responsible. It is they who must take corrective measures if the inflation is to be stopped. Naturally, the authorities want to shift the blame, so they castigate the rapacious businessman and the selfish labor leader. By approving guidelines, the businessman and the labor leader implicitly whitewash the government for its role and plead guilty to the charge. They thereby encourage the government to postpone taking the corrective measures that alone can succeed.

In the second place, whatever measure of actual compliance there is introduces just that much distortion into the allocation of resources and the distribution of output. To whatever extent the price system is displaced, some other system of organizing resources and rationing output must be adopted. As in the example of the controls on foreign loans by banks, one adverse effect is to foster private collusive arrangements, so that a measure undertaken to keep prices down leads to government support and encouragement of private monopolistic arrangements.

In the third place, "voluntary" controls invite the use of extralegal powers to produce compliance. And, in the modern world, such powers are ample. There is hardly a business concern that could not have great costs imposed on it by antitrust investigations, tax inquiries, government boycott, or rigid enforcement of any of a myriad of laws, or on the other side of the ledger, that can see no potential benefits from government orders, guarantees of loans, or similar measures. Which of us as an individual could not be, at the very least, seriously inconvenienced by investigation of his income tax returns, no matter how faithfully and carefully prepared, or by the enforcement to the letter of laws we may not even know about? This threat casts a shadow well beyond any particular instance. In a dissenting opinion in a recent court case involving a "stand-in" in a public library, Justice Black wrote, "It should be remembered that if one group can take over libraries for one cause, other groups will assert the right to do it for causes which, while wholly legal, may not be so appealing to this court." Precisely the same point applies here. If legal powers granted for other purposes can today be used for the "good" purpose of holding down prices, tomorrow they can be used for other purposes that will seem equally "good" to the men in power—such as simply keeping themselves in power. It is notable how sharp has been the decline in the number of businessmen willing to be quoted by name when they make adverse comments on government.

In the fourth place, compliance with voluntary controls imposes a severe conflict of responsibilities on businessmen and labor leaderers. The corporate official is an agent of his stockholders; the labor leader, of the members of his union. He has a responsibility to promote their interests. He is now told that he must sacrifice their interests to some supposedly higher social responsibility. Even supposing that he can know what "social responsibility" demands —say by simply accepting on that question the gospel according to the Council of Economic Advisers—to what extent is it proper for him to do so? If he is to become a civil servant in fact, will he long remain an employee of the stockholders or an agent of the workers in name? Will they not discharge him? Or, alternatively, will not the government exert authority over him in name as in fact?

V. Conclusion

Inflation being always and everywhere a monetary phenomenon, the responsibility for controlling it is governmental. Legally enforced price and wage ceilings do not eliminate inflationary pressure. At most they suppress it. And suppressed inflation is vastly more harmful than open inflation.

Guideposts and pleas for voluntary compliance are a halfway house whose only merit is that they can more readily be abandoned than legally imposed controls. They are not an alternative to other effective measures to stem inflation, but at most a smoke-screen to conceal the lack of action. Even if not complied with they do harm, and the more faithfully they are complied with, the more harm they do.

Nonetheless, we should not exaggerate either the problem or the harm that will be done by false cures. Prices will almost surely rise in coming months. We shall probably continue to experience inflationary pressure on the average over the coming years. The price rise, however, will be moderate. A major war aside, I cannot conceive that the monetary authorities will permit the quantity of money to rise at a rate that would produce inflation of more than, say, 3-to-10 per cent a year. Such inflation will be unfortunate, but if permitted to occur reasonably openly and freely, not disastrous. And, despite all the talk, prices and wages will be permitted to rise in one way or another. The guideposts will be more talked about than they will be voluntarily complied with or enforced by extra-legal pressure. Hypocrisy will enable effective evasion to be combined with self-congratulation. Debasing the coin of public and private morality is unfortunate, but in moderate doses not disastrous. The greatest harm will continue to be done by the measures taken to peg exchange rates. It is well to keep in mind Adam Smith's famous comment, "There is much ruin in a nation," but only to avoid overstating a good case, not to condone bad policy.

ROBERT M. SOLOW

The Case against the Case against the Guideposts

ROBERT M. SOLOW is professor of economics at the Massachusetts Institute of Technology and was senior staff economist of the Council of Economic Advisers in 1962, when the wage-price guideposts were first put forward by the Kennedy administration. He defends the limited but important role envisaged for the guideposts, stresses their importance as a means of education about wage-price-productivity relationships, and sees them as imperfect but better than any alternative so far suggested.

I choose this defensive-sounding title because it points to an important truth. The wage-price guideposts, to the extent that they can be said to constitute a policy, are not the sort of policy you would invent if you were inventing policies from scratch. They are the type of policy you back into as you search for ways to protect an imperfect economy from the worst consequences of its imperfect behavior. For this reason, it seems to me that the best way to start an evaluation of the wage-price guideposts is with recognition of the dilemma to which they are a response.

THE PROBLEM OF PREMATURE INFLATION: SOME OBVIOUS REMEDIES

The problem is that modern mixed capitalist economies tend to generate unacceptably fast increases in money wages and prices

41

while there is not general excess demand. No particular view of the economic process or of the determinants of demand need be implied by this observation. It is a fact, however, or at least it is widely believed to be a fact, that wages and prices begin to rise too rapidly for comfort while there is still quite a bit of unemployed labor and idle productive capacity and no important bottlenecks. This tendency creates a dilemma for public policy. Governments generally do not wish to acquiesce in an inflationary spiral; indeed, in our rather international trading world, governments may not be able to do so. On the other hand, governments value employment and output, for the very good reason that people value employment and output, so governments generally do not wish to choke off economic expansion while there is room for more.

This dilemma is not confined to the United States. Most of the advanced capitalist economies of the world have faced it, despite the differences in their wage- and price-making institutions. So far as I know, none of them has found a very satisfactory solution; and most of them have been driven to some form of "incomes policy," to something very like the wage-price guideposts. These policies have not been entirely successful either, but that may be too much to expect anyway.

It is no accident that the Council of Economic Advisers launched the local version of incomes policy in the January 1962 Economic Report, despite the fact that the unemployment rate was then near 6 per cent and manufacturing capacity only 83 per cent utilized, according to the McGraw-Hill survey. Wholesale prices were not then rising, nor did they begin to rise until 1965. But still the Council felt—with good reason—that it had to protect its flank against those who argued, even then, that an expansionary fiscal and monetary policy would dissipate itself almost immediately in inflationary wage and price behavior. The argument proved wrong; but that it could be seriously made suggests the nature and the seriousness of the problem of premature inflation.

Given the character of the problem, it is natural for an economist to turn elsewhere before he settles for anything so weak, so uncertain, and so uneven in its effects as exhortation. In particular, two possible policy lines present themselves as straightforward and natural. The first is simply to accept the universe: The appropriate remedy is either to restrict demand enough through fiscal and monetary means to keep the price level reasonably stable, or else to accept some inflation. The second approach is to recognize that the threat of premature inflation reflects significant departures from perfect competition in labor and product markets: The appropriate remedy is to create or restore competition by breaking up all concentrations of market power, whether in the hands of trade unions or large firms, and by eliminating all or most legal protections against domestic and foreign competition.

Both these suggestions have attractive aspects. The first promises that economic policy can be more or less confined to the impersonal tools of the fiscal and monetary policy that we know something about. The second caters to the economist's prejudice in favor of the mechanism of the competitive market. If there is a case against the case against the guideposts, part of it has to be that the first obvious remedy may be very costly, and the second obvious remedy is more than a little unrealistic.

The experience of the years 1958–64 certainly indicates that the economy can be run with quite a lot of slack, but not a catastrophic amount, so that the price level will more or less police itself. That is a possible policy. But it is not a costless policy. In the first place, one of the necessary concomitants of this policy is a pretty substantial unemployment rate. Since the incidence of unemployment is typically uneven, and the unevenness has no claim to equity, common decency requires that this policy be accompanied by a major reform and improvement of the unemployment compensation system, and possibly of other transfer payment systems as well. This is a budgetary cost, but not a real burden on the economy as a whole. In the second place, however, the maintenance of slack does represent a real burden to the economy as a whole in the form of unproduced output. It is not easy to make any estimate of that cost. The usual rule of thumb is that one-half point on the unemployment rate corresponds to something between 1 and 2 per cent of real GNP. In that case, the amount of relief from inflation that could be had by keeping the unemployment rate one-half point higher than otherwise desirable would have an annual cost of about $10 billion at 1965 prices and GNP. Just because that is a large number does not mean that the price is not worth paying. Everyone must choose for himself. But it does mean that an alternative policy capable of having the same restraining effect as a half point of unemployment is a preferable policy unless it imposes social costs of about that order of magnitude.]

The policy of heading off premature inflation by strengthening competition is in many ways the opposite of costly. Most economists, at least, have a preference for competition, free trade, mobility, and the like, on the ground that they promote economic efficiency, while any inequities that may result can be offset by other means. Most economists, therefore, would argue in favor of strengthening competition, free trade, and mobility even if there were no problem of premature inflation; all the more so, since there might be beneficial effects on the inflation front as well. But realism suggests that significant steps in this direction will be very slow in coming, if they come at all. In the meanwhile, the problem of premature inflation remains, and the unattainable best should not be allowed to become the enemy of the second best. To anyone who argues against guideposts that competition is the best policy, I reply: Yes indeed, and go to it, but meanwhile, . . .]

The logic of a guidepost policy is, I suppose, something like this. In our imperfect world, there are important areas where market power is sufficiently concentrated that price and wage decisions are made with a significant amount of discretion. When times are reasonably good, that discretion may be exercised in ways that contribute to premature inflation. (Institutions with market power may actually succeed in exploiting the rest of the economy temporarily or permanently, or they may see their decisions cancelled out almost immediately by induced increases in other prices and wages.) People and institutions with market power may, in our culture, be fairly sensitive to public opinion. To the extent that they are, an educated and mobilized public opinion may exert some restraining pressure to forestall or limit premature inflation.

The January, 1962, guideposts were intended to be a step in the educational process. Whatever else they have accomplished, or not accomplished, I think they, and the discussion they aroused, have surely made a dent on public thinking about wage and price behavior. I give an example: In 1962 it was often said that if money wages rose at the same rate as productivity and the price level were constant, labor would in effect appropriate all of the gains in productivity. There may still be people who don't realize that the effect would actually be to increase aggregate wages and aggregate profits at the same rate, preserving their proportional relations to one another. But there must be many fewer such people now.

The object of the guideposts was and is to hold up to the public—and to those participants in wage and price decisions who can exercise some discretion—a summary picture of how wages and prices *would* behave in a fairly smoothly functioning competitive market economy subject neither to major excess demand nor major deficiency of demand. The hope was that active discussion of the issues might induce the participants, in effect, to imitate a little more closely a few aspects of competitive price and wage behavior. If that happened, the expansion of real demand and the production of real output might be able to go a little further before unacceptable increases in the general price level would begin.

I think it is fair to say that no one connected with the guideposts expects or ever expected that they could have any major role to play either under conditions of generalized excess demand or under conditions of substantial slack in the economy. When unemployment is heavy and excess capacity is widespread, wages and prices are likely to police themselves. To expect the price level as a whole to fall is probably too much, but it is unlikely to rise, and if it does, not very much. Similarly, when demand is excessive in broad sectors of the economy, it is idle to believe that the price level can be talked out of rising. The guidepost idea does rest on the presumption that somewhere in between there is a zone of economic conditions, neither too tight nor too slack, in which there is some tendency toward inflation, but a weak enough tendency so that an informed and mobilized public opinion can have effect.

HAVE THE GUIDEPOSTS HAD AN EFFECT ON WAGES AND PRICES?

The most common criticism of dependence on wage-price guideposts is that they simply do not work and have no effect on either wages or prices. Some of these criticisms simply cancel one another: For every employer who complains that unions take the guidepost figure for a floor, there is a union leader who complains that employers take it for a ceiling. Such evidence is worth nothing. Better evidence can be had, but is in the nature of the case uncertain. We may not be able to tell whether the guideposts have had any influence on wage and price decisions: first because there is no way to measure the "intensity" with which the guideposts have been pressed; and second because we have no universally accepted quantitative doctrine about how prices and money wages are determined in the absence of guideposts. ✓

The best such quantitative explanation I know is that of Professor George Perry of the University of Minnesota. He reconstructs the percentage change in hourly wages in manufacturing from one quarter to the same quarter of the next year in terms of four determinants. The determinants are the unemployment rate, the accompanying change in the *Consumer Price Index,* the rate of profit on capital in manufacturing, and the change in the rate of profit. He finds, as you would expect, that wages in manufacturing will rise more rapidly the lower the unemployment rate; the faster the cost of living has been rising, the higher are profits, and the faster they have been rising. The precise relationship is based on the experience of the manufacturing sector from 1948 to 1960; it explains the course of money wages quite well during that period.

When Perry's relationship is used to explain wage changes in manufacturing after 1960, it tells an interesting story. In 1961 and the first half of 1962, wages rose faster than the theory would expect. Beginning with the third quarter of 1962, and without exception for the next fourteen quarters to the end of 1965, wages rose more slowly than the theory would expect. Runs in the residuals are not uncommon, but this run is uncommonly long. Moreover, although the overestimation of wage changes was initially small, it became substantial in 1964 and 1965. In 1965, the annual increase in wage rates was about 1.7 per cent lower than the 1948–60 experience would lead one to expect.

Is all of this difference attributable to the influence of the guideposts? Is any? I don't suppose any definite answer can be given. The timing certainly suggests that the guideposts had something to do with it. But econometric inference is rarely completely solid, and I have no doubt that someone who wanted strongly to resist that conclusion could produce a statistical model giving different results.

What does seem fairly clear is that manufacturing wages have gone up relatively slowly during the past few years, given the unemployment rate actually ruling, the good profits actually earned, and the increase in consumer prices that actually occurred. It is not farfetched to believe that the guideposts might have been an important factor in this structural change.

The object of the guideposts is to stall off premature inflation. Wages themselves are a matter of concern only because they bulk so large in total costs. If the guideposts served only to damp the increase in wages without holding down the price level, then their main result would simply be a transfer of income from wages to profits, and that is not their purpose. So the question arises whether there has been any visible change in price behavior.

All of the obstacles to clear-cut measurement of the wage effects apply equally to the price effects. Moreover, I know of no basic study like Perry's to serve as a starting-point for price behavior. I can report, however, on one small scale and partial experiment.

Year-to-year changes in the wholesale price index for all manufactures, between 1954 and 1965, can be explained moderately well in terms of the McGraw-Hill index of capacity utilization, and the accompanying year-to-year changes in labor costs per unit of output in manufacturing. As one would expect, the price index rises faster the higher the utilization of capacity and the faster unit labor costs increase. If one amends the relation among these variables to allow for a structural shift after 1962, the data suggest that wholesale prices rose about $7/10$ of a point a year more slowly after 1962 than before, for any given utilization rate and change in unit labor costs. (This suggestion just fails of statistical significance, but I suspect that lengthening the period and refining the data would correct that.)

Although this is the most tentative sort of conclusion, it is double-barreled. Even if there were no structural change in price behavior after 1962, it would mean that any reduction or slowdown in unit labor costs achieved through the guideposts was being passed on into prices to the usual extent. If in fact there was a structural change, it means that over and above the effect through labor costs there was a further tendency for prices to rise more slowly than earlier experience would suggest.

There is, as I have said, no firm reason to attribute these shifts in behavior to the guideposts. Nor is there any reason not to.

Would the Guideposts Freeze the Distribution
of Income and Interfere with Free Markets?

It is often remarked—as indeed I remarked earlier—that if wage rates on the average were to rise precisely as fast as productivity, while the price levels were to remain constant, then the proportions of the national income going to labor and to property would stay unchanged. To take some very round numbers, suppose production per man-year were $10,000 and the annual wage $7,500, so that $2,500 went to owners of capital. If productivity and the annual wage were both to rise by that famous 3.2 per cent, and prices were unchanged, then output per man-year would go to $10,320 and the wage $7,740. This would leave $2,580 in property income. Notice that the $320 of new output per man-year has been divided in the same 75–25 proportions as the original $10,000, so that the overall proportional distribution of the national income is undisturbed.

This algebraic fact has led to criticism of the guidepost concept. The argument is not at all about the equity or justice of the current distribution of income. The argument is that the distribution of income—before taxes and transfers—is part of the market process in our economy. Changes in incomes are supposed to guide efficiently the allocation of resources. To freeze the distribution of income in a pattern that may be suitable to current conditions can lead to distortions and inefficiencies if economic conditions change and call for a changed distribution of income.

It seems to me that this argument has no practical weight at all. It is rendered trivial by two facts. The first is that the division of the national income between labor and property incomes is among the slower-changing characteristics of our economy, or of any Western economy. The second is that neither the guideposts nor any other such quantitative prescription can be satisfied *exactly*. Suppose that wage rates do follow the guideposts exactly. Then if the price level, instead of remaining constant, goes up by, say, 1 per cent in a year, the share of wages in national income will fall by 1 per cent—that is, by about ¾ of one percentage point. If, on the other hand, the price level should fall by 1 per cent, the share of wages in national income would rise by ¾ of 1 percentage point. That may not seem like much, but actually it is quite a lot, more than enough to provide all the flexibility that our economic system is likely to need.

In the twenty years since the end of the war, the proportion of "compensation of employees" to national income has moved about within a narrow range, say from 65 per cent to 71 per cent. There is no reason to suppose that market forces will always want to keep the figure within those bounds, but there is every reason to believe that market forces will never, or hardly ever, want to move the proportional distribution of income very rapidly. As the numerical example shows, if wages adhered to the guidelines, the distribution of income could get from one end of its postwar range to the other in about eight years, with an annual rate of inflation or deflation never exceeding 1 per cent.

There is no practical question, then, of freezing the distribution of income. The normal amount of play in any such policy gives all the room needed for the market to operate. It would be possible to provide formally for more flexibility if that were needed. If the wages guideposts were expressed in terms of a fairly narrow range, say from 3.0 to 3.5 per cent per year, this would serve two purposes. For one thing, it would more nearly express the uncertainty in any estimate of the trend increase in productivity. And secondly, it would permit the outcome to be nearer the bottom or the top of the range, depending on "market forces." Even a steady price level would then permit some drift in the distribution of income.

Even apart from this question of distribution, one hears it said that the guideposts are a dangerous interference in the free market, even a form of price control. At least this criticism is inconsistent with the other one that claims the guideposts to be ineffective. With some ingenuity, one could probably cook up a set of assumptions under which the guideposts had no effect on wage-price behavior, yet managed to do harm to the market economy. But this seems farfetched to me. If they are a real interference with the market, they must be partially effective.

I would contend that it is also farfetched to describe the wage-price guideposts as anything remotely like a system of wage and price controls. But in any case I am not concerned with the way the guideposts have been used by this President or that President, but with the way they were intended. They were intended, as I mentioned earlier, as a device for the education and mobilization of public opinion. The January 1962 Economic Report said:

> Individual wage and price decisions assume national importance when they involve large numbers of workers and large amounts of output directly, or when they are regarded by large segments of the economy as setting a pattern. Because such decisions affect the progress of the whole economy, there is legitimate reason for public interest in their content and consequences. An informed public, aware of the significance of major wage bargains and price decisions, and equipped to judge for itself their compatibility with the national interest, can help to create an atmosphere in which the parties to such decisions will exercise their powers responsibly. . . . The guideposts suggested here as aids to public understanding are not concerned primarily with the relation of employers and employees to each other, but rather with their joint relation to the rest of the economy. (Pp. 185–86.)

It is no doubt inevitable that an activist President will want to help public opinion along. But that is still a far cry from wage and price control.

Moreover, by both intent and necessity, the guideposts can influence only those wage and price decisions in which the parties have a certain amount of discretion. Atomistic textbook competitors, having no discretion, will not be much influenced by either public opinion or the White House. But where there is enough market power, and hence enough discretion, for the guideposts to be a force, there is little or no reason to believe that the "free market" outcome will be in the public interest. The usual presumption against public interference in the market process does not hold. This conclusion does not depend on any very exact evaluation of the amount of competition to which the steel industry, or the aluminum industry, or the tobacco industry, or the United Automobile Workers, or the building trades unions are subject. It is enough that none of them is, and none of them thinks it is, selling against a nearly infinitely elastic demand curve.

Naturally, the fact that a concentrated industry and a strong union may make decisions not in the public interest does not automatically mean that what the guideposts suggest will be better. That question needs to be decided on its merits. Yet, the guideposts are intended to give a summary description of a well-functioning market economy; within limits they can be expected to represent the public interest fairly well. But it is much more important to realize that the public interest does need representation.

It is worth remembering, in this connection, that the guideposts are intended to have an effect on the general level of money wages and prices, not on relative wages and relative prices. Most of the things we expect free markets to accomplish are "real" things, more or less independent of the price level. Ideally, the guideposts should permit markets to allocate resources freely, insuring only that the price level not drift up in the process. The January 1962 Economic Report said: "It is desirable that labor and management should bargain explicitly about the distribution of the income of particular firms or industries. It is, however, undesirable that they should bargain implicitly about general price level." (P. 188.) In practice, one must admit, the guideposts will operate unevenly; relative prices and resource allocation may thus be affected. One can hope that these effects are second-order.

UNEVENNESS AND INEQUITY

This inevitable unevenness in operation strikes me as the main weakness in the guideposts. Public opinion is bound to have its greatest impact on markets that are centralized and conspicuous. That may not be all bad; centralization and discretionary power over prices and wages may be correlated. But there are obvious instances in which the correlation is broken, in which considerable market power in local markets goes along with decentralization and near-immunity to pressure from public opinion. The construction industry and the building trades unions are the standard illustration; parts of trade and transportation may provide other examples.

This weakness must simply be admitted. It is dangerous not only because it invites inefficient relative price effects, but because policy that tries to mobilize public opinion on behalf of the public interest will inevitably find its foundations sapped by obvious inequity.

There is probably no general solution to the problem. There may, however, be ad hoc solutions in special cases. If, as may well be the case, the Davis-Bacon Act is one of those legally enforced restrictions on competition whose main effect is to allow one segment of the labor market to exploit the others—and to hamper full-employment policy in the bargain—then repeal may well be in order.

Another possible solution to the problem of uneven impact might be to formalize the guideposts into some sort of advance-notice and/or public hearing procedure, perhaps through a committee of Congress. I am opposed to this sort of development. It would be a move away from the original conception of the guideposts as an educational device, in the direction of a system of semiformal price controls. It is unlikely that Congress would favor that much of a break with the past; if we are to espouse unlikely legislation, I would rather favor the promotion of competition and the reduction of tariff protection.

There is a different respect in which the involvement of Congress might be a good idea. Up to now, the burden of informing and mobilizing public opinion has fallen to the President and to the Chairman of the Council of Economic Advisers. This seems to be a mistake. The prestige of the President is probably too important a commodity to be spent in a way that invites occasional rebuff. And the prestige of the Council of Economic Advisers, taken by itself, is probably insufficient to carry the load. It might be helpful, therefore, if individual senators and congressmen would take part in the public debate, in their capacity as leaders and formers of public opinion. Even hearings are a possibility, provided they are hearings devoted to ordinary pieces of legislation—past or future— or to expert testimony and not to individual wage bargains or price decisions.

How Should the Guidepost Figure Be Set?

In principle, the guidepost figure for wages is supposed to be the trend-increase in productivity for the economy as a whole. This is a difficult thing to measure; indeed, the concept is not entirely free of ambiguity. For example, one clearly wants a figure free of the effects of short-term changes in capacity utilization in industry, because otherwise the result would be to transfer the risks of enterprise from profits to wages, and that is not the intent. This suggests using a long-run trend figure. On the other hand, it seems faintly ridiculous that the permissible wage increase today should be made to depend on what was happening to productivity a few decades ago. Actually, this particular problem is primarily a matter of measurement, not of ambiguity in principle. A group of technicians could probably come to reasonable agreement. The difficulty is, however, that this number produced by technicians needs to be believed and used by the public and others.

Consider the unedifying spectacle of earlier this year. Should the administration continue to promulgate last year's guidepost figure of 3.2 per cent per year, or should it continue to use the method by which last year's figure was calculated, which would yield 3.6 per cent for this year? The decision to stay with 3.2 per cent was clearly the right one in substance; nobody with any sense believes that the steady-state rate of increase of output per man-hour in the private economy is now 3.6 per cent annually. The whole difficulty was created by the explicit adoption of a five-year moving average as the "official" method for calculating the trend-increase in productivity. This is clearly not a technician's method; a technician would make a more explicit statistical decomposition into cyclical and secular productivity change. The five-year moving average was clearly a compromise expedient—a method anyone could understand, which happened to give the same numerical answer as the technicians' methods.

I am inclined to think that the technicians' methods should prevail. I realize that there are grave difficulties with this view. In the first place, the parties to collective bargaining are likely to resent being presented with a figure they had no part in setting. That is understandable. The trouble is that the parties' mutual relationship is naturally a bargaining one; presented with an opportunity to set or influence the guidepost figure, they will naturally bargain over it. But that would destroy any claim that the guidepost figure might have to be an objectively determined number. In the second place, I gather that some members of Congress would like to take a hand in guidepost-setting. Again, one can understand why. But in principle the guidepost figure is not something one sets, it is something that one finds out. Congress can investigate, of course, but it is far from clear that its methods are ideal for investigating the subtler properties of economic time series. I can imagine that every so often Congress might like to hear expert testimony on how the exercise is being carried out; that would be salutary. But that would be different from an airing of predictable majority, minority, and interested-party views.

There is another sort of problem which is not open to technical solution and on which exchanges of opinion might be useful. It was easy to begin talking about wage-price guideposts in 1962 because the immediate history was one of approximate price stability. But suppose prices have been rising, and suppose that it is very unlikely that they can be made to level out in one year. Then it is difficult for labor to acquiesce in a figure for money wage increases which would give the right real-wage increase only if prices were constant.

That would be to acquiesce to a subnormal increase in real wages and a supernormal increase in profits. On the other hand, to add the current rate of price increase to the rate of productivity increase would be to throw the entire burden onto profits or, more likely, guarantee that prices will continue to rise. What is needed is some target pace for slowing down the price trend over a couple of years. One can imagine rational discussion of such a problem in a small country with centralized and enlightened trade union and employer association leadership. (Even then I'm not sure one can imagine anything actually being accomplished on so difficult a matter.) It is less easy to imagine such discussion in the United States.

CONCLUSION

I have tried to convey the impression that wage-price guideposts are not an ideal or complete policy for the control of inflation. They may, however, under appropriate circumstances, offer a little help at even less cost. Alternatives sometimes proposed may be very costly or very unrealistic. Let me quote an English author, Henry Smith (*Lloyd's Bank Review,* January, 1966, p. 40):

> If the ideal answer is to allow the pricing system all the freedom that is possible, while creating an atmosphere which induces the maximum restraint on the use of strategic power capable of pushing up money wages and increasing prices, and this is probably the ideal solution, then out of the debate great good may come. If we go through the motions of working out what is called an incomes policy, although we cannot in reality put it into practice, then everybody on a position of strategic authority may think twice before using it. This may not seem to be a great deal. However, the agreed objectives of British economic policy — rising productivity, expanding exports, economy in the use of manpower, high employment— all depend for their success upon the containment of the inflationary forces which their pursuit may generate.

MILTON FRIEDMAN

Comments

Obviously, the title of my comments now must be "The Case against 'The Case against the Case against the Guideposts.'" And, of course, when Bob [Solow] replies, he will resort to exponents instead of to spelling out all the words.

I am delighted to join Bob on some of his suggestions and to find such a large measure of overlap with my own views.

In particular, I would like to commend him for suggesting that the Davis-Bacon Act be repealed, although I would urge that he extend his views to include as well the Walsh-Healy Act and minimum wage laws—all of which have the effect of producing unemployment. These are governmental actions whose *result*—not necessarily their *intention*—is to increase unemployment. It certainly would promote a more efficient use of our resources to eliminate them. The same is true of his comments on lower tariffs in international trade and greater competition at home. All are desirable and would promote the efficiency of the economy.

But, in my opinion, none of these items has very much to do with our present problem—the problem of *inflation*. They have to do with the average level of unemployment that is, in a sense, structural or normal or natural in a well-adjusted economic system. All of these measures would reduce that average level of unemployment and would make output higher, but none of them has very much to do with the problem of inflation, which is what the guideposts are supposedly concerned with.

I agree further with a point that is implicit in much of Bob's paper: that the analysis in the 1962 Report of the Council was extremely sophisticated—an analysis that, if rumor has it right, he was not unacquainted or unassociated with. It was in the main a correct analysis of the way competitive markets work and would serve as an admirable part of a text on the operation of labor markets.

But I do not believe one can defend the guideposts by defending that section. It was an exercise that was bound to have further consequences. If one is going to defend the guideposts of the 1962 Report, one must look not at the intentions of the author but at what consequences could be expected to flow from the approach outlined.

Those consequences have since then been spelled out very clearly. The relevant and appropriate qualifications in the 1962 statement have disappeared. The elements of flexibility and adaptability have gone beneath the surface. There has remained and has appeared above the surface a single *number* as a guide to the appropriate wage change, and a rigid notion that, except in really extraordinary cases, it is possible for somebody to consult some mystical set of figures about productivity and always come out with the finding that the correct number is 3.2.

Such consequences were to be expected. They were not an accident. It was to be expected that, if one is going to proceed with a policy which will tolerate the intervention of governmental officials in the setting of wages or in the setting of prices, then this must lead to relatively simple formulas combined with much give-and-take, not on the basis of academic economic considerations, but in response to political pressures.

I believe that we must go beyond the 1962 statement and look at the whole series of statements and at the present status of the guideposts. In doing so, let me try to analyze the logic that underlies the guideposts and that is expressed in Bob's paper, because I believe that logic is basically wrong.

What is wrong with the guideposts is not so much that there is no way of calculating what is the correct rise in productivity and not so much that they involve governmental intervention in the wage and price system, as that *they really have nothing to do with inflation*. They *cannot in any way,* in my opinion, have a significant effect under current or foreseeable conditions on the rate of price rise correctly measured.

I want to go to the logic underlying the guideposts. This logic is that there is market power lying around, and that, when times are reasonably good, market power is likely to be exercised in ways that contribute to premature inflation. One thing that always impresses me about this argument is how briefly it is alluded to *when* it is alluded to—at all. In paper after paper in the discussion of guideposts and cost-push inflation, or of market power as a source of inflation, you discover that there is but a sentence or two, and then the author goes on to other things. The reason for that is very clear—the logic of the analysis is wrong. Insofar as market power has anything to do with possible inflation, what is important is not the *level* of market power, but whether market power is *growing* or not. If there is an existing state of monopolies all over the lot, but the degree of monopoly has not been increasing, this monopoly power *will not* and *cannot be* a source of pressure for inflation. The argument made by those who assert it can be is that in the sector with market power, people with monopoly power will "naturally" push prices up, and these will rise while in the competitive sector prices are rigid, hence prices will not go down. The net effect, therefore, is said to be a general rise in prices.

But then you face the uncomfortable question: Why did these foolish monopolies charge such a low price before? Why were they so restrained? Why is it that in the past they haven't exploited their market power? Does anybody really believe that the carpenters and plumbers and all of the other long-standing unions have not all the time been getting the maximum—the maximum real income and real wage rate that they thought it was worth their while to get?

Historically, there is one case in American experience—outlined in my paper—which corresponds to the correct theoretical analysis of market power and of cost-push inflation.

From 1933 to 1938, there was a very rapid increase in the degree of market power: first, because of NRA and, second, because of what was happening on the labor front when you had the Wagner Act and other factors that produced growth in union power. In those circumstances, there was *growing* market power, *growing* monopoly, and therefore this sector did push their wages and their prices up relative to wages and prices in the rest of the economy. I believe that is one of the reasons why, in the period from 1933 to 1937, although national income went up very rapidly,

a large part of it was absorbed by rising prices—despite the very
high volume of unemployment. You had high unemployment all
along, yet prices rose. And this was because of a growing market
power. But today, there is no sign of any widespread growth in
market power. Monopolies are not on the increase. The degree of
union power is not increasing. In any event, the argument presented in Bob's paper is that market power alone—regardless of
whether it is growing—is a source of upward pressure on prices.
This seems to me almost entirely false. √

Another defect in the logic underlying the guideposts is the *confusion of part of the economy with the whole economy*. Let's suppose that the analysis were to some extent correct. Would it follow
that holding down wages or prices in one area did in fact reduce
inflationary pressures throughout the economy? That depends on
not looking at where the excess purchasing power that was available to hire the labor or buy the goods will go when it is diverted.

A third and, in my opinion, the most serious logical fallacy
underlying the analysis of cost-push inflation in the guideposts is
the *confusion of nominal magnitudes with real magnitudes*—of
dollars with real quantities or what a dollar will buy. This fallacy
is very deep and effects a great many current views. The basic fallacy is to suppose that there is a trade-off between inflation and
employment; that is, to suppose that by inflating more over any
long period of time, you can have on the average a lower level of
unemployment. This is the notion underlying the desire to maintain
a great deal of pressure on aggregate demand and, when you want
to avoid the symptoms of inflation, to try to suppress them by
guideposts, guidelines, and the like.

As in all such fallacies, there is an element of validity in it. The
correct argument is rather sophisticated, and that's why the simple
argument tends to be accepted. To suggest to you briefly why I
say this is a fallacy, I ask you to consider the experience of some
countries that have gone much further along this line than we have.
The most dramatic example I know of is Brazil which, two or three
years ago when the present government came into power, was
having price inflation at the rate of about 90 per cent a year.
Through "tight" monetary policies, they cut the rate of inflation
down to about 45 per cent a year—still, you would think, a fairly
healthy inflation. Unemployment rose to 15 per cent, at least for

a time. Now, by Bob's logic, you would say that this is a trade-off between inflation and unemployment, that the Phillips curve in Brazil is such that in order to maintain an acceptable level of unemployment, you have to have price inflation of 90 per cent a year. I think almost everybody would agree that that is an absurd statement. And so it is. What is true is that you have a trade-off between unemployment *today* and unemployment *tomorrow,* between unemployment now and unemployment later on.

Go back to the Brazilian case. They could have maintained unemployment low by going from 90 per cent to 100 per cent to 125 per cent to 150 per cent inflation. After a time, they would have gotten to a point where even acceleration of inflation would not keep unemployment low. When they cut it down to 45 per cent, they of course got temporary unemployment. If they cut it down to zero, they will get temporary unemployment. But if they then hold it at zero, employment will again increase as people get adjusted and adapted to it. As inflationary expectations are broken, you will come back to a higher level of employment.

It's the same way in the United States. By speeding up the rate of monetary expansion and aggregate demand, you can unquestionably increase output and employment temporarily. You *can* cut the level of unemployment down, but at what price? At the price of postponing the adjustment. What happens is that, as people get adapted to any given rate of price rise, as they come to anticipate a continuation of the price rise, the unemployment rate will creep up. Say you cut unemployment down to 3 per cent. Then, at the same rate of price rise, it will creep up. If you then try to hold it down by stepping up the rate of inflation from 3 per cent to 4 per cent or 5 per cent, you will again be able to cut down unemployment, but, again, only temporarily—only until people adjust their anticipations.

I grant you immediately that "temporary" may be a fairly long period, and I understand very well the political temptations to an administration that is in power for a fairly short period to try to postpone the evil day to a later date. That explains, in my opinion, why, worldwide, governments have over and over again had a tendency to go down this line. It is so tempting. But, from a logical point of view, the true trade-off is between unemployment today and unemployment at a later date. It is not between unemployment and inflation. There is no long-run, stable trade-off between inflation and unemployment.

Hence, the alleged case for the guidelines seems to me to rest on two basic fallacies: first, that market power is a source of rising prices, and second—on the belief that somehow or other you can fool the people all the time—that by increasing the rate of monetary expansion, you can thereby induce people to maintain a permananently lower level of unemployment.

In a way, these points need to be linked a little bit more closely to Bob Solow's argument, because it may not be clear to you that they really underly it. But his argument that there is a very narrow range within which it is possible to increase employment, while holding down inflation, will be seen to rest basically on these two propositions: on the first because, in his opinion, the danger of price rise exists only in these sectors where there is strong market power; on the second because he wants to cut out these price rises in order to be able to maintain a higher level of aggregate demand than would otherwise be consistent with price stability.

I might summarize this final analysis by putting it in terms which I think are appropriate and which to some of you will be very reminiscent of Wicksell's argument in another direction. In my opinion, there is what might be termed a "natural" level of unemployment in any society you can think of. This level of unemployment is the level at which there is no tendency for *real* wages to behave in a way different from that described in the 1962 Report.

The 1962 Report—if we go through it and analyze it in terms of real wages and not absolute wages—describes the circumstances under which unemployment would be at its "natural" level.

Let's suppose that this "natural" level is 4 per cent, just to use a number which comes from good sources. Measures such as the kind that Bob suggested—like repealing the Davis-Bacon Act, the Walsh-Healy Act, and minimum wages, lowering tariffs, and getting greater competition at home—would reduce the natural level of unemployment to something less than 4 per cent, say, to 3 per cent or to 2½ per cent. But for any given labor market structure, there is some natural level of unemployment at which *real* wages would have a tendency to behave in accordance with productivity. If you try, through monetary measures, to keep unemployment below this natural level, you are committed to a path of perpetual inflation at an ever-increasing rate. There is no other way in which you can keep unemployment indefinitely below this natural level. If, by contrast, you were to take as an objective of employment policy a level of unemployment higher than the natural level, you could achieve it, but only by perpetual deflation. Finally, there is an infinitely large number of monetary policies and price behavior which will keep unemployment at its natural level —once people's anticipations are adjusted to that pattern of price behavior.

ROBERT SOLOW

Comments

Milton and I seem to be talking about wholly different things; certainly, we are talking about them in a wholly different manner. My own attitude to the guideposts is not diametrically opposed to his: when I showed what I had written to my wife, she muttered something to the effect that if those guideposts have you for a friend, they have no need for an enemy.

I do tend to be a lot more tentative about most things than Milton. I think that part of the difference between our papers and our views is a matter of temperament. I have to admit that Milton reminds me a little of what Lord Melbourne is supposed to have said about Macaulay; namely, "I wish I was as cocksure about anything as Macaulay is about everything."

When you get right down to it, I have been trying to talk about the difference between a situation in which the wholesale price index is steady and a situation in which the wholesale price index is rising at 2 per cent or 3 per cent a year. I have been asking how much extra pressure on the price level it would generate if you tried to absorb another half million unemployed people. And Milton, on the other hand, is talking about Emperor Diocletian who evidently had a lot of trouble with the United Amber Workers, or UAW as they called it then, about the German and the Bolshevik and the Brazilian inflation, and about how the moral fiber of the nation is being ruined by guidelines. It really is not clear to me why extreme instances like this, or in what way extreme instances like this, are at all relevant to the problem that economic policy faces right now or has faced in the last couple of years.

It is true, I suppose, that Milton may reply that this is after all only the beginning, and great oaks from little acorns grow. Well, as anyone knows who has ever watched a great oak grow from a little acorn, it is not a whoosh! It takes a little while. I do think that our discussion ought to be confined to the rather small and marginal issues that economic policy is really about and has to be about.

Another difference between Milton and myself is that everything reminds Milton of the money supply. Well, everything reminds me of sex, but I keep it out of the paper.

I also think—and Milton has essentially conceded or almost conceded this point—that the question about the monetary character of inflation is irrelevant to the policy issue that we ought to be concerned with. Let's not worry about how it is done, about what in fact does control the level of demand, real and monetary, in the economy. Just imagine that there are two buttons in Gardner Ackley's office, one labeled "expand" and one labeled "contract." And let us suppose, which is equally unlikely, that Gardner sits there at the console of the mighty Wurlitzer and can play on these buttons. If you push the contract button, whether that means to reduce the money supply or make it grow at a very slow rate—it doesn't matter what goes on *inside* the machinery—you can have a situation in which money wages are falling or rising very slowly and prices are falling or rising very slowly.

If you push the button marked "expand" and push it hard enough, you will wind up with a situation in which prices are rising and money wages are rising and perhaps rising too fast. After you achieve a situation in which the money wage level and the price level are behaving the way you would like them to behave, you then take a look at the real part of the economy. And just suppose that, in order to get acceptable price and wage behavior, you find you must achieve a situation on the real side where unemployment is too high and output is too low and excess capacity is too high. In other words, in Milton's own phrase, the normal level of unemployment in the economy in this sense is too high for comfort, and the normal degree of excess capacity in the economy is too big for comfort. The question is: What do you do then? And that does seem to me to be the heart of the issue, and on this I do agree with Milton.

I also agree, as he pointed out, that there are a lot of long-run things that you can do. You can do many things to increase the degree of mobility and flexibility and competition in the economy. You can try to expose prices and wages to competition by allowing free entry into occupations and industries and by taking advantage of competition from abroad. You can do all sorts of things. But it may be that exhortation or education or even arm-twisting (I am more hot, as you will have gathered from the paper, for education than I am for arm-twisting) can also help to reduce, at least temporarily, the normal level of unemployment in the economy. And that, it seems to me, is what the policy is about.

I want to make this very clear. I am not resting my case on a theory of cost-push inflation. That's an issue by itself and one on which I have, as on most things, a little more uncertainty than Milton. The case it seems to me rests only on the *degree of tightness in the economy at which the price level begins to rise unacceptably rapidly.*

I also want to make another point clear. I don't think I'm guilty of the fallacy of which Milton charges me—of believing that inflation generates employment. I'm not arguing that. I'm arguing that demand pressure, whether it is generated by monetary or other means, generates both inflation and employment. And that is what creates the dilemma that this rather uneven, irregular, uncertain line of policy is trying to meet.

I take it as a fact that empirical inference is very difficult in these matters and not nearly so easy as Milton suggests. If we are talking sensibly, we're talking about small causes and small effects. We're talking about an extra half a point on the unemployment index and an extra 1 per cent or 2 per cent rate of inflation. I don't really think that you can answer those empirical questions by appealing to what happened at the time of the Bolshevik Revolution or by appealing to what Milton chooses to call a controlled experiment; namely, the difference between Germany after the First World War and Germany after the Second World War. (There were surely other differences between those periods, besides the fact that at one time the inflation was open and at the other time repressed. The degree of physical devastation is one.)

It is important to realize that, to judge the success of a policy, it is not sufficient to compare what actually happens with some ideal or target state of affairs. What you have to do is compare what actually happens with what would have happened had policy been different. And that is necessarily a difficult and conjectural matter about which reasonable men will disagree—again, because we're talking about small causes and small effects.

I think, in the most tentative sort of way, that there is some evidence that wages and prices have increased less in the last three years than previous history would have suggested to a reasonable man. I also think that there is some evidence of the existence of a band of economic conditions—and by economic conditions, I mean simply the relation between the pressure of aggregate demand and the capacity of the economy to produce goods and services—within which money wages and prices tend to rise.

Money and wage price movements may be fairly strong without the economy being tight. I have no way of knowing for sure whether wages and prices have risen more slowly in the last three years than a reasonable man might have been led by earlier but recent history to expect. And even if that is true, I have no way of knowing for sure whether the guidelines or guideposts policy has anything to do with it. But I think there is some evidence that it is so, and I take it as an open question as to whether the guideposts are in fact to get some credit.

There is, as Milton said, a good deal of agreement between us. For instance, I think we both agree that when there is genuine and widespread excess demand in the economy as a whole, guidelines are almost certain to be ineffective and, if they were effective, they might in fact not have entirely desirable effects.

Milton and I both agree, I think, that if we're talking about a mild inflation, it may well be both easier and better to have it open rather than repressed, provided—I would say, although Milton didn't say—that the weak, who can't protect their pensions and their savings against inflation, are in some way protected and provided for. Milton did say that the international financial policies that the country is pursuing must be capable of withstanding that degree of inflation.

I would like to mention a question that Milton didn't discuss, either in his comments or his paper—because he considers the issue settled long before one gets to that point. It is a question that was raised in John Dunlop's paper and in some of the discussion yesterday; namely, whether, if we are to have this sort of policy, the wage guideline ought to be set by some sort of tripartite, formal procedure, or whether in fact it ought to be laid down unilaterally by the Council of Economic Advisers, or by some agency of the government.

It's perfectly understandable to me that people who are exposed to such pressure—whether from public opinion or from the White House or from any place else—should feel resentful or uncomfortable about the fact that they have had no part in the formulation of this policy. I recognize that and I'm sympathetic with that view.

I have to admit that I don't have a lot of experience myself with tripartite proceedings. When I say I don't have a lot, what I mean is, I have none. So I am not the best person to judge the utility of such devices. I have my doubts, however. Remember that in principle you are trying to answer a delicate question: What average rate of increase in wage rates, accompanied by a fiscal and monetary policy which will achieve full employment, is likely to be compatible with rough price stability? That's a hard question to answer, and neither I, nor Gardner I imagine, would be inclined to argue that the Council of Economic Advisers is capable of giving an accurate, sharp answer to that question. But it's not at all clear to me that a tripartite procedure is a feasible way of getting an answer to that question. After all, in principle it is an analytical matter, not a bargaining matter. So if we are going to have to live with wage and price guideposts for a while, as we may in fact do—right or wrong, good or bad—I do recognize that there is this conflict between what would be a socially desirable way of arriving at a statement of what they ought to be, and the fact that you're faced with trying to find the answer to a very subtle question of fact and analysis. Tripartite proceedings are not necessarily the best way to achieve that kind of knowledge.

GARDNER ACKLEY

The Contribution of Guidelines

GARDNER ACKLEY, a distinguished economist, is now chairman of the President's Council of Economic Advisers. In these remarks delivered from notes at the conference, he points up the arguments for using guidelines, describes the serious problems that gave rise to them, and calls on those who criticize to develop acceptable and superior alternatives.

This conference raises fundamental issues not only of theory and philosophy, but also issues of crucial importance to current economic policy. I certainly cannot agree with a great deal of what has been written for and said during this conference. But I do feel that it is important that the conference has been held. I believe that it has served and will serve a useful purpose in forcing not only you in private life but those of us in the government to think about the questions that have been raised. I appreciate particularly the very thoughtful papers of John Dunlop and Harry Johnson, however critical they may be of what we have been doing.

In the time I have, it will surely not be possible for me to treat all of the issues that have been raised in the papers and the discussion. I will try to suggest what I think some of the issues are and to deal with a few of them. I shall speak mainly about the wage-price guideposts; but, at least by implication, some of what I say may be applicable to other types of voluntary controls.

It is certainly impossible to deal with all of the basic issues of economic theory which underlie a good deal of the argument about wage-price guideposts. Without going into the doctrinal matters that are involved, I shall merely assert my complete disagreement with Mr. Friedman's proposition that in any operationally meaningful sense inflation is caused by an excessive increase in the quantity of money and by nothing else. But as Mr. Solow asserted this morning—I think correctly—this doctrinal matter is only of limited importance to this discussion. Let me state a narrower proposition that I believe that Friedman would not have too much trouble with: if total demand in the economy exceeds the ability of the economy to produce goods and services with reasonably full employment of the available resources, then inflation is inevitable. Under such circumstances of generally excess demand, guideposts can play no significant part in avoiding inflation. And if they were to be seriously relied on under these circumstances, it could indeed mainly be to shift the blame for inflation away from the government policies that permitted total demand to be excessive. Of course, the definition of productive capacity, by comparison with which total demand may be excessive, is itself a significant issue.

INFLATION RESULTING FROM EXCESSIVE INCOME CLAIMS

First, however, let me deal with a closely associated issue. I believe the evidence is inescapable that we can have inflation without what *I* would call excess demand, as the result of excessive income claims by labor or business or both. Of course, one can define this possibility out of existence. If one defines the total productive capacity of the economy as that degree of utilization which, if exceeded, leads to rising prices, then all inflation becomes excess demand inflation and the issue disappears.

I would assert, as a meaningful proposition, that inflation *can* occur short of full utilization as a result of excessive income claims. Friedman is willing to admit that private market power can raise particular income claims short of full employment, or even short of excess demand pressures in the particular sector where the power exists. But he dismisses this by saying that the result can only be to change income distribution. If total demand is not excessive, the general price level will not be affected because other prices and incomes will necessarily fall.

But suppose they do not. Or suppose that efforts to raise income shares occur simultaneously in a number of sectors. Even then,

Friedman says, there will be no inflation unless the quantity of money increases to validate the higher average price levels (or, as I would prefer to say, unless aggregate demand is sufficiently stimulated by expansionary monetary or fiscal policies.) And so Friedman can *say* that inflation is still only owing to government policies and not to private behavior. If the government did not take the inflationary action, there would be no inflation.

This seems to me to evade the real questions. Suppose the government does not validate the higher income claims by demand expansion. Will the inflation just go away? Or will the economy merely operate with higher prices but at a lower level of output and employment? Is there not a *real* dilemma for government policy? Can the government indefinitely tolerate a serious underutilization of productive capacity? Can it accept the social distress and disorder which arise from reduced incomes and excessive unemployment, particularly when the burden falls on the most defenseless members of society?

It seems to me that Friedman has to assume the existence of an adequate degree of downward flexibility of incomes and prices in large sectors of the economy, and the almost unlimited willingness of these sectors to accept a relative redistribution of income against them as a consequence of market power in other sectors. If this flexibility and willingness really existed, the logical consequence would be continuous full employment of all resources. But this assumption seems obviously contradicted by the facts of our experience.

Beginning about 1955, the American economy began to develop an increasing shortfall of employment and output. By the Council's measurements, the shortfall of output was at an annual rate in excess of $25 billion at the business cycle peak in 1960, and in excess of $50 billion in early 1961. This shortfall did not disappear until the end of 1965. Perhaps Mr. Friedman might wish to dismiss this as the consequence of excessive income claims during 1955–57—based perhaps on inflationary expectations—which were purposely and properly not ratified by sufficient government stimulus to demand. This might satisfy Mr. Friedman; but it does not satisfy me. And I don't think it would satisfy the American people.

By our calculation the total shortfall of output over the years 1958–63 exceeds $200 billion. The average unemployment rate

during that six-year period was 6 per cent; it was still 5.5 per cent
at the end of 1963. Over this six-year period the wholesale price
index was almost perfectly stable. The consumer price index was
rising an average rate of 1.4 per cent a year. I don't know whether
Friedman would find this degree of inflation tolerable or not. I
would. But I wonder whether any of us would dare to describe
the combined results of private behavior and government policy
over this period as ideal or even acceptable.

In any case, we did continue with a relatively easy monetary
policy which, together with a massive tax cut and continued growth
in federal outlays, brought the unemployment rate down to 4 per
cent at the beginning of 1966. And, as everyone expected, this
brought some further exposure to inflationary pressures. The effective market power of many trade unions and of managements in
many industries was sufficiently enhanced so that it became easier
to stake out income claims that, if generalized, were inconsistent
with a stable price level. In addition, there were scattered instances
of demand curves moving to the right faster than supply curves,
with markets clearing only at somewhat higher prices.

In short, we had moved further into the band in which inflationary pressures exist, even though the economy was still short of
what could reasonably be called full employment of resources.
Within this band, pressures toward inflation become more intense,
the higher the degree of utilization. It is within this band, not
beyond it, that the guideposts are intended to be effective.

It is, to me, a striking fact that average hourly earnings in manufacturing have increased in every single year since 1933. (Incidentally, this was not true prior to 1933.) The amount of the
annual increase in wages since 1933 is not uniform. Econometric
studies for the postwar period show that the increase depends on
such factors as the prior increase in the cost of living, on profits,
and on the extent of unemployment. Cross section studies, in which
the cost of living is not relevant, show a dependence on profits,
degree of unionization, or industrial concentration. But every
regression of wage rate changes on changes in the supposed causal
factors shows a large constant term—reflecting the tendency for
wages to increase every year, independently of anything else. This
tendency of wage rates to increase every year, no matter what, can
only have an institutional explanation, in the broadest sense of that

term. And the wage guidepost is intended to be an institutional counterforce to this institutional inflationary bias.

Similarly, on the side of prices, there may well be an institutional bias toward inflation. Friedman admits the existence of monopoly elements which enable producers to hold prices above a purely competitive equilibrium. He says, however, that this could only explain high prices and not rising prices, unless the degree of monopoly is increasing. I once repeated this particular bit of doctrine myself. But I am convinced that it is wrong, because it fails to take account of the interactions of prices and costs and the downward rigidities that surely exist and that explain why prices don't fall indefinitely in a period of slack.

Since Friedman asked for the theoretical underpinnings of this idea, I will give it. My model of price-making can be sketched somewhat as follows. A plausible theory of oligopolistic-pricing behavior suggests that the margin over costs that producers in strategic industries can attempt to earn varies with the strength of demand in their markets. Although their ideal monopoly price may be no higher, their ability to realize it will strengthen as excess capacity is reduced. Thus as the economy expands, producers in these industries attempt to raise their margins over cost by lifting their prices. In the absence of effective downward flexibility in other prices and in wage rates, the average level of prices is thereby raised. But the higher prices in turn affect the general level of costs, both through increases in the cost of purchased materials and through the impact of the cost of living on the cost of labor. Prices will consequently be raised again in these industries, and in others, in an effort to restore the desired and competitively feasible margin, even without any further increase in the overall degree of utilization in the economy, and without any increase in industrial concentration. And then we can be off to the races.

In short, at high utilization, the income claims of labor and business can add up to more than 100 per cent of the total product, giving rise to a built-in inflationary spiral. Whether or not one calls income claims on the side of business an institutional factor, they are surely amenable to an institutional counterforce, which the price guidepost is intended to supply.

I had intended at this point to deal with the question whether, in the current situation, aggregate demand in fact now exceeds our ability to produce without excessive strain, or threatens to do so in the near-term future. In view of the limitations of time, and because I have expressed myself on this question elsewhere, I will omit this. I will only summarize what I would have said by asserting my view that the economy is now still within the area for which guideposts can be reasonably expected to apply. I will go on to deal instead with some of the questions that have been raised here. Can guideposts work? Have they worked? Are they inefficient or unfair?

Contribution of Guideposts to Price Stability

You will not hear from me any extravagant claims for the effectiveness of the guideposts. I think that they have made and can make a modest but significant contribution to price stability. They make this contribution not exclusively, I think, in the way many people assume. It is not so much, in my view, that workers and employers come up to a wage negotiation and say, "Let's see now, the government says the guidepost is 3.2 per cent. Perhaps we should settle for that figure because that's what the government says we should do." Nor, on the side of prices does the most important effect come when firms are making price decisions and some executive says, "Well, let's see now, productivity in our industry is advancing at 4.8 per cent a year. The government says we should therefore reduce prices. So I guess that's what we should do." Sometimes, of course, if it is a sufficiently important case, the government may be standing there, looking on, making noises about guideposts, remonstrating a bit. Or the parties may fear that there will be unpleasant remonstrances after the fact. But this direct effect relates to a fairly small number of important cases.

The larger influence of the guideposts is more indirect. For five years we have been hammering home some fairly simple arithmetic about the relations among wages, productivity, and costs; and between individual actions and overall results. Leaders of labor, I think, increasingly understand that wage increases in excess of productivity gains raise costs and therefore prices, and in the end do labor no good. And they know that what one powerful union gets away with influences what other unions try to achieve. As a result of this educational effort, the labor unions, at least in many cases, are bringing a different attitude to the bargaining table. And the public, too, has learned about this arithmetic, and a somewhat different public attitude surrounds the negotiations. *Suffice it to*

Business has learned some simple arithmetic, too. If overall prices are to be stable, all individual prices cannot rise. And if prices generally rise when costs are stable, costs will not remain stable and business will not gain in the end. Indeed, by forcing the government to adopt more restrictive policies, business may lose. Cooperation with the guideposts on the part of business is partly a matter of doing what's good for business generally, because in the long run it will be good for my business. But I think something more than that is involved. *gain in interim*

It seems clear to me that corporate presidents and executives are more than mere stewards of their stockholders. They clearly distribute part of the stockholders' profits to universities, hospitals, community chests, and other worthy causes. They accept responsibility for the welfare of the communities in which they are situated, they hire teenagers in the summer, they support symphony orchestras, they sometimes support the John Birch Society and sometimes the NAACP. Some economists may not approve it, and many at Chicago refuse to believe it, but the fact is that corporations accept a degree of social responsibility. What the guideposts and the guidelines attempt to do is harness this sense of social responsibility to the national interest in price stability or balance-of-payments equilibrium.

I have talked with many businessmen about their prices. I am surprised—I was almost going to say shocked—by the fact that never once has one of them said to me, "It is none of your business." Rather, without exception the answer has been, "I accept the objectives of your program. I recognize my responsibility." This does not mean that the businessman always, or even often, agrees with what I suggest. But I know of many instances in which prices have not been raised, or were raised less, or were raised on a smaller range of products. In a few instances, prices have acually been reduced.

Why do businessmen respond? I have suggested that it is from a sense of social responsibility, or a wish to participate in a national consensus. But is it also through coercion or fear of coercion? That question has been repeatedly raised here.

Let me say flatly that I know of no instance in which anyone has been deprived of property or opportunity as a result of violating the guideposts. Indeed, I know of no instance in which one has been deprived even of an invitation to a White House dinner! The allegation that I heard last night that antitrust prosecution or tax investigation may have been used as a method of persuasion is based, so far as I know, on the sole authority of an article in *The Wall Street Journal* which gave no names or cases. But if it is not threats, if it is not deprivation of property or of opportunity, then we are given to understand that it's the result of what has here been called "ear-twisting" (elsewhere referred to as ear-stroking or arm-twisting) or "thunderbolts" from on high.

Now, I have been trying to find out what people here mean by "ear-twisting." Is it, on the part of the President, being effective, persuasive, even passionate in private conversation? Is that really bad on the part of the President? Do we want an inarticulate, unpersuasive, incoherent spokesman for what he believes in? "Thunderbolts?" What thunderbolts? Last evening, Mr. Livingston quoted several statements by the President and by Walter Heller, all intended, apparently, to be amusing because of their milk-toast quality. The strongest statements that have been made on specific cases, I think, and that may have offended the sensibilities of some people were statements I have made—one or two of which, on reflection, slightly offended my own sensibilities. But the President's choice of language, in my view, has been untraditionally moderate for a political leader. I recall some of Theodore Roosevelt's vivid phrases; Franklin Roosevelt's "economic royalists"; or Harry Truman "giving them hell." I have heard no one who has here referred to "thunderbolts" quote any offensive statement that President Johnson has made about guidepost violators.

We have also heard here about the entering wedge thesis—that guideposts started as education but have progressively moved toward coercion and that the worst is still ahead. This thesis seems hardly supported by history. The worst confrontation on wage-price guideposts, marked by the least temperate· language, was in the 1962 steel case. Since then the dialogue has been improving, and it still is. I don't think anyone enjoyed the recent confrontations over steel or aluminum. The confrontations, the conversations, and the "reasoning together" are increasingly moving behind closed doors and toward polite friendly discussions. I am not absolutely sure that this is an improvement. I will admit it is considerably more pleasant.

There have been occasions when price increases have not seemed justified and when federal agencies, as buyers, have sought lower priced supplies. On other occasions, stockpiles have been released to keep prices from rising. These involve purchases and sales no different from those of private companies faced with price increases. If this is coercion, it is the coercion of the market place. If the federal government is in the market place—and it inevitably is—it seems to me that there is every reason for it to promote price stability by its market actions, rather than the contrary. Indeed, if the government did the opposite it would, I think, properly be subject to criticism.

Finally, the point has been made repeatedly that the guideposts are inequitable, because they are adhered to primarily by large firms or conspicuous industries. This burden of bigness is viewed as unjust and unfair. I agree that this is one of the more vulnerable aspects of the guideposts. It surely would be unjust if there were penalties attached to violation. Nevertheless, it seems obvious to me that it is more important that the guideposts be honored—to the extent that they may be—in strategic industries and in pattern-setting wage negotiations. As in other things, more is asked of those who have more to contribute. We invite all to be responsible. All have the same opportunity to respect the public interest. Because some may flout it is no reason why it is unfair to request that it be respected.

Let me turn very briefly to the argument about the effects of the guideposts on economic efficiency. In broad outline, the guideposts—including the exceptions—describe the price and wage behavior of a competitive economy in the long run. And—especially if one emphasizes the exceptions—they describe how it would tend to work even in the relatively short run. So far as labor markets are concerned, I doubt that a guidepost wage structure, even with no account for the exceptions, could be described as less efficient than the pattern of wage movements actually observed in modern labor markets. Indeed, I would argue the contrary.

So far as prices are concerned, the guideposts suggest that price trends should reflect divergent secular trends in costs, in just the way that a competitive economy would tend to do. I do not think that the price structure would be more efficient today if steel prices had been successfully raised in 1962, and had been raised in 1963, 1964, and 1965 by more than they were. But if they had been, I am convinced that not only steel prices but the whole price level would now be higher.

One might argue that the price structure would be more efficient today if copper prices were higher. But again, given long-run costs and availability of resources, it is quite possible that the greater short-run efficiency would have been purchased by a greater long-run inefficiency—as well as by a higher general price level. This conclusion gains support from the efforts of the producers themselves to stabilize prices rather than to clear the market or to maximize short-run profits.

ARE THERE ACCEPTABLE ALTERNATIVES?

In evaluating the guideposts, one has to recognize that they are very imperfect instruments, with many undesirable aspects. But a judgment about them must be made in terms of the available alternatives. I will not dignify the argument that open inflation is a superior alternative, because it is not an alternative to guideposts: It is an alternative to inappropriate monetary and fiscal policies. But would a higher degree of unemployment and underutilization be an acceptable alternative? Would a creeping price inflation be an acceptable alternative? This could create the same kind of expectations and speculative pressures and imbalances as arise from an excess demand inflation, and could thereby impair the chances of sustaining a balanced prosperity. Is breaking up monopolies or oligopolies a feasible alternative?

John Dunlop has suggested some alternatives or supplements to guideposts, many of which we are indeed trying to pursue. His suggestions are at least aimed at the same problem as are the guideposts. Some of the other suggestions—particularly from the lawyers—have been to make the guideposts more formal, more legal, more procedural. I wonder if we are really sure that is what we want. I think we ought to take a pretty hard look at it. I agree that due process is necessary before depriving people of property and civil rights. But I do not quite see the role of due process before a public official exercises his jaw in private persuasion or public dialogue, nor its role in assuring less offensive rhetoric. Among other things, Mr. Livingston suggested that participation by Congress might be appropriate in designing the guideposts. I wonder if this is really feasible. In the case of most economic legislation in these areas, Congress has not found it possible to set up detailed standards for administrative action. For example, the legislative standards provided in the Price Control Act of 1942 were, as I recall, that price ceilings should be "fair and equitable and effectuate the purposes of the Act." I do not at this moment see how the Congress could effectively participate in the establishment of specific guideposts.

Others want to submit guideposts to some form of collective bargaining. It may very well be that the Labor-Management Advisory Committee—or some other tripartite group—should participate in the setting or administration of guideposts. The Labor-Management Advisory Committee was active during the first three years of the existence of the guideposts. I do not believe that it made any constructive contribution, although some of us hoped that it would. In contrast with a specific bargaining situation, there were no clear economic or other pressures on the contending parties to arrive at a constructive policy solution. Unfortunately, at least up until now, both sides have been generally opposed to guideposts. The one thing on which they could agree is that we should not have them. I think that the tripartite discussion that has taken place here at this conference has tended toward that same consensus. If it were possible to achieve tripartite agreement by labor and management on guideposts or an effective substitute for them, I certainly would be completely in favor of it. If labor and management failed to agree—and indeed condemned such an approach, with no constructive alternative—I am not prepared to recommended that the government should necessarily relinquish its leadership.

In 1962 the Council of Economic Advisers proposed the present guideposts and laid them on the table for public discussion. In my view, no very effective or widespread public discussion has ensued; and such discussion as has occurred has not been particularly constructive. *This* conference was not held in 1962 or 1963; nor was there any other as far as I know. And I am not clear that the discussions here have advanced us very far toward even the faint outlines of a consensus on a constructive alternative. Nor did the conference on the same subject sponsored a few weeks ago by the American Bankers Association, nor the one a little earlier sponsored by the U.S. Chamber of Commerce. If consensus on guideposts or an alternative to them could be achieved—through tripartite discussions or otherwise—I think it would be a great and useful achievement. I certainly hope that something of this sort can emerge from the revival of the Labor-Management Advisory Committee.

In conclusion, it is my contention that the voluntary controls are aimed at *real* problems: the problems of the balance of payments and of an inflationary bias of the economy at full employment. These problems will not just go away. If we do not like the present voluntary controls, we need alternatives which are constructive and superior. All of us in the government will appreciate your participation in helping us to find them.

PART II

Experience with Guidelines

JOHN T. DUNLOP

Guideposts, Wages, and Collective Bargaining

JOHN T. DUNLOP is professor and chairman of the Department of Economics at Harvard University and is heavily involved in the labor relations of a wide range of industries, especially the construction industry. He recognizes the problems with which wage-price guideposts are designed to deal, argues that they are not working, and presents his own alternative solution to the problems.

The time has come to transform the national wage and price policies—as they are officially stated, as they are being administered, and as they are understood in newspaper and popular discussion. There are at least these three sets of guideposts, and they do not all point in the same direction.

The wage and price guideposts have ceased to be viable—economically or administratively. This state of affairs should come as no surprise since specific incomes policies have been short-lived in all advanced countries. A policy, including related administrative arrangements, appropriate to an economy starting from excess capacity and high unemployment is not likely to be ideally suited to sustained high level employment. We do not expect fiscal or international economic policies to be invariant, and there is no reason to expect wage and price policies—and their administration—to be more permanent.

It is my hope that this conference will make a contribution to the reformulation of wage and price policies appropriate to a period of sustained high employment. This is a relatively new problem confronting the country; it was not an insistent question when the guideposts were formulated. In my view, a wide range of structural adaptations in government policies, in collective bargaining, and in other private decisions are requisite to a greater degree of wage and price stability at sustained high level employment. Public discussion and governmental leadership should be devoted to achieving these changes rather than arguing about the guideposts.

This paper is divided into four sections. The first briefly appraises the contribution of the guideposts to economic policy in recent years. The second section states briefly and sharply the major defects of the policy. The third section sets forth some basic problems which every form of wage and price policy must resolve to remain viable in our society, and the final section proposes an alternative or transformed wage and price policy for high levels of utilization. Each section is organized to make a series of points.

I. Give Credit Where Credit Is Due

(1) The guideposts were developed as an integral part of an expansionist policy, to help move the economy toward its full employment potential. They were aimed at "segments of the economy where firms are large or employees well organized or both" and where "there is considerable room for the exercise of private power and a parallel need for the assumption of private responsibility." They were designed to prevent sectors with strong market power from dissipating expansionary measures into wage and price increases while the system as a whole operated with considerable slack. The analyses of Schultze[1] and Eckstein and Fromm[2] on the role of steel prices in the inflation of the late 1950's, and concern with the basic steel wage negotiations in 1962, underscored the

---

[1] Charles L. Schultze, "Recent Inflation in the United States," Study Paper No. 1, Joint Economic Committee, *Study of Employment, Growth and Price Levels* (Washington, D.C.: U.S. Government Printing Office, 1959).

[2] Otto Eckstein and Gary Fromm, "Steel and the Postwar Inflation," Study Papers No. 2 and No. 3, Joint Economic Committee, *Study of Employment, Growth and Price Levels* (Washington, D.C.: U.S. Government Printing Office, 1959).

need for a wage-price policy at the early stages of the new administration.

The guideposts were also formulated to mitigate the fears of conservative elements—in Congress, in the administration, and in the business community—who were not naturally attracted to the analysis of the new economics or its policy prescriptions. Later, the advocacy of a tax cut could point to the guideposts as evidence of a concern for the dangers of inflation. The unwarranted fears of inflation were a major deterrent to expansionist policies. As Mr. Slichter said to a bankers' association in the spring of 1959: "The greatest harm and waste caused by inflation and the fear of inflation is that they have made both government and industry afraid of expansionist policies and have deprived the country of billions of dollars of production and millions of man years of employment which the country could have had if it had not made a fetish of a stable price level."[3] The guideposts were designed to mute some of the opposition to expansionist policies.

(2) The guideposts have probably played a role, on the price side anyway, in mitigating the psychological and speculative elements of inflationary pressures in recent years. Prices are influenced by anticipations and expectations of future prices. A rise in uncertainty over the prospects of holding current prices and an increase in the probabilities of price increases may be an independent factor influencing current price stability. The guideposts as popularly conceived, backed by a few cases of dramatic confrontation between the White House and industry, have probably exerted a measure of constraint on these factors influencing prices. The anticipations of inflation, expectations and uncertainty in price making, have been mitigated to a degree, and stability has thereby been enhanced. The guideposts have also helped to educate the community that every rise in wage rates does not provide a justifiable basis for increasing prices by the same percentage or amount. In enterprises that have a measure of control over price, and where price decisions are prominent and publicly exposed, it appears that a degree of additional caution and care, and increased subtlety, has been introduced by the guideposts. My impression is that the

[3] *Potentials of the American Economy, Selected Essays of Sumner H Slichter* (Cambridge, Mass.: Harvard University Press, 1961), p. 149.

guideposts to date probably have constricted price increases to a small degree.

On the wage side, it is my considered judgment that the guideposts probably have had no independent restraining influence on wage changes in private industry. They have been used to insist upon smaller increases for federal government employees than might otherwise have been enacted by Congress; but even here the independent effect of the guideposts is unclear. I know of no person actually involved in wage setting on the side of industry, labor organizations, or as a government or private mediator or arbitrator who thinks that the guideposts have had on balance a constrictive influence; and I have discussed the issue in detail with scores of such persons in the past six months.[4] There have been no confrontations on wages as on prices.[5] The evidence from statistical studies of the Phillips curve, relating wage changes and unemployment, appears to me inclusive both to what has happened and the reasons for any possible change.

(3) The guideposts were adopted in part out of concern with the balance of payments. While international competition has been a factor in particular sectors affecting price and wage making in the United States from colonial times, the guideposts helped to emphasize the interdependence of the economy of the United States with those of other advanced countries. The guideposts helped to popularize the balance of payments factor in the consciousness of many groups and organizations for the first time. The Trade Expansion Act was being discussed at about the same time. Regardless of any constraint the guideposts may have had on wages and prices, these developments required for many some attention to policy changes that might be necessary because wages and prices in the United States are not set in a closed economy. It is a little strange that the balance-of-payments problem has been so little discussed in conjunction with the guideposts in recent years.

(4) The guideposts were in part initiated as economic discus-

---

[4] At the conference meetings two participants with experience in negotiations volunteered that they thought the wage guideposts had had on balance a slightly constrictive influence, but they cited no specific cases.

[5] I do not exclude the basic steel settlement. The *Newark Operating Engineers* case is a sport.

sion and education in the community. The 1962 Economic Report of the President stated: "How is the public to judge whether a particular wage-price decision is in the national interest? No simple test exists, and it is not possible to set out systematically all of the many considerations which bear on such a judgment. However, since the question is of prime importance to the strength and progress of the American economy, it deserves widespread public discussion and clarification of the issues. What follows is intended as a contribution to such a discussion." This report proposed no "rule" but a "guide"; the guideposts did not "contribute a mechanical formula for determining whether a particular price or wage decision is inflationary"; they were "general guideposts" to which "specific modifications must be made to adapt them to the circumstances of particular industries." While the guideposts have become a rigid 3.2 formula since 1962, in the views of many newspapers, they started out in part as a contribution to a public dialogue on economic policy. There were many earlier advocates of such an annual discussion of the economic setting and criteria for wage and price decisions.[6]

II. THE BRICKBATS

(1) It is strange that the same policy makers who were so successful in selling the country a major change in fiscal policy should be so unsuccessful in securing assent to its guideposts. As I size up the situation, as they relate to wages the guideposts enjoy the active opposition of organized labor, of most business spokesmen, except as they may be advocated to constrict wages, of mediators or arbitrators whether public or private; and they enjoy little respect among industrial relations specialists in universities. It may be said that such a state of affairs should not be surprising since the Council of Economic Advisers is representing public interest against special interests. But in our society, the guideposts must command widespread respect and assent among decision makers—which they do not—to be viable.

The government economic policy makers did not devote much

---

[6] John T. Dunlop, "Policy Problems: Choices and Proposals" in *Wages, Prices, Profits and Productivity,* edited by C. A. Myers (New York: American Assembly, 1959), pp. 137–60.

time or energy to sell the guideposts policies. They were understandably preoccupied with fiscal policies which warranted top priority. The guideposts were generally less urgent with underutilized resources and stable prices. The Council was better equipped and staffed to deal with macro-economic issues than with wage and price decisions in a wide variety of particular sectors. Decision makers on fiscal policy are more prominent and concentrated than those who make wage and price decisions in sectors with substantial market power. When the guidepost policies came to be most needed in 1965 and 1966, they could not be counted an effective policy tool. The superb performance of securing support for the fiscal policy has not been matched in efforts or results in the wage-price area.

(2) The wage and price guideposts are not expressed in criteria that are meaningful to private decision makers. The "trend rate of overall productivity increase" and the relative rate of an industry's increase in productivity compared to the average are scarcely standards which are meaningful to decision makers on wages and prices. These concepts are not congenial or directly applicable in their operating experience. Wage decisions are typically argued in terms of comparative wages, living costs, competitive conditions, labor shortages, ability to pay, specific productivity, job content, and bargaining power. Negotiators and their constituents understand these concepts. Pricing decisions are considered in terms of specific competitive prices, quality, advertising, market prospects, responses to changes in other prices, costs, and the like. The diffuse structure of collective bargaining and pricing makes the standards of the guideposts appear remote and unrealistic. The guideposts simply "do not come through." The macro-standards not only have no simple application to specific wage or price decisions, they do not appear relevant, controlling or decisive to micro-decision makers. You cannot effectively prescribe micro-decisions with macro-precepts. I suggest that unless guidepost standards are formulated in terms much more directly applicable and specific for decision makers, in terms they ordinarily utilize, the guideposts will command neither respect nor application.

(3) One of the most serious shortcomings of current wage-price policy, as it has been administered, is that the Council of Economic Advisers is being forced reluctantly in the direction of becoming

an administrative agency. It is ill equipped for the purpose. There is danger that its concentration on a growing number of wage-price cases may divert it from the formulation of general economic policy which it has performed with great distinction. The Council has a very small staff; the Council and its staff turn over frequently. At the early stages of the expansion, only a few cases were likely to arise. But it is the nature of an economy near full employment that inflationary pressures on wages and prices arise at many points. The Council is not designed or equipped to deal with a substantial volume of actual wage-price decisions. Neither is the White House. The prestige of the President is too valuable an asset to be dissipated in a growing number of wage or price confrontations. As the economy tightens, the present wage-price policy does not appear to be administratively viable.

(4) The actual administration of the guideposts, not in the form of general preachment but rather in the mobilization of governmental pressures in particular cases, raises two groups of questions of deep concern. (a) Why were particular situations selected for confrontation rather than others, and what criteria are to be used in the selection of such cases in the future? (b) What review of the facts and arguments regarding wage and price decisions is to be made, and in what forum, in advance of the conclusion that the "guideposts have been violated" and that a wage or price decision is "against the public interest"? Certainly not all wage increases in excess of 3.2 per cent a year, to use the popular view of the guideposts, or all wage increases that violate the more flexible language of the 1962 guideposts have been seriously scrutinized. Neither have all prices been reviewed, and those situations in which prices might have been reduced or quality improved pose almost impossible administrative difficulty.

I am personally disturbed by the absence of due process in the administration of the policy. I have looked at thousands of wage decisions in my time and have been involved in such decisions as mediator, arbitrator, fact-finder, or administrator of wartime controls. I am always impressed with how different a case may look after it has been presented in a forum which permits full review of the facts and contending arguments as compared to the reports of government or academic experts. The judgment that a wage or price increase in our economy is violative of the public interest is a serious conclusion that should warrant dispassionate review with full opportunity for the presentation of contesting views. The present policy does not afford this elementary right.

(5) There are a number of questions of analysis that can be raised with the guideposts. The neutrality of the guideposts with respect to the distribution of income does not appear to hold if the requisite price reductions do not take place. It is not clear what is the "general guide" for compensation in the event that the price guideposts are not achieved nor what is the "general guide" for prices if the wage guideposts are not achieved.

The relation of the guideposts to patterns of wages and prices during cyclical fluctuations raises a number of questions. If one starts with an economy moving upward from low levels of utilization to high levels, it appears that average wage or compensation rates increase slowly at first and then more rapidly. Deferred increases and settlements in 1966 continue to show a more rapid rate of increase than in earlier years. Average productivity, in contrast, appears to increase more rapidly during early stages of the upswing than can be sustained over the long pull at peak levels. At present levels of utilization, the further hiring of the unemployed and the large attraction of additional women and youth into the labor force should be expected to accelerate an increase in labor costs. The higher recruitment and training costs and generally lower productivity will increase labor costs and may be expected to offset overhead reductions at peak operations. The consequences of these wage rate, labor cost, and productivity movements is not price stability at sustained high levels of utilization, but rather price increases. It is by no means clear that some average level of productivity increase over recent years is a reliable measure of the rate of productivity increase at sustained high employment. The relevant question is an old one—how much price drift at sustained high employment?

As an economy approaches any practicable definition of full employment, the relative argument for concentrating wage and price policy on "segments of the economy where firms are large or employees well organized or both" would seem to be less appropriate. The competitive sectors and bottlenecks, generally, in competitive or more concentrated sectors become more significant. The guideposts may be more appropriate to moving toward practical full employment than defining wage and price policies appropriate to sustained full employment.

III. Some Basic Problems

In my view a wage-price or incomes policy does not consist primarily in proclaiming each year the ideal or utopian world in which wages and prices so move that the average level of prices is stable, average wages rise by average productivity, and there are suitable adjustments in the structure of wages and prices. That ideal has been portrayed and preached for many years, and it was popular before the Council existed. A policy is to be judged rather in terms of the implementation of these objectives and in the administrative arrangements suitable and practicable to achieve the goals.

It has been suggested earlier that policies and administrative arrangements suitable during an upswing toward potential output are not necessarily suitable for continuing levels of sustained full employment, defined in practicable terms including "appropriate" regard for other objectives of public policy.[7] It is important now to identify a few of the basic problems of establishing and sustaining wage and price policies for full employment.

(1) Any viable policy must command in our society the respect and allegiance of the leaders of labor organizations and the business community as well as governmental agencies and the press. In order to secure such consensus it is clear that the policy can only be expressed in rather general terms. But one should not underestimate the significance of such general statements and shared ideas in influencing specific behavior, at least to some degree. The policy statement which was drafted on "Sound Wage and Price Policies" by the President's Committee on Labor-Management Policy[8] in the first part of 1963, but never consummated, would be illustrative of what I have in mind.

---

[7] These other objectives include economic growth, employment of marginal groups of workers, industrial peace, the absence of formal wage and price controls, distributional equity, price stability, balance-of-payment objectives, and so forth.

[8] See, Jack Stieber, "The President's Committee on Labor-Management Policy," *Industrial Relations,* February, 1966, pp. 1–19.

Business and labor leaders have little respect for the current guideposts, in part because they had no role in drafting them. This is one of the major defects with the guideposts. In our society interest groups must have a role—not a controlling role—in the formulation of wage-price policy if they are to conform to it. Any new or reformulated wage-price policy must be developed with the active participation of business and labor leaders.

(2) A specific illustration of the significance of participation in policy formulation concerns the use of economic force, the strike and the lockout. A wage policy is not likely to be effective, nor will be related policies concerning price setting, if parties feel no qualms about using force against the policy. The acid test of a wage policy is what happens to a strike in defiance of the policy. In an industrial relations system, such as ours, with decentralized bargaining and with little direct control by confederations of labor and employers over constituents, the difficulties are substantially increased of achieving a viable wage and price policy. The high value placed in the community (and in legislation) on rank and file control is a further significant factor imparting an upward influence on wage settlements. The achievement of consent by leaders of labor and management is indispensable to a viable wage-price policy. Participation in the policy formulation is decisive to consent and to disavowal of economic action against the policy, at least in the absence of legal controls. Any new or reformulated wage-price policy must be prepared to deal with the strike or lockout against the policy.

(3) The federal government is poorly equipped and coordinated to facilitate a viable wage-price policy at high employment. The statistical and other data on price schedules, quality, margins, productivity, wage rates, compensation, labor costs, and the like are simply not available by detailed sectors for these policy purposes. Neither are there generally available the experts in government with detailed knowledge of market structures, price schedules and wage setting in specific sectors adequate to the detailed policy issues. The price and wage sectors, moreover, do not well correspond. The data and expertise required for policy judgments are of a very different order than required for general economic reporting and indicators. Any new or reformulated wage-price policy

must give careful attention to more appropriate administrative arrangements.

(4) The relations between government officers charged with settling labor disputes and those charged with stabilization objectives seriously need to be clarified. The basic questions have not been confronted. The discussion proposed by the Council in 1962 might well have started at home. What are the obligations of a mediator, if any, to the guideposts? Should he make mediation proposals to the parties outside the guideposts? Who is to determine what the guideposts mean specifically in a particular case? Can such determinations be made in advance or as negotiations proceed? Is it really possible to compress a complex settlement, including pensions and work rules, into a single percentage figure? Do not some different estimates arise from legitimate institutional needs of the parties? Why not let the Council try its hand at dispute settlement? Should the Council criticize the parties after a settlement which it regards as obnoxious? Should the criticism extend to the mediator? Should a mediator express views about the relations of a settlement to the guideposts? What are the obligations of a member of a fact-finding board appointed by the government, with power to make recommendations, to the guideposts? Is this responsibility to be specified to the parties and the board in advance of any appointment? When boards are appointed pursuant to statutory authority, as in the railroad and airlines industries, what weight should be given to the guideposts, and whose interpretation is to be determinative if any weight is given them? Should a fact-finding board express the view that it does not regard itself bound by the guideposts if one of the parties requests or insists upon the views of the board on this question, although it might indicate general economic conditions have always been taken into account by boards?

I trust you are aware that all these questions are not hypothetical. One set of government agencies exists to settle disputes and another to be concerned about stabilization and inflation. They do not speak the same language, and it is difficult to find a basis for any collaboration. In our pluralistic society this state of affairs may not seem unusual or serious. Yet, it is having some dangerous consequences for both collective bargaining and stability. In situations in which employers may fear that settlements are likely to run high, some have rushed to seek the assistance of the White House, the Council of Economic Advisers, or the Secretary of Labor, or all three, "to enforce" the guideposts. The resulting inept private bargaining and strike have frequently produced larger and more unstabilizing settlements. There have also been cases in which a union in a relatively weak bargaining position has sought to interpret the 3.2 figure as one to which it was entitled by government declaration. The guideposts have held out unavailable and ineffectual government assistance in negotiations, resulting in more inflationary capitulations or routes after shutdowns. Any new or reformulated wage-price policy must clarify the relation of mediation and fact-finding to general economic policy.

IV. AN ALTERNATIVE APPROACH

The discussion which follows is concerned with the spectrum of wage-price policy between pure preachment on the one hand and the introduction of wage and price controls on the other. It concerns an economy operating near full employment, however that may be exactly defined. This is the zone of experience of the past six months and would appear to be, on most estimates of economic and military events, the zone of likely experience in the several years immediately ahead. It approaches the problem of wage-price policies at continuing full employment.

The terrain of wage-price policy between formal controls on one side and pure macro-preachment on the other is very large and has been relatively underdeveloped. It is this range of policies which needs formulation if there is to be a lesser degree of price inflation at high utilization. It is also the zone in which there should be identified alternative policies, with greater or lesser degrees of stringency, so that wage-price policies, in addition to fiscal and monetary policies, may be adapted to changes in inflationary pressures.

It may be useful to distinguish at least five types of policy approaches in this vast terrain: (1) Do nothing extraordinary to interfere with the operation of labor and product markets. This approach would not preclude improvements in public and private employment services and more training in the labor market or continued anti-trust policies in product markets. But no accelerated policies are advocated to deal with full employment. (2) Use executive power to pressure particular price or wage decision makers to reduce or rescind increases already made or in prospect. This has been the approach of recent years. (3) Use executive power under established legislation to reduce inflationary pressures by such measures as variations in stockpiles, constriction of expenditures or procurement in sensitive sectors, adjustments in tariff schedules and the like. These methods have recently been utilized in a few situations. (4) The identification of a few major bottleneck sectors and the development with industry and labor of comprehensive programs to reduce price and wage pressures in these sectors. This approach is explored later in this section. (5) The legislative authorization for advance reporting of certain price and wage changes and the establishment of a machinery for pre- or post-review of price and wage situations. This approach has been used abroad and has its advocates here.

There are no doubt other alternatives and variants in this terrain, and social inventiveness to create others is to be encouraged. It is appropriate to hold that the present approaches are to be appraised in terms of alternative policies. But the choice is not wage and price controls or the present policy approach and practices. There are more options, and we need to use our ingenuity to invent even more.

The basic suggestion of this section is that the wage-price policy be reformulated to concentrate private and public policy on expanding supplies (and constricting demands) in a limited number of bottleneck sectors which are likely to contribute most substantially to increases in wage rates and prices. Aside from continuing general preachment, government policy should give up the attempt to review by administrative decision and to pass judgment on various private wage and price decisions and try to compel by administrative pressure changes in those decisions. It should concentrate its energies rather on the problems of a few of the most important bottleneck sectors.

The proposal for the abandonment of the present use of administrative pressure is not derived from any lack of concern with the prospects of inflationary pressures at high utilization nor from an absolute preference for employment compared to stability. My judgment is based rather on the views developed in section II that

the present approach is no longer viable administratively or economically, and that some transformation of wage-price policy is
urgently needed. Moreover, my judgment is that the vigorous pursuit of the bottleneck approach advocated will yield larger results
in contraints on prices and wage rates. The proposed policy transformation should be developed through a reconstituted President's
Committee on Labor-Management Policy to secure the requisite
consensus.

The major activities of the government in such a bottleneck
oriented program would be as follows:

(*a*) The identification in the short run and in the longer period
of the major priority bottlenecks in the economy. This
process would require both a good deal of technical ingenuity in estimating forward demands and supplies and
capacities by time periods, substitution possibilities, and
the like, and also the exercise of judgment in the selection
of a limited number of priority sectors.

(*b*) The development of detailed private and public policies
in the bottleneck sectors to mitigate inflationary pressure
by increasing supplies and constricting demands. This policy
development would require close collaboration of labor
managements, and operating government agencies at the
state and federal level. The government would require
interagency task forces or committees to develop and to
follow the variety of policies developed for each of the
priority sectors. But there must be central direction and
authority to resolve conflicting governmental policies, perhaps an office of economic stabilization.

(*c*) The range of policies developed for each bottleneck sector
would involve continuing interchange of discussion, statistics and appraisal of the outlook by private parties and
government representatives designed to review measures
to reduce inflationary pressures, and the prescription of
wide range of private and public activities. It is clear that
the appropriate and practical policy is highly variable and
specialized to a sector.

This approach is not inconsistent with the 1966 report of the
Council; indeed, it there specified a few "selected problem areas"

—food, non-ferrous metals, machinery, construction, and medical services. In my view, this approach requires much higher priority, much more careful formulation, the development of program for each sector with business and labor and operating government agencies, and most of all the establishment of mechanisms to secure the execution of government policies and the cooperation of private policies in each of these critical sectors.

The government is not now organized to effectuate such an approach. A few paragraphs of advice in an annual report to an industry will not produce results; the need in these trouble spots is for detailed studies for working with the sectors, coordinating diffuse and often conflicting government policies, a number of specific administrative or legislative actions, leadership, and a sense of persistence and urgency. Structural changes in organizations, in ways of making decisions, and in criteria of internal success typically come about very slowly, and yet, these institutional changes are likely to be most decisive in achieving greater stability in wages and prices at high degrees of utilization.

The list of the sectors which are likely to be most critical to wage and price stability over the next five years or so, in my view, would include some branches of transportation, medical and hospital services, construction, local government services, certain professional services, and perhaps automobile manufacturing should be added. Most of these trouble spots are not the concentrated sectors which are the focal concern of the guideposts. In each of these sectors detailed, but coordinated, studies should be in process of inflationary pressures and bottlenecks. Consultations on a continuing basis should be under way under coordinate government leadership with business and labor leaders, and a consistent range of policy suggestions should be explored.

If one takes the construction industry as only one example, the scale of the problems and the inadequacy of the government to contribute to the solution of bottlenecks is apparent. I do not wish to excuse the management and labor organizations from failures as well. There has been no census of construction since 1939. The data are most inadequate on prices, costs, and productivity on an overall basis or by branch of the industry. Regional data are highly inadequate. The general quality of almost all statistics is poor. Any careful review of the problems of this industry would suggest a need for long-term improvement in the collective bargaining and dispute settling machinery of most branches of the industry to bring more national responsibility to unresolved local issues; a strengthening of the integrity of employer bargaining groups; reforms to make pension and health and welfare benefits transferable from one locality or region to another to improve mobility; improvements in quantity and quality of training programs of many branches of the industry; consensus on estimates of forward manpower needs by categories; changes in tax credits for travel allowances to encourage mobility; greater attention to measures to reduce seasonality; the development of measures to control in some degree the rates of expenditures of governmental agencies on construction in the light of market conditions; the adaptation of credit policies in housing to inflationary pressures; the coordination of the policies of the new HUD department to the major tendencies in construction; the need for greater research and development expenditures, and so forth. I intend no definitive program here, and it should be observed that a number of steps in some of these directions have been advocated and some are under way in consultation between the industry and the Secretary of Labor.

A listing of measures and the preparation of supporting studies (and these do not exist) in each of the bottleneck sectors does not automatically produce results. Where is there responsibility in the federal government to discuss these problems and their solutions on a continuing basis? How is one to unify a highly diffused, feuding, and decentralized labor and management? How should the government be organized to pursue these questions to assist in securing changes in private and public policies to reduce inflationary pressures and achieve higher utilization?

A wage-price policy—between preachment and controls—at high levels of utilization comes down to detailed micro-problems. No general phrasing will substitute. Government leadership which takes the form of conference, persuasion, study, catalyst, and regulation can only be effective through continuing activity related to these problems as a group. No mechanism now exists for such coordinated policy development and implementation in major bottleneck sectors. A wage-price policy for high employment involves the development of programs to break through bottlenecks (and constrict demand) rather than to roll back wages and price changes that may appear to have exceeded a generalized macro-yardstick.

ARTHUR M. ROSS

Guideline Policy —— Where We Are and How We Got There

ARTHUR M. ROSS is Commissioner of Labor Statistics in the United States Department of Labor. In his prior role as professor of economics at the University of California (Berkeley), he wrote widely on issues in labor economics. Here he draws on his wide knowledge to provide an overview of incomes and guidelines policies in many countries of the free world, including the United States. He appraises the success of these policies as "limited to poor" but expresses hope that they will prove more workable in the future.

I. INTRODUCTION

Wage and price restraint programs in Western Europe and the United States during the past two decades have often been criticized as a refusal to make difficult choices, a desire to have the best of both worlds. But simple moralisms of this type are not always the best guide to economic policy. The persistence of these endeavors in the face of the generally discouraging reception from labor and management and the generally adverse judgment of pro-

AUTHOR'S NOTE: I have prepared this paper as an economist concerned with wage problems, rather than in my present official capacity as Commissioner of Labor Statistics in the Department of Labor. I should like to acknowledge, however, useful suggestions from staff members of the Bureau, including Kurt Braun, John Creane, Harry Douty, Peter Henle, and William Shelton.

97

fessional economists expresses a conviction that it ought not to be necessary to choose between excessive unemployment, unacceptable inflation, and burdensome regulation of all private decisions. Thus the repeated attempts, since the publication of *Full Employment in a Free Society*[1] over two decades ago, to square the circle and reconcile the seemingly irreconcilable objectives of full employment, price stability, and economic freedom.

The theoretical ambiguities and factual uncertainties surrounding the enterprise are also notable, but here again they should not necessarily be counted against the entrepreneurs. Still, it is well to be conscious of these ambiguities and uncertainties in commencing an exploration of the topic.

1. *What is the employment objective?* What is the full employment and what is the price stability which are to be reconciled with each other?

The classic definition of Sir William Beveridge is that a country has full employment when the number of job vacancies equals or exceeds the number of unemployed workers. This concept is a little oversimplified because it says nothing about the characteristics of the vacancies or the unemployed. Ten vacancies for heavy construction workers are not exactly equal to ten unemployed middle-aged women. It is of interest, however, that experimental job-vacancy surveys in the United States indicate that vacancies and unemployment in a labor market area tend to be equal in a range of 2.0 or 2.5 per cent of the labor force.

A second concept, more familiar to American economists, is that full employment is reached when there is no lack of effective demand. In such case the residual unemployment reflects movement in and out of the job market, labor turnover, and seasonal fluctuations, together with a residue of hard-core unemployed whose handicaps are so great that they are unacceptable to employers even when labor is scarce. Some reasonable calculations based on American data yield a rate between 2.5 and 2.8 per cent corresponding to a "full effective demand" concept of full employment.

Actually, however, the concept is not so self-contained as it may

---

[1] William Henry Beveridge, *Full Employment in a Free Society* (New York: W. W. Norton & Company, 1945).

seem. Seasonality of production is distinctly related to the strength of effective demand. The same is true of the rate of labor turnover as well as the length of time it takes to move from one job to another. There is no clear line between employability and unemployability; much depends on what the alternatives are as seen by the employer. Moreover, the "irreducible minimum" also depends on the extent of governmental assistance and control in the operation of the labor market. During World War II, for example, the unemployment ratio fell to about 1 per cent in a regime of compulsory controls over hiring and job-seeking. Germany and Sweden, which have unusually well-developed manpower institutions, maintained unemployment rates of less than 2 per cent for many years without permitting unit labor costs to get out of hand.

A third concept of full employment has been most important from an operational standpoint in the United States. In this view, full employment is attained, for practical purposes, when inflationary tendencies become so strong as to require fiscal and monetary policies which slow down the economy. The Eisenhower administration thought the economy was overheated in 1957, when the unemployment rate fell to about 4 per cent. This is now almost universally viewed as a mistake; but some conservative economists stated in February, 1966, that the dangers of inflation were so great that unemployment should not be pushed below the most recently reported 4 per cent rate—which had actually fallen to 3.7 per cent. There is an element of the "practical limit" concept in the "interim target" of the Council of Economic Advisers, which was inferentially lowered to about 3.5 per cent in the 1966 Economic Report.

2. *What is the price-level objective?* Likewise there is no objective definition of price stability but rather a range of policy judgments. Of course there are some conservatives who interpret the phrase literally, and perhaps even some romantics who believe that the benefits of economic progress should be dispersed in the form of lower prices while incomes remain stable. But it is more to attach explicit or unspoken modifiers, under which the goal becomes reasonable, substantial or virtual price stability. During the "creeping inflation" debate of the 1950's, Sumner Slichter and like-minded economists were thinking in terms of 2 or 3 per cent

annually. A popular rule of thumb today is that 2 per cent isn't too bad, but 3 per cent would be unacceptable. Actually it is difficult to evaluate a given rate of advance without knowing two additional pieces of information: whether prices are increasing less rapidly, or even more rapidly, in other countries, and whether consumers and businessmen expect the movement to escalate or decelerate. The first is important from the standpoint of international payments, and the second from the standpoint of speculative market behavior. It follows that a really valid determination of an acceptable rate of price increase would depend upon the situation of a particular country at a particular time.

3. *What is the relationship between the employment level and the price level?* That rising economic activity will exert upward pressure on the price level while manpower resources and industrial capacity are not fully utilized is generally conceded. Yet, the exact relationship has been difficult to establish, to say the least. A. W. Phillips' celebrated article concluded that "if aggregate demand were kept at a value which would maintain a stable level of product prices the associated level of unemployment would be a little under 2½ per cent," and that "if demand were kept at a value which would maintain stable wage rates the associated level of unemployment would be about 5½ per cent."[2] Although Phillips assumed only a productivity trend rate of 2 per cent per year, his estimates seem much too modest for modern conditions. In his equally famous "Study Paper No. 1," Charles Schultze concluded that "a 4 per cent unemployment rate . . . seems to imply an annual [wage] increase of some 5 per cent in the postwar period," but that "the relationship between wage rates and unemployment breaks down once unemployment falls below 5 per cent."[3] Samuelson and Solow paired 3 per cent unemployment with a 4 to 5 per cent price rise.[4] Meanwhile, about half of

[2] A. W. Phillips, "The Relation between Unemployment and the Rate of Change of Money Wage Rates in the United Kingdom, 1861–1957," *Economica* 25 (Nov., 1958): 299.

[3] Charles L. Schultze, *Recent Inflation in the United States,* Joint Economic Committee (Washington: U.S. Government Printing Office, 1959), pp. 61–62.

[4] Paul A. Samuelson and Robert M. Solow, "Analytical Aspects of Anti-Inflation Policy" (1959 AEA meetings), *American Economic Review* 50 (May, 1960): 177–94.

all Ph.D. candidates in economics have been doing Phillips-curve thesis research, but the problem remains elusive.

4. *Is cost-push a significant cause of inflation?* Under the traditional quantity theory, the price level was governed by the quantity of money. Keynesian theory also presented a demand-pull explanation, although emphasizing aggregate spending rather than the stock of money. The cost-push version became respectable and influential about 1960, inspired by the 1955–57 inflation in the United States when prices rose substantially with no evidence of excess demand. A. P. Lerner developed a theory of "sellers' inflation" which arises along a spectrum of market inflexibility. ". . . We have the situation where prices not only refuse to fall when there is a deficiency of demand, but tend to *rise* if there is a level of demand that provides a satisfactory level of employment. Prices will then be stable only if there is considerable unemployment. In the absence of this degree of depression, wages and prices will be rising in a sellers' inflation, with labor blaming the wage increases on price increases, and business blaming the price increases on wage increases."[5] Perhaps the most authoritative statement was contained in *The Problem of Rising Prices,* written by William Fellner and others for OEEC, "Where collective bargaining results in wage increases greater than supply and demand forces alone would have yielded, and at the same time greater than the increase in labour productivity in the economy, it must be regarded as an independent factor contributing to the rise in prices."[6] The authors held that postwar inflation in France was dominated by excess demand; that wage increases did not outrun productivity in Austria, Belgium, Germany, Italy, or Switzerland; but that "excessive wage increase constituted both an important and independent inflationary force" in Norway, Sweden, Denmark, the United Kingdom, and the United States—especially in the last three.[7]

Thus there is impressive support for the idea of cost-push inflation, although some economists such as Professor Milton Friedman would still deny its validity. But large uncertainties remain.

---

[5] A. P. Lerner, "On Generalizing the General Theory," *ibid.* 50 (March. 1960): 135.

[6] Fellner *et al., The Problem of Rising Prices* (Paris: OEEC, 1961), p. 45.

[7] *Ibid.,* p. 46.

There is no empirical test to ascertain whether cost-push is dominant in a particular inflationary episode. As Samuelson and Solow emphasize, the fact that money wages rise faster than productivity proves nothing; this happens in the purest of demand inflations. And the fact that expenditures increase more rapidly than real output is only the simple arithmetic of any kind of inflation. The timing of wage and price changes is not a reliable test since we do not have a zero time from which all changes begin.[8]

It is correspondingly difficult to define the circumstances under which wage and price restraint, as distinguished from regulation of effective demand, becomes the critical policy variable. Cost-push will not emerge until the margin of unused manpower and industrial capacity narrows to a certain width. But when it narrows still more, demand pressures begin to swamp the situation and cost-push becomes part of a cumulative, vicious circle process. Thus guidepost policies are not necessary up to a certain point; and a little bit further, they become ineffective. The location of this intermediate band, and its width, undoubtedly vary from one country to another, and from one period of time to another even in a given country. It is no wonder there is so much argument about it. Neither is it any wonder that there is so much disagreement concerning the effectiveness of wage and price restraint policies.

II. European Experience in the Postwar Period

Wage and price restraint policies—or "incomes policies," as they are called outside the United States—have been used in five different contexts: (*a*) as one aspect of total economic mobilization during World War II; (*b*) as one method of dealing with the scarcity of resources in the European postwar reconstruction programs of 1945–50; (*c*) as one feature of economic planning in the developing countries; (*d*) as one technique of coping with the limited economic pressures of the Korean War and the Vietnam War in the United States; and (*e*) as one means of facilitating economic growth and high employment, both in Europe and the United States, in the 1950's and 1960's.

The fourth and fifth of these situations are most relevant to

[8] Samuelson and Solow, "Analytical Aspects," pp. 177–94.

the purposes of this conference. My review of European policies will therefore deal mainly with the period after the immediate urgencies of postwar reconstruction had abated. Likewise, my discussion of American experience will be centered largely—although not entirely—on the period since 1950.

A. GENERAL COMMENTS ON EUROPEAN EXPERIENCE

As in the United States, European incomes policy is based on the rubric that increases should not exceed productivity growth; and the prevailing practice is to use the trend rate in the national economy rather than rates in specific enterprises or industries or year-to-year fluctuations in the national rate. But in a number of countries, productivity is not the sole criterion. "Guidelines" or "norms" indicating the rate of increase consistent with wage and price policy rather are based on official estimates of the total economic situation and its further development. This is increasingly done in connection with national economic planning or "indicative programming," which is spreading in Europe.

This section of the paper will review the experience in Austria, Denmark, France, Germany, the Netherlands, Norway, Sweden, and the United Kingdom. In the majority of these eight countries, incomes policy has been combined with price policy. In fact, guidance for non-wage incomes has been largely combined with price policy, a fact which reflects not only inadequacies of data concerning non-wage incomes but also the difficulty of devising criteria for appraising them.

In particularly serious situations, some countries have requested or imposed a temporary wage (or wage-price) "pause." This was the case in the United Kingdom during 1961 and in Austria during 1962. Denmark took legislative measures in 1963 which amounted almost to a complete "stop" in incomes and prices. Nowhere, however, have such emergency measures been effective for any extended period of time.

None of the various systems of wage and price control has been intended to replace general monetary and fiscal policies or special measures designed to affect demand and supply.

In Europe, income and price policies are viewed as part of general economic policy. In some of the European countries, general economic policy is developed by public bodies known by various names such as Social and Economic Council, National Economic Development Council, Council of Economic Experts, Economic Council, and the like. There is a strong trend toward tripartite composition of these bodies. Sometimes they also include representatives of consumers, farmers, and other special interests.

In addition, special institutions have been developed in the Netherlands, Austria, and the United Kingdom to seek the implementation of wage and price policies formulated by the economic councils. These organizations may also participate directly or indirectly in the development of policies. They tend to be bipartite or tripartite, in order to secure the voluntary cooperation of affected parties. The objective of preserving industrial peace is interwoven with that of attaining price stability.

The Dutch system was established in 1945, although it has been revised on several occasions. The Austrian setup dates from 1957, and the British arrangements have been developing gradually since the wage pause of 1961.

B. COUNTRIES WITH SPECIAL INSTITUTIONS TO IMPLEMENT
   INCOME AND PRICE POLICIES

1. *The Netherlands.* The 1945 statute established a government-appointed Board of Government Mediators to determine whether collective agreements were consistent with the national interest and to approve or reject them accordingly. The decisions of the Board were enforceable in court. Prior to their submission to the Board, collective agreements were examined by a joint body of employers and trade unions called the Labor Foundation. In 1951 a tripartite agency—the Social and Economic Council—was set up to advise the government on matters of overall economic policy, including wage and price developments. From then on, demands for wage increases were first discussed in the Labor Foundation, and were then referred to the Social and Economic Council, which submitted a report to the government. The government then decided whether there should be a mandatory or a permissive wage increase or none at all. A permissive wage increase was implemented through collective bargaining, subsequent examination of the resulting agreements by the Labor Foundation, and, finally, approval by the Board of Government Mediators.

A revision of the system became effective in 1963. Authority to approve collective agreements was transferred from the Board of Government Mediators to the Labor Foundation. If the Board of Government Mediators believed that a wage settlement would result in price increases or otherwise impair the national economy, it could warn the Foundation and advise the Minister of Social Affairs to nullify it wholly or partly.

Efforts to develop a more satisfactory long-range system are continuing. Meanwhile, organized labor, management, and the government have reached a transitional agreement on the method which will be used in 1966 to determine whether negotiated wage increases are excessive. (The government has defined a "danger zone" of 7 per cent for the guidance of the parties.) Under this transitional agreement, the Labor Foundation no longer evaluates collective contracts but merely transmits them to the Board of Government Mediators for review. If the mediators regard the increase as excessive, they may either return the contract to the Labor Foundation for further review or else request the Minister of Social Affairs to suspend it. If the Minister does so, the Labor Foundation then returns the contract to the parties for reconsideration. Unless the latter take appropriate action (as a rule within two weeks), the Minister invalidates the contract.

In its early postwar decisions, the Board of Government Mediators relied largely on the concept of a socially just minimum wage. Subsequently, it applied the principle that, to prevent price increases, wage raises must not exceed productivity gains in the various industrial branches and sectors concerned. Since the revision of the central control system in 1963, appraisals of the economic situation, based on estimates of the Central Planning Bureau and the national economic plan, have replaced productivity as the decisive criterion for wage movements.

2. *Austria.* A 1957 decree of the Council of Ministers established a Wage-Price Commission, composed of representatives of management, labor, and the government, as an advisory body to help combat inflation through voluntary action. The Commission's authority has been augmented by an agreement in 1961 between the presidents of the Chamber of Commerce and the Austrian Trade Union Federation and by legislation enacted in 1962.

Since the execution of the 1961 agreement, the Commission has performed its function of preventing excessive wage and price demands with the help of two subcommittees—one for wages and a second for prices. The subcommittees handle applications submitted to the Commission by parties seeking approval for wage or price increases. They are guided by the principle that wage raises should be held within the limits of productivity gains and that exports must not be jeopardized.

Actually the Commission has no power to force entrepreneurs or trade unions to submit applications or to abide by its decisions. It has been able to influence wage and price developments to some extent, however. According to the Minister of Social Administration, the system has been workable largely because of the high degree of organization among both employers and employees, the major role played by the government in economic policies, and the fact that the Austrian state itself is an important consumer and producer of a wide range of goods and services.

3. *United Kingdom.* The tripartite National Economic Development Council is responsible for studying and appraising general wage and price movements. In addition there is a Board of Prices and Incomes with a neutral chairman, a number of neutral members, a businessman, and a trade unionist. Like the Austrian Wage-Price Commission, the Board operates two divisions, one for prices and the other for incomes. Its function is to examine, when requested by the government, whether specific price and wage changes are consistent with the national interest. In particular, it is authorized to investigate cases where prices should have been lowered, in the opinion of the government, but were not.

The Council's income guidelines were agreed upon by the Trades Union Congress, the Confederation of British Industry, and the NEDC. A White Paper published in 1965 spelled out the standards.

For incomes in general, the norm is in terms of an average annual increase in per capita money income consistent with stability in the general price level. The present norm is 3 to 3.5 per cent. It is subject to reconsideration by the government in the light of reviews conducted from time to time by the NEDC.

The White Paper holds that the long-term productivity trend must take precedence over other factors such as supply and demand for different kinds of labor, the movement of profits, comparisons with wages in other occupations, and changes in the cost of living.

Moreover, account must be taken also of increases in labor costs resulting from reductions in working hours without loss of pay, higher overtime rates, and other improvements in fringe benefits.

Increases in compensation above the norm are warranted only where exceptional treatment is required in the national interest and should be balanced by increases below the norm.

Some of the other incomes such as those of farmers and landlords are determined to a considerable extent by government policy. Income of government-owned industries accrues directly to the community, but the prices charged are susceptible to the general considerations of policy. Incomes of self-employed persons should be guided by the same considerations and may therefore be referred to the Board. Where the growth of profits or dividends is based on excessive market power, this could indicate scope for price reductions; and such cases can also be referred to the Board.

An "early warning" system is operated on a voluntary basis. It provides for advance notice of claims for wage or price increases, so that the government can decide whether they should be referred to the Board. To implement the system, the Trades Union Congress has established a committee which makes comments and suggestions regarding proposed wage claims of member unions. On the management side, the Confederation of British Industry has agreed to collect information and pass it on to the government, but it refuses to judge the information against guideline criteria or intervene in specific decisions made by its members.

In February, 1966, the government submitted to the Parliament a bill aimed at supplementing the present voluntary system with a mandatory system. The bill proposes that prices and charges included in an official list may not be increased without prior notification to the government and increases may not be put into effect until thirty days thereafter unless they have been approved. The bill proposes further that if the matter is referred to the Board, the increase may not become effective until the Board's report has been published (or until three months after the referral, whichever is earlier). Likewise, no wage settlement may be placed in effect during thirty days after notification to the government, unless consent is given; and if the case is referred to the Board, the three-month waiting period also applies.

The bill provides for penalties in case of non-compliance with these procedural rules, but the report of the Board will only be advisory. Thus the effect of the bill would be to give the government and the Board four months in which they can attempt to exert their influence.

C. COUNTRIES WITHOUT SPECIAL INSTITUTIONS TO IMPLEMENT
   WAGE AND PRICE POLICIES

1. *Federal Republic of Germany.* For at least a dozen years after the war, German unions pursued a cautious wage policy. But with high profits, endemic labor shortages, and rapid productivity gains, employers granted wage increases far above those required by the collective bargaining contracts. Toward the end of the 1950's, unions began to argue that they were entitled to more generous treatment. Chancellor Adenauer, as well as the authorities of the German Central Bank, replied that improvement in wages and working conditions must be kept in close relationship with increased national income. By 1960, the government was urging that wage increases be held to 4 per cent annually, but employers almost universally disregarded this advice.

In 1964 a Council of Economic Experts, composed of five neutral specialists, was appointed. Its duty was to "analyze periodically the overall economic development of the Federal Republic of Germany and to facilitate the formation of public opinion as well as decision-making in all agencies responsible for economic policies."

In its first report, the Council recommended that wages should not be raised by more than the expected average increase in productivity. It added, however, that this rule could not be strictly applied in the absence of monetary equilibrium and other necessary conditions. Management and labor could not be saddled with responsibility for the stability of the economy. In this spirit, the chairman of the public mediation agency suggested that in a case before him, the basic wage increase should not only include allowance for the productivity gain to be expected in the current year but also a supplement to compensate for probable appreciation of the price level.

In commenting on the Council's report, the federal government urged that wage and salary increases in 1965 should not exceed the estimated productivity growth of 5 per cent. The government rejected the notion of an increment to cover anticipated price increases. Actually, average hourly earnings in manufacturing rose by more than 10 per cent between 1964 and 1965.

2. *France.* The first four national economic plans in France did not include any formal statement of income policy, although prime ministers occasionally urged employers to hold the line. The fifth Economic Development Plan, to run from 1966 through 1970, does include elements of incomes policy designed to correct strong inflationary tendencies.

In preparing this plan, the government underlined the importance of maintaining the growth of income at a rate compatible with stability of production costs. (Unit labor costs had risen rapidly between 1960 and 1963.) The plan apparently deals with full incomes of various economic groups, rather than only wage rates or other unit measurements of income. According to the calculations, income of farmers should not grow at a rate exceeding 5.3 to 5.5 per cent; that of entrepreneurs, 3.2 to 3.4 per cent, that of upgraded workers, 3.2 to 3.4 per cent, including wage drift; and that of other workers, 2.8 to 3 per cent.

A committee has been established in the Planning Commissariat to follow the movement of cost and incomes so as to establish a base for a more elaborate policy. As in the United Kingdom, the public sector of the economy is quite large in France, which permits the government to exert a considerable indirect influence on wage development in the private sector.

3. *Denmark.* Denmark has an elaborate and highly centralized collective bargaining system focused on biennial general wage negotiations. Up to 1960, government intervention was based on the objective of industrial peace rather than explicit incomes policy goals. In 1962, however, shortly before the beginning of national negotiations, Parliament established an Economic Council, consisting of twenty-five members representing all important interest groups (including trade unions, employers, civil service, agriculture, industry, and the handicrafts), with three neutral persons acting as a Board of Chairmen. After discussions within the Council, the chairmen were empowered to issue advisory opinions.

Wage bargaining proceeded but without a successful outcome. In February, 1963, the government submitted a package of eleven bills to enforce a temporary "income stop" for a two-year period in order to avoid an impending balance-of-payments crisis. Legislation was carried by a narrow vote. It extended existing collective agreements for two years.

This action did not in itself prevent wage drift, because many important contracts establish only the minimum wages and have no direct bearing on individual rates. The central organizations of unions and employers, however, were able to neutralize wage drift to a considerable extent by rejecting widespread demands for increases above the levels fixed in national agreements. Wage escalator clauses were retained, but direct and indirect taxes were removed from the cost-of-living index governing the application of escalators.

Additional legislation restricted dividend payments and executive compensation to the levels of prior years. Prices and profit margins were frozen unless permission should be secured from the Monopolies Board on the basis of higher production costs.

This emergency legislation expired in 1965. In the meantime government officials have been holding talks with top leaders of management and labor, while the Economic Council is searching for a solution to the problem of incomes policy. In 1965, reports of the Economic Council on national economic development, production trends and income distribution were used as the basis for national negotiations. The parties also agreed that if no settlement were reached in direct negotiations, the government mediator would be asked to render advice based on general economic considerations.

D. TRADE UNION ATTITUDES IN EUROPE

In many European countries, trade unions have been inclined to accept national wage and price policy in one form or another. The reasons include their experience with disastrous inflation in earlier times, the desire to protect employment opportunity in the export industries, participation in formulating and executing policy through membership in bipartite or tripartite boards, and close relations between the trade union movement and labor parties.

On the other hand, other European unionists express continued distaste for wage restraint policies. They argue that workers should have the same freedom to determine the price of labor as sellers enjoy fixing the prices of products, that free collective bargaining should not be impaired, and that workers should be able to obtain what they can from prosperous firms willing to pay generously to attract and hold scarce manpower. There is particular opposition against policies which are limited, as a practical matter, to restraint of wages and salaries without regulating profits, rents, dividend interest, and farm incomes.

As in the United States, unions frequently argue that the trend of national productivity cannot be the only factor in wage determination. Workers should be permitted to seek a higher proportion of national income. And as in the United States, they point out that price increases occurring for reasons independent of wage costs have depressed the advance of real wages below the productivity trend and have reduced labor's share of total income.

Although it is difficult to generalize about so many national labor movements, probably there is some tendency toward acceptance of economic planning institutions and incomes policy criteria. A case in point is the British Trades Union Congress, which is participating in the wage and price plans of the Labour party government after many years of reluctance. The Trades Union Congress joined with British management in signing a Declaration of Intent containing a pledge to raise productivity, keep prices stable and use the growth of national output as a guideline for increases in money incomes. In its 1965 convention the Trades Union Congress argued that real incomes can rise more rapidly if prices are stable, and that incomes policy will permit greater social justice not only as between workers and the rest of the population but as between groups of wage and salary earners.

E. MANAGEMENT ATTITUDES

European employers generally express distaste for outside interference in labor relations, and many tend to regard incomes policies as representing a drift toward compulsion. Opposition to such policies, however, is weaker in management circles than among the trade unions. One reason is that as a practical matter the policies are concerned with wages more than other forms of income. Another reason may be that the majority of employers are free to pay higher wages than those specified by the industry-wide collective bargaining agreements.

The Confederation of British Industry has given the Labour

Party's National Development Plan, with its incomes and price policies, a guarded reception. The Confederation has indicated that it wants to offer support, but only so long as such support does not conflict with vital interests of its members. Willingness to cooperate in the plan for advance notification of intended price increases was made dependent on the condition that the Confederation would not be asked to take any position regarding them.

Some European employers argue that wage increases should be held below the trend rate of productivity in order to meet the challenge of the competition in foreign markets, provide a greater stimulus to investment, encourage risk-taking, and the like. Labor costs actually did decline in some European countries until the late 1950's, but are generally increasing at the present time.

F. THE PROBLEM OF WAGE DRIFT

European incomes policies were established as long as twenty years ago. All the plans have been changed repeatedly, however; frequently they have been dropped and then picked up at a later point; they are still in an experimental stage everywhere. Under these circumstances, any attempt to sift out their results from all the other influences on incomes, costs, and prices would be very difficult indeed.

It is clear, however, that a principal problem has been the phenomenon of wage drift. As noted above, wage restraint policies, intended to choke off a "cost-push" inflation, can easily be swamped by demand pressures. This has generally been the case in the postwar European prosperity.

The essence of wage drift is that employee earnings become dissociated from contractual wage rates. The instrumentalities of wage drift have differed from one country to another. In the United Kingdom, loose incentive rates, systematic overtime, and special agreements between shop steward councils and employers have been instrumental. The majority of strikes in Britain have been "unofficial" or unauthorized stoppages designed to improve on the terms of the formal agreement.

When I made a brief study of wage drift in Italy during 1961, I found that the mechanisms included job evaluation piecework compensation and merit rating. Job classifications in the national agreements were frequently obsolete, and many larger factories were using more sophisticated plans of their own. While incentive rates were regulated to some extent by collective agreements, specific production standards were being determined by management, either unilaterally or in consultation with works councils. About 20 per cent of the firms were using merit rating to adjust individual wage rates.

Wage drift was not so prevalent in France. It was very pronounced in the metalworking industries, however. Among skilled metal workers in the Paris district, hourly earnings were 35 to 40 per cent above the negotiated rates. The increments were taking the form of unilateral bonuses and premiums or systematic assignment of overtime, and thus did not emerge from the collective bargaining process.[9]

The payment of wage rates in excess of contract minima has been traditional in Germany, but the gap between contractual rates and actual hourly earnings widened greatly during the 1950's. The premium wages, supplements, bonuses, and welfare payments were generally unilateral. Employers were prepared to pay them so long as economic conditions were favorable, but reserved the right to eliminate them. Job evaluation plans, adopted unilaterally or in agreement with works councils, sometimes included occupational rates twice as high as those in the regional agreements. Eventually, however, unilateral wage drift became incorporated in subsequently negotiated wage increases. In 1960, for example, while the government and the Employers Confederation were imploring that settlements be held to 4 per cent, increases of 8 to 15 per cent were being negotiated. There is no doubt that this movement represented, in considerable part, a recognition and incorporation of increases which had already been granted in local plants. In other words, previous wage drift was being legitimized at the same time as original increases were initiated.[10]

[9] A. M. Ross, "Prosperity and Labor Relations in Western Europe: Italy and France," *Industrial and Labor Relations Review* 60 (October, 1962): 68–69, 77.

[10] A. M. Ross, "Prosperity and Labor Relations in Europe: The Case of West Germany," *Quarterly Journal of Economics* 76 (August, 1962): 342–56.

III. Experience in the United States

A. WORLD WAR I

 Many years after the termination of World War I, Bernard Baruch described in his autobiography the problems he encountered in attempting to obtain voluntary cooperation from industry in the mobilization effort of 1917–18.

> In 1917, the principle that a sound mobilization program must adapt the law of supply and demand to the needs of the war was considered revolutionary. Because we ignored this principle, we floundered during the first year of the war while shortages developed, production lagged, prices rose, and many profiteered.[11]

Even after its reorganization in 1918, the War Industries Board could not fix prices but could only seek to negotiate with industry representatives. Even this limited authority lacked a firm legal basis. Fortunately the war ended before the unsolved problems could come to a head.

B. WORLD WAR II

Although the United States was involved in lend-lease activities and defense production for almost two years prior to Pearl Harbor, inflation was not a serious threat because of the large amount of unused manpower and industrial capacity. President Roosevelt established the National Defense Advisory Commission in May, 1940, with price stabilization and consumer protection divisions to watch the impact of the defense program on the price structure. Some scattered price problems began to appear in the fall of that year. At first they were handled informally. After the Office of Price Administration and Civilian Supply was established, selective price orders were issued. At that time public opinion was not prepared for comprehensive price control, since the country was not yet at war and the full magnitude of the defense effort could not be predicted. Moreover, Congress had not yet been persuaded that statutory powers should be granted to a price-control agency.

---

[11] Bernard M. Baruch, *The Public Years* (New York: Holt, Rinehart & Winston, 1960), p. 54.

The first formal price schedule, relating to second-hand machine tools, was issued in February, 1941. As 1941 wore on, the tempo of formal actions increased, so that nearly 50 additional schedules were promulgated between February and December. Another 58 schedules appeared during the two months between the attack at Pearl Harbor and passage of the Price Control Act on January 30, 1942.

After this law was enacted, the Office of Price Administration continued to extend selective price controls; and by the end of March, nearly one-third of the commodities covered by the BLS Wholesale Price Index had been brought under control.

These piecemeal measures were not accomplishing the job, however. Wholesale and consumer prices continued to advance rapidly, until OPA issued a general freeze order in the form of the General Maximum Price Regulation of April 28, 1942. This was the most important single step in the field of price control during the war. With a few exceptions, every seller was held to the highest price charged in March, 1942, for any given commodity to any given class of consumer. From then on, price increases could be made only with permission of the Office of Price Administration.

Wage control received little attention until 1942. It took many months to absorb the large volume of unemployment at the beginning of the period. As production levels rose, the level of profits advanced, so that wage increases put little pressure on profit margins. So far as labor policy was concerned, the government was concentrating on the prevention of industrial disputes which might interfere with the defense effort.

During 1941 the relationship between wages and prices began to receive more attention, but the government hoped that price control would make wage dealings unnecessary. As a result, the Emergency Price Control Act of January, 1942, did not provide for control over wages. Dispute settlement was still the principal theme of labor policy.

Ten days after the attack on Pearl Harbor, a Labor-Management Conference met at the President's request and agreed to a no-strike, no-lockout agreement for the duration of the war. Then the President appointed the National War Labor Board—with representatives of labor, management and the public—to settle industrial disputes, including wage disputes referred by the Secretary of The Department of Labor. Thus the National War Labor Board did have power to fix wage rates, but only in those cases that could not be settled peacefully through collective bargaining. There was no control over the wage increases granted voluntarily by employers, and most increases occurred in this manner because of the growing manpower shortages.

In July, 1942, the Board adopted the "Little Steel" formula: workers who had not received a 15 per cent increase in hourly wages since January 1, 1941, were entitled to make up the difference. The Little Steel formula was based on the fact that the cost of living index had risen about 15 per cent between January 1, 1941, and May, 1942. The Board made it clear that even though the cost of living might rise above the May, 1942, level, the 15 per cent formula would not be revised. Otherwise, wage claims would be considered only for workers whose pay was substandard (below 50 cents per hour), or who were receiving less than the "going rate" for the same kind of work in the same labor market area.

Once these general principles had been stated, the President moved to bring all wages within the control of the National War Labor Board. Congress approved proposed amendments to the Emergency Price Control Act; and on October 3, 1942, the President issued Executive Order 9250, prohibiting wage changes without the approval of the Board. Thus, all voluntary as well as disputed wage increases, with the exception of those in agriculture and on the railroads, were brought within government control for the first time.

The character of wage stabilization was affected by several important decisions made early in the period. First, some flexibility was preserved through continuation of the Little Steel formula, the inequity principle, and permission to eliminate substandard rates. Second, control over fringe benefits was looser than the limitation of hourly wage increases. Unions therefore were able to concentrate on benefits long enjoyed by white collar workers and executives such as vacations, paid holidays, and sick-leave allowances. Third, wage control was kept separate from price control. Wages were not automatically adjusted for changes in the cost of living, nor were the wage decisions of the Board normally influenced by possible effects on prices. Likewise, except in a few cases, wages were dissociated from manpower considerations.

There was considerable wage drift during this period, for perhaps the only time in American history, and fringe benefits were permitted to increase more rapidly than wage rates. Yet, the wage and price controls, supported by measures to sterilize excess demand, were highly successful on the whole. Prior to October, 1942, both wages and the Consumer Price Index had been increasing at rates approaching 1 per cent per month. In contrast, the consumer price trend was cut to about 0.4 per cent per month, and the wage trend to about 0.25 per cent per month, during the period between October, 1942, and August, 1945.

At the end of the war with Japan, labor's strong discontent with wage controls came to the surface. It was generally anticipated that there would be considerable unemployment during the reconversion period and that wage controls would not be necessary. Executive Order 9599, issued by President Truman on August 18, 1945, permitted wage increases without prior government approval so long as they were not used as the basis for seeking higher price ceilings. Comprehensive price controls continued, but as would have been expected, it was not practical to liberate some workers from wage control and restrain others. After strikes in the automobile, steel, and coal industries, the wage line was broken in February, 1946. This in turn gave impetus to the attack on price control, which disintegrated for all practical purposes by June, 1946. Formal decontrol followed within the next few months.

A "demand-push" inflation ran rampant in 1946 and 1947 as wartime savings were liquidated, taxes were sharply reduced, and consumer borrowing multiplied. Whether wage and price controls could have been effective in the face of such unlimited demand is certainly questionable, although many economists believe they should have been continued. After the Consumer Price Index had risen 15 per cent between 1946 and 1947, President Truman asked for authority to reimpose price and wage ceilings. Congress refused to grant such authority; and the supply of goods and services caught up with the demand soon afterward.

Meanwhile, many wage disputes had been referred to presidential fact-finding boards, but their recommendations were based on bargaining equities rather than stabilization criteria.

C. THE KOREAN WAR

Inflationary possibilities were underrated at the outset of the Korean War. The government believed that the increased defense expenditures could be met without serious disruption of the civilian economy and without the need for direct wage and price controls. Since taxes were being raised and credit was being tightened, the theory was that deficit spending with its inflationary consequences could be avoided.

Deficit spending was avoided, but nonetheless there was a frantic splurge of private spending by householders and business firms, actuated by expectations of shortages and higher prices to come, fears of World War III, and plain uncertainty. To these speculative influences was added the "marking up" of wages and prices in order to get under the wire before controls were imposed. The Wholesale and Consumer Price Indexes rose 10 per cent between 1950 and 1951, while average hourly earnings in manufacturing advanced 9 per cent.

Meanwhile, in September, 1950, Congress authorized price and wage controls in the Defense Production Act. Several important months were lost, particularly after China intervened late in November, 1950. Appeals for voluntary restraint were not heeded in the atmosphere of inflationary psychology. By the time that a general wage and price freeze was adopted by the end of January, 1951, the structure of wages and prices was already out of balance and could be stabilized only at a higher level.

The freeze order gave the country sufficient pause to realize that World War III was actually not impending. The splurge of spending rapidly subsided. It was no coincidence that consumer buying diminished immediately, or that inventory accumulation tapered off soon afterward, or that all observers noted a softening of inflationary pressures even as the government spending program gathered steam. The pressures were largely of a psychological character and the freeze was effective in handling them.

The conduct of wage and price controls in the 1951–53 period was largely a matter of leveling off the distortions which had been created prior to the freeze. There was no comprehensive economic planning; there was little acceptance of the need for controls by labor and management; unlike World War II, a no-strike, no-lock-out pledge had not been given. Under these circumstances, there was little alternative to a defense in depth. The controls thus were applied too late and too weakly, and may have been inflationary on balance. Nevertheless consumer prices rose only 3 per cent between 1951 and 1953, while wholesale prices declined.

Looking back on the situation, it may be concluded that direct controls over wages and prices were needed at the outset of the Korean War because of the substantial increases and realignments in output, drastic changes in economic expectations, vivid memories of World War II shortages, and great uncertainty over the meaning of the new situation. Controls, however, were established too late and continued too long on a comprehensive basis. They could have been removed when the major economic shifts had been accomplished, the community had become psychologically adjusted to the Korean War, and fiscal and credit policies had had time to become effective. Specifically, they could have been eliminated by the fall of 1951 except for price ceilings on a few scarce materials.

D. THE WAGE-PRICE GUIDEPOSTS

The "Guideposts for Noninflationary Wage and Price Behavior" were systematically expounded for the first time in the 1962 Report of the Council of Economic Advisers. But as early as 1952, President Truman's Council held that wage increases should be limited by the gain in productivity, which was then considered to be in the range of 2 to 3 per cent. During President Eisenhower's administration, the Council repeatedly endorsed this proposition in general terms. As already noted in Part II of this paper, the productivity trend was fast becoming the central theme of incomes policy in Northern European countries. Moreover, the theory of "cost-push" inflation began to emerge at the end of the 1950's in writings which have already been mentioned.

In 1959 the Joint Economic Committee sponsored a special inquiry into "Employment, Growth and Price Levels." Extensive hearings were held, and special papers and studies prepared under the direction of Otto Eckstein. The major conclusion was to endorse the proposition that the United States had been suffering from cost-push inflation. Particularly influential on this point were the papers, "Prices and Costs in Manufacturing Industries," by Charles L. Schultze and Joseph L. Tryon, and "Steel and the Postwar Inflation," by Otto Eckstein and Gary Fromm. These monographs, together with Thomas A. Wilson's "Analysis of Inflation in Machinery Prices" laid the groundwork for subsequent CEA policy statements.[12]

The original formulation in the 1962 Report was as follows:

> The general guide for noninflationary wage behavior is that the rate of increase in wage rates (including fringe benefits) in each industry be equal to the trend rate of overall productivity increase. General acceptance of this guide would maintain stability of labor cost per unit of output for the economy as a whole—though not of course for individual industries. . . . The general guide for noninflationary price behavior calls for price reduction if the industry's rate of productivity increase exceeds the overall rate—for this would mean declining unit labor costs; it calls for an appropriate increase in price if the opposite situation prevails; and it calls for stable prices if the two rates of productivity increase are equal.[13]

These were advanced as "general guideposts." The CEA recognized that "to reconcile them with objectives of equity and efficiency, specific modifications must be made to adapt them to the circumstances of particular industries." The most important exceptions cited in 1962 were the following:

> (1) Wage rate increases would exceed the general guide rate in an industry which would otherwise be unable to attract sufficient labor; or in which wage rates are exceptionally low compared with the range of wages earned elsewhere by similar labor, because the bargaining position of workers has been weak in particular local labor markets.
>
> (2) Wage rate increases would fall short of the general guide rate in an industry which could not provide jobs for its entire labor force even in times of generally full employment; or in which wage rates are exceptionally high compared with the range of wages earned elsewhere by similar labor, because

---

[12] Shultze and Tryon, "Prices and Costs in Manufacturing Industries," Joint Economic Committee, Study Paper No. 17 (Washington, D.C.: U.S. Government Printing Office, 1960), 58 pp.; Eckstein and Ott, "Steel and the Postwar Inflation," Joint Economic Committee, Study Paper No. 2 (Washington, D.C.: U.S. Government Printing Office, 1959), pp. 1–38; Wilson "An Analysis of the Inflation in Machinery Prices," Joint Economic Committee, Study Paper No. 3 (Washington, D.C.: U.S. Government Printing Office. 1959), pp. 41–81.

[13] *Economic Report of the President, together with the Annual Report of the Council of Economic Advisers* (Washington, D.C.: U.S. Government Printing Office, 1963), p. 189.

the bargaining position of workers has been especially strong.

(3) Prices would rise more rapidly, or fall more slowly, than indicated by the general guide rate in an industry in which the level of profits was insufficient to attract the capital required to finance a needed expansion in capacity; or in which costs other than labor costs had risen.

(4) Prices would rise more slowly, or fall more rapidly, than indicated by the general guide in an industry in which the relation of productive capacity to full employment demand shows the desirability of an outflow of capital from the industry; or in which costs other than labor costs have fallen; or in which excessive market power has resulted in rates of profit substantially higher than those earned elsewhere on investments of comparable risk.[14]

The guideposts were not intended to be substituted for vigorous fiscal and monetary policies, nor considered applicable in all circumstances. Kermit Gordon, a member of the Council of Economic Advisers when the guideposts were first enunciated, stated at the recent Employment Act Symposium: "It was thought that there existed a band of unemployment rates, above which the guideposts were superfluous and below which they would be largely ineffective. While neither the width nor the position of this band could be defined with precision . . . it was felt that within the band the guideposts would have a constructive influence in restraining inflationary wage and price behavior."

The guideposts attracted immediate and wide attention. Numerous questions of meaning and interpretation soon arose.

First, were the guideposts only a means of assisting the general public in appraising the wisdom of private wage and price decisions, or were they subject to enforcement through the exercise of executive power? The Council's Report insisted that the guideposts were intended as a contribution to "public discussion and clarification of the issues." But President Kennedy and Secretary Goldberg each stated on more than one occasion that the government could not stand idly by when the public interest needed protecting.

Second, how were the exceptions to be applied? When are wage rates "exceptionally high" compared with wages earned elsewhere by "similar" labor? When is labor's bargaining position in a particu-

[14] *Ibid.,* p. 189.

lar labor market "weak" or "especially strong"? How much would costs other than labor have to rise in order to justify a price increase? What is the basis of judging whether an industry has attracted "sufficient" capital?

Third, how was the productivity test itself to be applied? (Actually no percentage figure was specified, but a table was supplied showing growth of output per man-hour in various parts of the economy during various periods. Since 3 per cent was the average increase for the total economy between 1947 and 1960, the report was widely interpreted as establishing a "three per cent productivity limit.") On this point there were three chief possibilities:

(*a*) The first was the one urged by the Council: that average wage increases should not exceed average productivity gains, but that specific adjustments might deviate upward or downward in accordance with the suggested criteria. The critieria themselves had some startling implications, such as the notion that wage increases under free collective bargaining could be inversely proportional to the workers' bargaining power. But there was an even more fundamental problem: how could a desired ex post statistical result be converted into thousands of ex ante wage decisions? Has the Council provided a policy guide or a tool of economic analysis?

(*b*) A second possibility was that wage increases should not exceed 3.0 or 3.5 per cent. Although the Council strived to obviate such an interpretation, the administration contributed to it by publicly praising significant wage settlements "within the limits set by productivity," and remaining silent on those exceeding 3.0 or 3.5 per cent.

(*c*) The third—and most realistic—interpretation was that the guideposts provided a serviceable tool which the administration might use in a few key situations such as steel. As Solicitor General Archibald Cox observed at the time, "the trick may be to pick out those few situations which have the same potential as steel for setting off a chain reaction." Actually the more important problem was to identify those prices and wages which had strategic importance and which the government could put its finger on. This soon created problems of equity, notably the government's inability to put its finger on the construction industry with its highly decentralized bargaining structure.

The first year's experience was somewhat equivocal. The steel wage settlement was praised for being noninflationary, and the administration staved off what would have been a damaging increase in steel prices. The wage settlement for non-operating railroad employees won a presidential blessing; but if the guideposts had been taken seriously the increase would have been smaller, considering the rapidly declining employment trend in the industry. In any event it is doubtful that the increase would have been any larger in the absence of the guideposts. In the shipping and airline industries, wage settlements far out of line with the guideposts were developed with the assistance of federal mediators, emergency boards, and special representatives. In the construction industry, large annual increases were negotiated in contracts running from three to five years in duration.

In 1963, as in 1962, the principal guidepost incidents involved the steel industry. In April the major producers made some selective price increases amounting to a 1 per cent advance in the industry's price level. President Kennedy commented that they had "acted with some restraint," and expressed the hope that other companies—"particularly in the oil industry," as well as the Steelworkers' Union—would do likewise. In June the Steelworkers accepted a new contract, to run from July 30, 1963, to May 31, 1965. There was no wage increase and the fringe benefits did not amount to more than 3 per cent per year.

Under the circumstances of 1962–63, with the unemployment rate hovering close to 6 per cent, it is doubtful that inflation was such a serious threat to justify active emphasis on wage and price restraint. At the beginning of 1964, however, it seemed apparent that the income-tax cut would soon be enacted. The Council endeavored to tighten up the exceptions to the guideposts, lest they become the general rule. "The general guideposts can cover the vast majority of wage and price decisions. . . . The modifications of the guideposts still apply, but it must be emphasized that they are intended to apply to only a relatively few cases."

In addition, the 1964 Report included the well-known 3.2 per cent, described as the "average annual percentage change in output per man-hour during the last 5 years." This immediately became the de facto standard of wage increases, and the exceptions faded into the background. Likewise the language concerning price cuts became part of the background music.

The important applications of the price guideposts in 1964–66 (at least those which have been the subject of public discussion) have been mainly in basic raw material industries—steel, aluminum, copper. In the latter two cases, government-owned stockpiles were available to stabilize the market. The principal wage cases have been the 1964 auto contracts, the 1965 steel agreement, and the federal employees' pay bill of 1965. The annual cost of the auto settlement, including fringe benefits, was something over 4 per cent; President Johnson hoped that "other industries with profits below the high levels in the automobile industry will not use the auto settlement as a pattern." The steel settlement was consistent with the guideposts when all the complications of timing were taken into account, while the federal pay bill provided an average increase of 3.6 per cent.

In its 1966 Report, the Council decided to drop the five-year moving average of productivity changes in the private economy.

> Now that the economy is at the end of its fifth year of uninterrupted expansion, a five-year moving average no longer gives a reasonable approximation of the true productivity trend. The last recession year (1960) drops out of the average; yet the unsustainable productivity gains of a year of recovery (1961) and four years of improving utilization of productive capacity are retained. . . . It appears that the long-term trend, independent of cyclical swings, is slightly over 3 percent.[15]

On these grounds the Council recommended that the 3.2 per cent wage guidepost be continued.

E. ATTITUDE OF LABOR AND MANAGEMENT IN THE UNITED STATES

The official pronouncements of the AFL-CIO and the leading business organizations concerning the guideposts are distinctly negative.

The most recent statement of the AFL-CIO Executive Council, made on February 24, 1966, stressed the following objections: (1) Increased living costs have not been taken into account, with the result that a 3.2 per cent guidepost for money wage increases

---

[15] *Economic Report of the President, together with the Annual Report of the Council of Economic Advisers* (Washington, D.C.: U.S. Government Printing Office, 1966), p. 92.

does not yield 3.2 per cent in real purchasing power. (2) If the trend rate of productivity must be the ceiling, average wage increases will be less than the productivity increase because of the weak bargaining position of many workers. (3) The guideposts weigh more heavily on workers than on employers because wage increases can readily be compared with the 3.2 per cent, while there is no standard for profits and dividends; and industries with higher than average productivity gains have not reduced their prices. (4) The credibility of the guideposts was destroyed when the moving-average formula was changed in 1966. This action has accelerated the shift of income from wage and salary earners to other groups.

The National Association of Manufacturers, in commenting on the President's Economic Report for 1966, said that the wage guidepost has some value as an educational device, but tends to become a floor rather than a ceiling for wage changes. Other business objections are that price increases are dealt with more harshly than wage increases, as shown by recent situations in steel, aluminum, and copper; that prices ought to be set by competitive forces; and that the Council of Economic Advisers should not act as a part-time enforcement agency without statutory powers or administrative procedures.

Official utterances tend to be dogmatic and seldom tell the whole story. Despite labor's deep and genuine discontent with the present policy, it is significant that the AFL-CIO has not expressed categorical opposition to wage and price restraint policies as such. There may be a recognition that oversized wage increases could result in the abandonment of expansionary policies on the part of government. Likewise, despite the anti-interventionist theme of NAM and Chamber of Commerce expressions, it seems evident that many large corporations are willing to recognize that, because of their size and importance, they have acquired the status of "semi-public utilities." If faced with a practical choice between formal controls and informal guideposts, there might be an inclination to prefer the latter.

Thus it is necessary to distinguish between the principle of wage and price restraint and the format which has been developed up to now. Dissatisfaction with the present format does not necessarily mean rejection of the principle.

IV. THE RECORD OF WAGES, COSTS, AND PRICES

Economic data for leading industrial countries (including some not specifically discussed in this paper) are set forth in Tables 1–6 at the end of this article. These tables include measures of money wages, real wages, unit labor costs, consumer prices, wholesale prices, and unemployment rates. There are additional details for the United States in Tables 7–11.

The essential purpose of wage and price restraints is to minimize increases in unit labor costs and price levels. Yet, it is very difficult to find any perceptible correlation between the existence of formal wage-price or incomes policies, on the one hand, and the degree of cost and price stability on the other. Neither does the existence of special bipartite or tripartite machinery appear to affect the results in any systematic way. Emergency actions of a mandatory character, such as the price freeze in France in recent years, do show up in the statistics. But it does not seem possible to isolate the effect of informal controls of the guidepost variety. For example, two of the European countries with the most elaborate organization for incomes policy have been the Netherlands and the United Kingdom. They have the highest labor cost indexes (on a 1953 base) with the exception of France and are in the upper half of countries in terms of consumer price indexes.

Italy, Germany, and Japan were the countries with the most stable labor costs and the most stable wholesale prices in the period up to 1960. Incomes policy was not emphasized in any of these countries prior to 1960, although the German government has made some ineffective pronouncements in more recent years.

The difficulty of interpreting the statistics does not prove that incomes policies have been insignificant. An alternative explanation would be that the impact has been overshadowed and outweighed by other influences on costs and prices. Among these would be the following:

1. *Unemployment rates*. Since 1958 the United States has had the best record of any country in the world with respect to stability of labor costs. Comparisons are difficult, however, because of high unemployment levels in this country until 1965. It might be added that the relationship between incomes policy and cost-price stability is not at all clear even for countries with comparable unemployment rates. As Table 1 indicates, Sweden and Japan have had

unemployment rates in the area between 1 and 2 per cent (adjusted to American concepts and definitions). There has been more talk about incomes policy in Sweden, but costs and prices have remained lower in Japan.

2. *Productivity growth.* Comparable productivity statistics are not available, but it is known that the percentage increase in output per man-hour has been extraordinarily high in Italy, Germany, and Japan during the postwar period. The reason is that these countries began from such low levels after their military defeat in World War II. Indexes of hourly earnings and real earnings have also been among the highest, and for the same reason. It is no coincidence that these countries were able to combine low unemployment with cost-price stability for about fifteen years after the war.

3. *Labor force growth.* Labor force growth is an additional factor affecting the degree of cost and price stability in an era of rapid economic expansion. In this respect, Germany has had the advantage of high birth rates during the 1930's, as well as the resettlement of the Sudeten Germans, the influx of refugees from the East, and large-scale importation of labor from Greece, Italy, Spain, and elsewhere. France, in contrast, has had difficulty maintaining labor force growth because of low birth rates in the prewar period.

4. *Mixed purposes.* Cost-price stability is not the only objective of wage-making institutions and not the only basis on which they have been judged. The much discussed collective bargaining systems in Sweden, Norway, and Denmark, for example, are often discussed in terms of incomes policy. But the fact is that subsequent to the early period of postwar reconstruction (during which austerity was practiced with considerable success, as in the United Kingdom), the principal theme of the Scandinavian systems has been the maintenance of industrial peace through highly centralized negotiations between authoritative confederations of labor and management. There are some minor strains of incomes policy, it is true. For instance, it is said that Denmark's purpose is to have about the same amount of inflation as its trading partners, and that a prediction of wage drift becomes an element in the bargaining between Swedish employers and unions. But the Scandinavian systems are primarily addressed toward industrial peace.

V. CONCLUDING COMMENTS

Wage and price restraints acquire meaning only in a larger policy context. They are only one aspect of increasingly active government intervention throughout the advanced industrial countries in furtherance of an increasingly strong commitment to full employment and economic growth. While the degree of concern over inflation varies from one country to another, it is not in the cards that a country can assume permanent responsibility for the employment level and remain persistently indifferent to costs and prices. The fact that full employment, price stability, and economic freedom have not yet been satisfactorily reconciled does not mean that the search can or will be abandoned.

The unsatisfactory state of affairs and the prevalent controversy concerning wage and price guideposts in the United States is no reflection at all on the authors or guardians of the guideposts. On the contrary, it reflects the fact that they have been operating at the frontier of economic policy. It ought to be comforting that the posture is equally uncomfortable in most other countries, and more so in some.

The fact is that despite many years of experimentation, the problem is still in an experimental stage. Each country will have to answer a somewhat different set of questions in light of its own particular history, ideology, and institutions. I should like to conclude this paper by listing some of the principal questions which have to be considered in the United States:

1. What is wage-price policy or guidepost policy or guideline policy or incomes policy anyway? The problem is still at a stage where there is a real need to clarify concepts and definitions. Every survey of incomes policy includes a somewhat different set of countries and programs. I take it we are not speaking of mandatory regulation of wages and prices in their full detail, supported by large-scale administrative and enforcement apparatus, such as we imposed during World War II, or the temporary absolute freeze of prices and/or wages in a military or economic emergency, such as we used in 1951 and the French in 1963. Our present preoccupation is with informal more than formal regulation, and with long-term more than short-term efforts. On the other hand, it need not be assumed that the scope of guidepost policy is necessarily limited to rates of wages and to unit prices, nor that the productivity trend

must necessarily be the sole or principal fulcrum of policy.

2. Can greater public acceptance of an overriding national need justifying restraints on private behavior, even the absence of a major war, be secured? Traditionally the level of economic understanding in the United States has not been high, but the situation has greatly improved in the past decade. I personally think that discussion concerning the guideposts has contributed to a better understanding of economic relationships and has had some informal influence on wage and price determination even in cases where specific pressure has not been exerted. Knowledgeable leaders of management and labor recognize that even if the war in Vietnam were to end tomorrow, they would not have heard the last of wage and price restraint. But we are still a long way from a consensus on the policy needs.

3. How can the leaders of industry, labor, and other affected interest groups be associated with policy formulation without the sacrifice of policy objectives? It is surely unlikely that effective wage and price restraint can be imposed on business firms and unions from the outside, especially in the absence of a national emergency. If policy is to be developed through consultation with the principal interest groups, there must be a potent consultative mechanism capable of producing an authoritative consensus. But there is always a real danger that consensus will be achieved at the expense of objectives.

4. How can guideposts be made effective in a wider sector of the economy without formal and mandatory control? As noted above, pressures have been exerted largely on national unions and oligopolistic firms in the primary metal industries, and on federal pay adjustment legislation. Could effective compliance be secured elsewhere through industry councils, or centralized collective bargaining structures, or special dispute settlement mechanisms, or consultation with professional associations, or in some other fashion?

5. Is a controlled wage *level* compatible with a flexible wage *structure* which can respond to special factors affecting particular industries, establishments, trades, and professions?

6. Is it possible to build a better bridge between long-run economic relationships and short-run wage and price decisions? Is it possible to have a wage policy, incorporating other elements beyond the trend rate of productivity, which is neither too rigid to be

enforceable nor too limber to be significant? Likewise, can standards of price determination be devised which are more closely related to price theory and policy than those presently set forth in the guideposts, without establishing a rule of "anything goes"?

7. If average wage increases are held to a level of the trend productivity rate, and consumer prices continue to creep upward, how can workers receive the real wage increases to which they are entitled in accordance with guidepost theory? Even if average labor costs are kept from rising, this is no guarantee that consumer prices will remain stable. Real hourly compensation in the American economy has risen by 3.2 per cent or more in only one year since 1959. This appears to have occurred in 1963–64 (see Table 7), and there are reasons to suspect the accuracy of the statistics for that year. Real hourly compensation rose only 2.1 per cent in 1964–65. The increase will probably be less than 2 per cent in 1965–66.

Traditionally, real wage rates have increased less than productivity in periods of boom and more than productivity in periods of recession. There is a shift to profits in the boom and a shift away from profits in the recession. If we are successful in avoiding recessions—which is the central purpose of the New Economics—when should real wages catch up? Attaching a cost-of-living escalator clause to the guideposts, under circumstances like those of the present, would not only contribute to a wage-price spiral but also yield a target figure beyond the reach of all but the most powerful unions. Guideposts of 6 per cent or more would hardly be a stabilizing device in today's economy. But labor will understandably be less than enthusiastic about a permanent wage gap and a chronic shift to profits. Does this mean that complete and literal stability of consumer prices must be obtainted? Is there an appropriate time and place for real wages to catch up with productivity in the absence of recessions?

It may be that the problem is insoluble so long as wage and price policies are tied so closely to a single criterion, the trend productivity rate; and that the appropriate terms of wage and price restraint will have to be redefined from time to time on the basis of intensive study of the entire economic situation. Such an examination might provide a format for intimate consultation among leaders of government, industry, and labor.

TABLE 1

Unemployment Rates in Eight Major Industrial Countries, 1960–65[1]

	United States	Canada	France[2]	Germany (Federal Republic)	Britain	Italy	Sweden	Japan
1960	5.6	7.0	2.6r	0.7	2.4	4.3	[3]	1.4
1961	6.7	7.1	2.3r	0.4	2.3	3.7	1.5	1.3
1962	5.6	5.9	2.5	0.4	2.9	3.2	1.5	1.1
1963	5.7	5.5	2.8r	0.5	3.4	2.7	1.7	1.1
1964 (preliminary)	5.2	4.7	2.3r	0.4	2.4r	3.0r	1.6	1.0
1965 (preliminary)	4.6	3.9	2.8	0.4	2.2	3.9	1.2	1.0

[1] Adjusted to United States labor force concepts and definitions.

[2] Includes unemployed repatriates from Algeria. Beginning in late 1962, a large number of repatriates entered France, adding an estimated 200,000 to 250,000 persons to the labor force. Most of these repatriates experienced some unemployment. If the unemployed repatriates are excluded, France's adjusted unemployment rates would be about 2.0 per cent in 1962, 1963, and 1964 and about 2.6 per cent in 1965.

[3] Not available.

Note: r = revised.

Sources: Neef, Arthur F., "International Unemployment Rates, 1960–64," in *Monthly Labor Review* 88, No. 3 (March, 1965): 256–259; and ILO, OECD, and national statistical publications. Some data are based partly on estimates.

Prepared by: U.S. Department of Labor, Bureau of Labor Statistics, Division of Foreign Labor Conditions (BIC), April, 1966.

TABLE 2

Indexes of Unit Labor Cost in Manufacturing for Selected Countries, 1953–65
(1953 = 100)

Selected countries	1953	1954	1955	1956	1957	1958	1959	1960	1961	1962	1963	1964[1]	1965[1]
National currency basis													
All employees:													
United States—Series A[2]	100	102	99	104	108	111	109	110	109	109	108	107	106
Series B[3]	100	102	100	108	111	114	114	118	118	116	117	117	...
Canada	100	102	98	101	109	110	109	113	112	111	112	112	114
France	100	102	109	115	125	140	143	144	153	164	176	177	(185)
Germany (F. R.)	100	99	99	106	108	111	110	113	120	128	132	133	(139)
Japan	100	103	104	104	98	104	98	96	98	107	111	109	(116)
The Netherlands	100	104	109	118	129	132	137	129	139	143	153	163	(170)
Sweden	100	104	109	114	114	116	115	117	121	129	132	133	...
The United Kingdom	100	101	105	115	119	125	124	125	135	139	138	139	(142)
Production workers:													
United States—Series A[2]	100	99	96	99	102	102	99	99	96	97	96	96	96
Series B[3]	100	99	97	103	105	104	104	106	105	103	105	104	...
Germany (F. R.)	100	96	99	106	106	108	106	108	114	121	123	124	...
Italy	100	96	94	95	94	93	86	85	87	93	102	107	...
Sweden[4]	100	105	108	113	113	113	111	111	114	118	120	119	...
The United Kingdom	100	101	105	114	117	120	119	121	128	130	128	129	...
United States dollar basis[5]													
All employees:													
Canada	100	103	98	102	112	112	112	115	108	102	102	102	104
France	100	102	109	115	116	108	102	103	109	117	125	126	(132)
Germany (F. R.)	100	99	99	106	108	111	110	113	124	134	139	139	(146)
The Netherlands	100	104	109	118	129	132	127	129	147	151	162	172	(179)
Production workers:													
Germany (F. R.)	100	96	99	106	106	108	106	108	119	127	129	130	...

[1] Preliminary. Data in parentheses are estimates that may be considerably revised.
[2] Based on Federal Reserve Board index of manufacturing production.
[3] Based on estimates of gross national product originating in manufacturing, published by the U.S. Department of Commerce, Office of Business Economics.
[4] Manufacturing and mining.
[5] Adjusted for changes in the official or commercial exchange rate. Until 1961, the Canadian dollar had no par value and was allowed to fluctuate freely in international exchange markets. Adjustments for France are based upon changes that occurred in 1957 and 1958. Adjustments for Germany and the Netherlands are based upon changes in par value that occurred in March, 1961.
Prepared by: U.S. Department of Labor, Bureau of Labor Statistics, Division of Foreign Labor Conditions (BLC), April, 1966.

TABLE 3

Average Hourly Earnings and Indexes of Earnings in Manufacturing in 12 Countries, Selected Years, 1953–65

Year	United States Dollars	Belgium Francs	Canada Dollars	Denmark Kroner	France Francs	Germany, (Federal Republic) DM	Italy Lire	Japan Yen	Netherlands Guilders	Sweden Kronor	Switzerland Men Francs	Switzerland Women	United Kingdom Men Pence	United Kingdom Women Pence
Currency unit:	Dollars	Francs	Dollars	Kroner	Francs	DM	Lire	Yen	Guilders	Kronor	Francs	Francs	Pence	Pence
Average Hourly Earnings in National Currency Units														
1953	1.74	21.31[1]	1.36	4.06	1.41	1.59	169	77.9	1.03	3.79	2.81	1.83	49.2	29.5
1957	2.05	26.63[1]	1.61	5.03	2.02	2.09	207	94.9	1.49	4.90	3.21	2.06	65.3	37.7
1960	2.26	29.59	1.78	6.03	2.59	2.62	232	109.3	1.75	5.77	3.61	2.29	76.8	44.0
1962	2.39	33.26	1.88	7.49	3.03	3.23	286	140.2	2.17	6.78	4.13	2.61	84.9	49.0
1963	2.46	36.20	1.95	8.11	3.29	3.46	334	155.9	2.33	7.29	4.48	2.82	88.7	51.0
1964	2.53	40.74	2.02	8.84	3.50	3.73	371	169.9	n.a.	7.76[1]	4.83	3.03	95.5	54.6
1965	2.65	42.72	2.15	9.21	n.a.	4.15	n.a.	n.a.	n.a.	n.a.	n.a.	n.a.	99.9	56.8
	(Dec.)	(Apr.)	(Oct.)	(Mar.)	(July)	(July)							(Oct.)	(Oct.)
Indexes of Hourly Earnings (1953 = 100)														
1953	100.0	100.0	100.0	100.0	100.0	100.0	100.0	100.0	100.0	100.0	100.0	100.0	100.0	100.0
1957	117.8	125.0	118.3	123.9	143.3	131.4	122.5	121.8	144.7	129.4	114.3	112.6	132.5	127.9
1960	129.9	138.9	130.9	148.6	183.7	164.8	137.4	140.3	169.9	152.4	128.6	125.2	156.2	149.2
1962	137.4	156.1	138.2	184.5	214.9	203.0	169.4	182.2	210.7	179.0	147.1	142.7	172.7	166.2
1963	141.4	169.9	143.3	199.8	233.4	217.6	197.8	200.1	226.3	192.5	159.5	154.2	180.4	173.0
1964	145.4	191.2	148.5	217.7	248.3	234.6	219.6	218.0	260.2	204.9[1]	172.0	165.7	194.2	185.1
1965	152.3	200.5	158.0	226.9	n.a.	261.0	n.a.	n.a.	276.0	n.a.	n.a.	n.a.	203.2	192.7
	(Dec.)	(Apr.)	(Oct.)	(Mar.)	(July)	(July)								

[1] Estimated.

Note: Data for Belgium, Netherlands, and the United Kingdom represent October each year; data for France represent September each year.

Source: Statistical Supplements, *International Labour Review*, selected early years, *Bulletin of Labour Statistics*, 4th Quarter 1965, and the *Year Book of Labour Statistics*, 1964, International Labour Office (ILO), Geneva; and national statistical publications.

Prepared by: U.S. Department of Labor, Bureau of Labor Statistics, Division of Foreign Labor Conditions (BIC), April, 1966.

133

TABLE 4

Consumer Price Index, 12 Countries, 1953–65
(1953 = 100)

Year and month	United States	Belgium[1]	Canada	Denmark[2,3]	France	Germany (Federal Republic)	Italy	Japan	Netherlands[3]	Sweden[3]	Switzerland	United Kingdom
1953	100.0	100.0	100.0	100	100.0	100.0	100.0	100.0	100	100	100.0	100.0
1954	100.4	101.1	100.6	101	99.7	100.2	102.8	106.5	104	101	100.7	101.8
1955	100.1	100.8	100.8	108	100.8	101.8	105.2	105.3	106	104	101.6	106.4
1956	101.6	103.7	102.3	114	102.8	104.4	108.8	105.7	108	109	103.2	111.6
1957	105.2	106.9	105.5	115	105.4	106.6	110.2	109.0	115	113	105.1	115.8
1958	108.0	108.3	108.3	115	121.5	108.8	113.3	108.5	117	119	107.2	119.3
1959	108.9	109.6	109.5	117	128.9	109.9	112.8	109.7	118	120	106.4	120.0
1960	110.6	110.0	110.8	118	133.6	111.5	115.4	113.6	121	124	107.9	121.2
1961	111.8	111.0	111.9	123	138.0	114.3	117.2	119.6	123	127	110.0	125.3
1962	113.0	112.6	113.2	133	144.7	118.3	123.3	127.8	127	133	114.7	130.6
1963	114.4	115.0	115.2	140	151.6	122.0	132.5	137.5	132	137	118.7	133.2
1964	115.9	119.9	117.2	144	156.7	123.8	140.3	142.7	136	141	122.2	137.6
1965:												
June	118.1	124.9	120.3	151[5]	162.6	128.7	146.3	153.9	146	146	126.3	145.0
	119.1	126.4	121.4	158	161.7	129.5	147.7	154.8	145	151	129.2	146.2
	(Dec.)	(Nov.)	(Nov.)	(Oct.)	(Nov.)	(Nov.)	(Sept.)	(Nov.)	(Nov.)	(Nov.)	(Nov.)	(Nov.)

[1] Excluding rent.

[2] Excluding rent. Inquiry at beginning of quarters; annual indexes are centered by averaging five quarters from January to January.

Note: The country indexes are not strictly comparable because of different methods and concepts used in their construction.

[3] From published rounded indexes.

[4] New national index (259 commodities) linked in 1962 to Paris region index (250 commodities).

[5] April.

Source: *Statistical Bulletins, Main Economic Indicators*, May, 1964, and January, 1966, (Paris: Organization for Economic Co-operation and Development (OECD), and national statistical publications.

Prepared by: U.S. Department of Labor, Bureau of Labor Statistics, Division of Foreign Labor Conditions (BIC), April 1966.

134

TABLE 5

Wholesale Price Index, 12 Countries, 1953–65

(1953 = 100)

Year and month	United States	Belgium	Canada	Denmark¹	France	Germany (Federal Republic)	Italy	Japan	Netherlands	Sweden¹	Switzerland	United Kingdom
1953	100.0	100.0	100.0	100	100.0	100.0	100.0	100.0	100.0	100	100.0	100.0
1954	100.2	99.0	98.3	100	98.3	98.4	99.1	99.2	101.4	99	100.8	100.3
1955	100.5	101.0	99.0	103	98.1	100.1	100.0	97.5	102.2	103	101.0	102.9
1956	103.8	103.6	102.2	106	102.4	101.5	101.7	101.8	104.5	108	103.4	107.3
1957	106.8	106.3	103.0	106	108.2	103.4	102.7	104.9	107.4	110	105.1	110.7
1958	108.3	101.7	103.1	105	120.7	103.0	100.9	98.0	105.2	107	101.8	111.4
1959	108.5	101.3	104.5	105	126.5	102.2	97.9	99.0	105.8	107	100.2	111.8
1960	108.6	102.6	104.6	105	129.7	103.4	98.8	100.1	103.2	111	100.8	113.3
1961	108.2	102.4	105.7	107	132.4	104.9	99.0	101.1	102.5	113	101.0	116.3
1962	108.5	103.2	108.7	109	136.0	106.1	102.0	99.4	103.3	115	104.5	119.0
1963	108.2	105.7	110.9	113	141.0	106.7	107.3	101.2	106.0	119	108.5	120.6
1964	108.4	108.9	111.2	117	142.4	107.7	110.9	101.4	112.4	126	110.5	121.7
1965: June	110.9	110.2	113.3	127	143.1	109.7	112.5	101.6	115.5	129	110.7	126.7
	112.3²	110.9	114.8	124	143.8	111.1	113.8	103.2	116.5	130	113.9	127.2
	(Dec.)	(Oct.)	(Nov.)	(Oct.)	(Nov.)	(Dec.)	(Nov.)	(Dec.)	(Nov.)	(Oct.)	(Nov.)	(Nov.)

¹ From published rounded indexes.   ² Provisional.

Note: The country indexes are not strictly comparable because of different methods and concepts used in their construction.

Source: *Statistical Bulletins, Main Economic Indicators,* May, 1964, and January, 1966, (Paris: Organization for Economic Co-operation and Development (OECD), and national statistical publications.

Prepared by: U.S. Department of Labor, Bureau of Labor Statistics, Division of Foreign Labor Conditions (BIC), April, 1966.

TABLE 6

Indexes of Real Hourly Earnings in Manufacturing in 12 Countries, Selected Years, 1953–65

(1953 = 100)

	United States	Belgium	Canada	Denmark	France	Germany (Federal Republic)	Italy	Japan	Netherlands	Sweden	Switzerland Men	Switzerland Women	United Kingdom Men	United Kingdom Women
1953	100.0	100.0	100.0	100.0	100.0	100.0	100.0	100.0	100.0	100.0	100.0	100.0	100.0	100.0
1957	112.0	116.8	112.1	109.1	135.9	123.3	111.1	111.9	125.9	115.1	108.8	107.2	114.4	110.5
1960	117.4	126.2	118.0	126.9	137.5	147.8	119.0	123.6	140.8	123.2	119.2	116.1	128.8	123.2
1962	121.4	138.6	122.2	141.2	148.5	172.7	137.2	142.6	169.8	135.0	128.4	124.4	132.2	127.2
1963	123.4	147.5	124.4	144.1	153.8	180.0	149.2	145.6	174.3	141.5	134.7	130.1	135.4	129.8
1964	125.3	159.5	126.7	152.0	158.3	189.4	156.4	152.8	188.7[1]	145.8	140.8	135.6	141.0	134.5
1965	128.6 (Apr.)	162.9 (Apr.)	131.3 (Nov.)	163.6 (June)	n.a.	201.8 (July)	n.a.	n.a.	192.9[1]	n.a.	n.a.	n.a.	141.0 (Apr.)	133.7 (Apr.)

[1] Estimated.

Sources: International Labor Office: *Year Book of Labor Statistics,* 1964, *Bulletin of Labor Statistics,* 3rd Quarter 1965, and *International Labor Review,* statistical supplements, selected issues; Organization for Economic Co-operation and Development (OECD), *Statistical Bulletins, Main Economic Indicators,* May, 1964, and January, 1966; and national statistical publications.

Prepared by: U.S. Department of Labor, Bureau of Labor Statistics, Division of Foreign Labor Conditions (BIC), April, 1966.

TABLE 7

Labor Compensation, Labor Costs and Prices Total Private Economy
Annual Percent Changes, 1947–65

Year	Compensation per Man-hour	Output per Man-hour	Unit Labor Costs[1]	GNP Deflator	Percent Change		Real Hourly Compensation[2]
					Wholesale Price Index	Consumer Price Index	
1947–48	8.8	4.2	4.4	+6.7	+ 8.3	+7.7	1.0
1948–49	1.7	3.2	−1.5	−0.6	− 5.0	−1.0	2.7
1949–50	7.0	8.3	−1.1	+1.4	+ 4.0	+1.0	5.9
1950–51	9.9	2.9	6.7	+6.7	+11.4	+8.0	1.7
1951–52	6.2	1.9	4.3	+2.2	− 2.8	+2.2	4.0
1952–53	6.4	4.1	2.0	+0.9	− 1.4	+0.8	5.5
1953–54	3.0	2.3	0.8	+1.5	+ 0.2	+0.4	2.6
1954–55	3.2	4.4	−1.2	+1.5	+ 0.3	−0.3	3.5
1955–56	5.8	0.1	5.6	+3.4	+ 3.2	+1.5	4.2
1956–57	6.4	3.0	3.3	+3.7	+ 2.9	+3.5	2.9
1957–58	4.2	2.9	1.2	+2.6	+ 1.4	+2.8	1.3
1958–59	4.6	3.7	0.9	+1.6	+ 0.2	+0.8	3.8
1959–60	3.9	1.6	2.2	+1.7	+ 0.1	+1.6	2.2
1960–61	3.7	3.4	0.3	+1.3	− 0.4	+1.1	2.7
1961–62	4.4	4.6	−0.3	+1.1	+ 0.3	+1.2	3.1
1962–63	4.0	3.5	0.6	+1.3	− 0.3	+1.2	2.7
1963–64	5.1	3.6	1.4	+1.7	+ 0.2	+1.3	3.8
1964–65	3.7	2.8	0.9	+1.8	+ 2.0	+1.7	2.1

[1] Index of compensation per man-hour divided by index of output per man-hour.

[2] Index of compensation per man-hour divided by Consumer Price Index.

TABLE 8

GNP IMPLICIT PRICE DEFLATOR, 1947–65

Seasonally adjusted quarterly totals at annual rates
(1958 = 100)

Year	4th Quarter Index	Percent Change 4th Qtr.—4th Qtr.
1947	77.0	
1948	80.3	+4.3
1949	78.9	−1.7
1950	82.3	+4.3
1951	86.7	+5.3
1952	88.3	+1.8
1953	88.4	+0.1
1954	89.8	+1.6
1955	91.6	+2.0
1956	95.4	+4.1
1957	98.5	+3.2
1958	100.6	+2.1
1959	102.1	+1.5
1960	104.0	+1.9
1961	105.1	+1.1
1962	106.2	+1.0
1963	107.8	+1.5
1964	109.6	+1.7
1965	111.7	+1.9

Source: *Survey of Current Business* August, 1965, 4th Quarter 1965 from *Economic Report.*

TABLE 9

WHOLESALE PRICE INDEX

Per cent Change from December to December

Year	All Commodities	Farm Products and Processed Foods	Industrial Commodities
1947–48	+ 1.4	− 6.8	+ 4.9
1948–49	− 6.1	− 8.9	− 4.9
1949–50	+14.7	+17.0	+13.9
1950–51	+ 1.3	+ 3.5	+ 0.4
1951–52	− 3.5	− 8.3	− 1.4
1952–53	+ 0.4	− 2.3	+ 1.5
1953–54	− 0.5	− 2.6	+ 0.2
1954–55	+ 1.6	− 6.4	+ 4.3
1955–56	+ 4.5	+ 6.1	+ 4.1
1956–57	+ 1.9	+ 4.2	+ 1.1
1957–58	+ 0.6	− 0.3	+ 0.9
1958–59	− 0.3	− 4.4	+ 1.1
1959–60	+ 0.5	+ 3.9	− 0.6
1960–61	− 0.2	− 0.6	− 0.1
1961–62	0.0	+ 0.6	− 0.2
1962–63	− 0.1	− 2.1	+ 0.5
1963–64	+ 0.4	0.0	+ 0.6
1964–65	+ 3.4	+ 9.6	+ 1.4
1965	—	—	—

Source: U.S. Department of Labor, Bureau of Labor Statistics, Washington, D.C. 20212, February, 1966.

TABLE 10

Per cent Change in Selected CPI Components 1947–65

Year ending December	All items	Food	Non-durable commodities less food	Durable commodities	Services
1948	2.7	—0.9	5.0	6.9	6.1
1949	—1.9	—3.7	—4.9	—2.5	3.5
1950	5.8	9.7	5.3	6.1	3.7
1951	5.9	7.4	4.7	4.6	5.2
1952	0.9	—1.1	—0.6	—0.1	4.6
1953	0.6	—1.2	1.8	—1.5	4.2
1954	—0.4	—1.7	—0.6	—2.1	1.9
1955	0.3	—0.9	1.1	—1.2	2.2
1956	2.9	3.1	2.8	2.2	3.1
1957	3.0	2.8	2.2	2.3	4.5
1958	1.7	2.2	—0.3	1.8	2.8
1959	1.5	—0.8	2.5	0.6	3.6
1960	1.6	3.1	0.9	—1.7	2.8
1961	0.6	—0.9	0.3	1.1	1.9
1962	1.2	1.5	1.0	0.5	1.7
1963	1.7	1.8	1.2	1.0	2.2
1964	1.1	1.4	0.4	0.4	1.8
1965	2.0	3.5	2.0	—1.0	2.7

TABLE 11

Gross Average Hourly Earnings, Selected Industries, 1947–65

			Manufacturing							Retail trade		Finance, insurance, and real estate		
Date	Mining	Contract construction	Total Gross	Total Straight-time	Motor vehicles and equipment	Motor vehicles	Basic steel	Textile mill products	Wholesale trade	Total	Limited price variety stores	Total	Banking	Hotels, tourist courts, and motels
December — Average Hourly Earnings														
1947	$1.588	$1.632	$1.274	$1.22	$1.560	—	$1.528	$1.099	$1.260	$0.923	—	—	—	—
1948	1.729	1.780	1.377	1.34	1.683	—	1.667	1.188	1.335	.980	—	—	—	—
1949	1.701	1.827	1.384	1.35	1.713	—	1.657	1.189	1.369	1.005	—	—	—	—
1950	1.827	1.948	1.517	1.45	1.865	—	1.843	1.304	1.483	1.060	—	—	—	—
1951	1.98	2.08	1.61	1.54	1.98	—	1.91	1.34	1.56	1.13	—	—	—	—
1952	2.13	2.22	1.70	1.63	2.14	—	2.13	1.36	1.65	1.18	—	—	—	—
1953	2.16	2.36	1.77	1.71	2.18	—	2.20	1.36	1.73	1.24	—	—	—	—
1954	2.15	2.43	1.81	1.75	2.26	—	2.27	1.36	1.78	1.28	—	—	—	—
1955	2.26	2.50	1.90	1.83	2.33	—	2.48	1.41	1.87	1.33	—	—	—	—
1956	2.42	2.65	2.02	1.95	2.50	—	2.64	1.46	1.98	1.38	—	—	—	—
1957	2.49	2.79	2.08	2.03	2.51	—	2.74	1.49	2.06	1.46	$0.98	—	$1.71	$1.06
1958	2.51	2.91	2.17	2.10	2.74	$2.83	2.98	1.51	2.13	1.53	1.01	—	1.76	1.11
1959	2.62	3.01	2.24	2.17	2.77	2.85	3.08	1.58	2.20	1.56	1.05	—	1.82	1.14
1960	2.62	3.17	2.29	2.23	2.83	2.91	3.05	1.61	2.26	1.61	1.05	—	1.90	1.19
1961	2.69	3.30	2.37	2.29	2.99	3.10	3.25	1.65	2.34	1.68	1.13	—	1.97	1.23
1962	2.74	3.41	2.43	2.34	3.11	3.22	3.24	1.69	2.41	1.74	1.16	—	2.03	1.24
1963	2.78	3.53	2.51	2.42	3.22	3.32	3.31	1.76	2.48	1.81	1.21	—	2.08	1.24
1964	2.86	3.63	2.58	2.47	3.32	3.44	3.39	1.83	2.55	1.77	1.31	$2.34	2.08	1.35
1965	2.97	3.76	2.66	2.54	3.43	3.52	3.44	1.91	2.65	1.85	1.41	2.43	2.16	1.40
Percent Change														
1946–47	—	—	11.7	11.0	11.5	—	15.9	—	7.7	10.4	—	—	—	—
1947–48	8.9	9.1	8.1	9.8	7.9	—	9.1	8.1	6.0	6.2	—	—	—	—
1948–49	-1.6	2.6	.5	.7	1.8	—	-.6	(1)	2.5	2.6	—	—	—	—
1949–50	7.4	6.6	9.6	7.4	8.9	—	11.2	9.7	8.3	5.5	—	—	—	—
1950–51	8.4	6.8	6.1	6.2	6.2	—	3.6	2.8	5.2	6.6	—	—	—	—
1951–52	7.6	6.7	5.6	5.8	8.1	—	11.5	1.5	5.8	4.4	—	—	—	—
1952–53	1.4	6.3	4.1	4.9	1.9	—	3.3	(1)	4.8	5.1	—	—	—	—
1953–54	-.5	3.0	2.3	2.3	3.7	—	3.2	(1)	2.9	3.2	—	—	—	—
1954–55	5.1	2.9	5.0	4.6	3.1	—	9.3	3.7	5.1	3.9	—	—	—	—
1955–56	7.1	6.0	6.3	6.6	7.3	—	6.5	3.5	5.9	3.8	—	—	—	—
1956–57	2.9	5.3	3.0	4.1	.4	—	3.8	2.1	4.0	5.8	—	—	—	—
1957–58	.8	4.3	4.3	3.4	9.2	—	8.8	1.3	3.4	4.8	3.1	—	2.9	4.7
1958–59	4.4	3.4	3.2	3.3	1.1	.7	3.4	4.6	3.3	2.0	4.0	—	3.4	2.7
1959–60	(1)	5.3	2.2	2.8	2.2	2.1	-1.0	1.9	2.7	3.2	(1)	—	4.4	4.4
1960–61	2.7	4.1	3.5	2.7	5.7	6.5	6.6	2.5	3.5	4.3	7.6	—	3.7	3.4
1961–62	1.9	3.3	2.5	2.2	4.0	3.9	-.3	2.4	3.0	3.6	2.7	—	3.0	.8
1962–63	1.5	3.5	3.3	3.4	3.5	3.1	2.2	4.1	2.9	4.0	4.3	—	2.5	(1)
1963–64	2.9	2.8	2.8	2.1	3.1	3.6	2.4	4.0	2.8	-2.2	8.3	—	(1)	8.9
1964–65	3.8	3.6	3.1	2.8	3.3	2.3	1.5	4.4	3.9	4.5	7.6	3.8	3.8	3.7

1 No change.

NOTE: Dashes indicate data not available.

Source: U.S. Department of Labor, Bureau of Labor Statistics.

E. H. PHELPS BROWN

Guidelines for Growth and for Incomes in the United Kingdom: Some Possible Lessons for the United States

E. H. PHELPS BROWN is professor at the London School of Economics and a participant in current British efforts to develop a workable incomes policy. He describes this development, its conceptual under- pinning and operational approach, and offers us some lessons which may be useful for policy-makers in the United States.

I. THE MOVEMENT TOWARD GUIDELINES

The United Kingdom has not adopted its guidelines out of any doctrinal conviction. Governments have developed the pol- icy by successive acts of expediency: they have been driven into it by force of circumstances and the lack of practicable alternatives. As an abstract principle it was repugnant to accepted notions. The first Labour government after World War II, in introducing what proved to be a two years' standstill in wages, salaries, and divi- dends, declared that "it is not desirable for the Government to interfere directly with the income of individuals otherwise than by taxation. To go further would mean that the Government would be forced itself to assess and regulate all personal incomes according to some scale which would have to be determined. This would be an incursion by the Government into what has hitherto been regarded as a field of free contract between individuals and organisations."[1] The instigation to a return to economic planning came not from socialist circles but from top management. The decisive steps of setting up new institutions, one to plan economic growth and the other to pass pay rises in review, were taken by a Conservative government dedicated to the restoration of a "free for all."

The circumstances that forced these uncongenial measures upon governments were mainly those of the foreign balance. A sharp, adverse movement of the terms of trade through the war years, and the loss of income from overseas investments sold during the war, obliged the United Kingdom to increase its exports greatly if it was only to pay for its prewar volume of imports. By 1956 it had in fact succeeded in doubling the volume of its exports. But this was not enough. With the growth of the home economy, imports continued to mount; increasing payments overseas were needed for aid and defense; with the freeing of capital markets, investment overseas grew too. Although the total value of British exports doubled between 1950 and 1964, the rate of rise proved too low to prevent deficits in the balance of payments recurring whenever an upturn of domestic activity brought a surge of imports. These deficits were more embarrassing than they would have been in a country whose currency was not used as an international reserve. The experience of 1957 showed that a loss of confidence could put sterling under pressure without any current deficit in the balance of payments; when a deficit was evident and persistent, a run on the pound became inevitable.

The countermeasures were traditional: higher interest rates, quantitative and qualitative restriction of credit, and a check on government spending together with higher taxes. These proved effective in meeting the crisis of the foreign exchanges. But at home they were associated with checks to investment and output, and a rise in unemployment. A sharp political reaction expressed the disquiet of public opinion. Governments did not wait to see whether the continuance of monetary and fiscal constraints would prove compatible with a renewed rise of physical output but

[1] Statement on Personal Incomes, Costs & Prices (Cmd. 7321, Feb., 1948).

loosened the constraints as soon as they dared. Activity responded for two years or so; but then once more the balance of payments gave concern, and on went the brakes again. Periods of fairly rapid growth of industrial production—1953–55, 1959–60, and 1963–64—alternated with periods of little growth or none—1956–58, 1960–62, and 1965.

These fluctuations were not greater than those of some other Western economies, and we cannot be sure that if governments had not used controls correctively the course of growth left to itself would have been steadier or more rapid. The modulation of investment in the public sector, indeed, served at times to offset an investment cycle in the private sector such as previous experience suggests would have tended to assert itself in any case. But at particular points controls impinged to set up fluctuations. The effect was conspicuous: it was stigmatized as "Stop and Go." The manufacturers of automobiles and other consumer durables resented the concentration upon them of the abrupt changes in demand brought about by variation of the hire purchase regulations. For managers generally, the opening and closing of the financial throttle, and the variations of their current sales, were disturbing to the programming of investment over five or more years ahead that they found needful in their own businesses. Observers increasingly aware of the low standing of the United Kingdom in the international "league table" of economic growth attributed it in great part to this upsetting of investment plans.

An influential section of management found the remedy in guidelines for investment. In November, 1960, the Federation of British Industries held a conference on "The Next Five Years." The report of the group that considered "Economic Growth in Britain," presented by the managing director of Guinness, Sir Hugh Beaver, urged that there was "room for a more conscious attempt to assess plans and demands in particular industries for five or even ten years ahead," and asked whether government and industry together might not be able "to agree on an assessment of expectations and intentions which should be before the country for the next five years." In April, 1961, the National Institute of Economic and Social Research organized a conference in London at which a French delegation headed by M. Pierre Massé, director-general of the French planning organization, expounded its methods in principle and practice. In July of the same year the independent Council on Prices, Productivity and Incomes, under the chairmanship of the former chairman of Unilever, Lord Heyworth, stressed "that effective investment needs to be programmed. This carries at once an implication for public policy. There is little point in a programme that is subject to interruption, but hitherto it is investment that has had to bear the greater part of the cutting back when restraints are imposed." But not merely should the investment programs of business be left undisturbed, they should be coordinated and stimulated. "When any one firm or industry draws up such a programme . . . it has to assume a certain rate of growth in the rest of the economy; but this depends in its turn on the investment being undertaken there—the actual rate of growth in each sector depends on the expected rate of the others. . . . A consensus may establish itself in this way, through which a low or equally a high rate may impose and justify itself. The present need for the United Kingdom is to form a consensus about a higher rate. This might be done if the programs from the main sectors were collected and collated in a national projection of investment intentions. Through the discussion of this it would be possible to assure those concerned both that they were not heading toward overlapping and excess capacity in their own sector, and that they were keeping in step with other sectors; and if in the aggregate the programme seemed too small, those who drew up particular programmes could be invited to expand them in the knowledge that they would not be moving forward alone." In France, these functions "have been undertaken for the whole economy by the Commissariat du Plan. It has been claimed for the French procedure that the exchange of information has made better forecasting possible; that the collation of programmes has made it possible to avoid both unemployment and surplus capacity that would otherwise have arisen at particular points; and that the interchange of ideas has changed attitudes and imparted a stimulus to growth. We think that the United Kingdom has something to learn from this experiment."[2]

These observations appeared just at the time of a run on sterling. The government decided to accompany the immediate application

[2] Council on Prices, Productivity and Incomes, Fourth Report, July, 1961, pars. 47, 48.

of restraints with two measures designed to improve the performance of the economy in the longer run, by speeding up the rise of
productivity and slowing down the rise of pay. In the pursuance of
the first aim it set up a National Economic Development Council.
In performance of the second, it promulgated a wage pause, followed it by laying down an upper limit within which subsequent
rises should be contained, and set up a National Incomes Commission to help apply that limit. Before we ask how the Development Council set about its task, let us consider how the government
came to commit itself to limiting the rise of rates of pay.

It would have said that this commitment was forced upon it by
the troubles of the balance of payments. These could not be put
down to the export performance alone, but at least they would not
have come about had exports risen as much as the record of other
manufacturing countries suggested that they should have done.
That they had not might be ascribed to a number of factors, but
again comparison with other countries suggested that a major cause
was a relative rise in British costs. Both comparisons are illustrated
in Table 1. This indicates that export promotion depends on more
than costs and prices alone, but that these have exerted a powerful
influence. It was therefore disquieting that the rise in wage costs
per unit of output in manufacturing had been greater in the United
Kingdom than in any of the other countries: between 1951 and
1952 the rise has been estimated to have been some 50 per cent in
the United Kingdom but little more than 10 per cent on the average
of the other main exporters of manufactures.

Hence the search by successive British governments for a means
of slowing down the rise of money earnings. This rise was at the
root of the troubles of the balance of payments: these in turn
cause periodic setbacks to production and investment—if money
incomes had risen slower, real incomes would have risen faster. It
was this effect, and not any wasteful or inequitable outcome of
inflation internally, that led to guidelines for incomes in the United
Kingdom.

The question then was, why had money incomes risen so fast?
It was always clear that their unprecedented rise had been possible only in the presence of an unprecedentedly high prevailing
level of demand and low level of unemployment. The study of
year-to-year changes also showed that the rate of rise, both of

negotiated rates and of that component of earnings which is added by "wage drift," varied to a great extent with the level of demand. To a great extent, but not entirely: in years when the rate of unemployment (as reckoned in the United Kingdom) lay between 1.7 and 2.0 per cent, for instance, the recorded rises in weekly earnings ranged from 3.5 to 8.5 per cent. This diversity came to be seen as the effect of variations in the expectations prevailing among the parties to negotiations. The consensus they reached was recognized as a distinct factor in determining the amount by which earnings would rise in the presence of a given high level of demand and as capable, moreover, of maintaining rises even under a restrained demand.

TABLE 1

CHANGES IN EARNINGS, PRODUCTIVITY, AND UNIT WAGE COST IN MANUFACTURING, AND IN PRICES AND QUANTITIES OF MANUFACTURED EXPORTS

	1953–55 to 1959–61 Manufacturing: percentage change in			1953–61 Exports of manufactures: percentage change in	
	Earnings $ U.S. (1)	Output per Man-Hr. (2)	Wage Costs per Unit of Output $ U.S. (3)	Prices $ U.S. (4)	Quantities (5)
Italy	33	n.a.	n.a.	− 21	345
Japan	48	63	− 8	− 9	290
Germany	55	39	11	5	191
Sweden	43	n.a.	n.a.	12	120
Netherlands	55	29	20	5	114
France	20 †	46	− 18	− 1	111
Belgium	34	21	11	− 5 *	86 *
U.S.A.	26	23	2	20	33
U.K.	43	17	22	14	32
Canada	25	10	15	3	27

† Rise in francs, 69 per cent.
* Including Luxembourg.

SOURCE: *Export Trends* (U.K. National Economic Development Council, 1963), Tables 11, 12.

The evidence for this conclusion was provided in great part by knowledge of what actually went on when rates of pay were raised. In the United Kingdom most collective bargaining is industry-wide; the agreements usually specify only changes that are widely applicable because simple in form, and much remains to be determined firm by firm and job by job; a substantial part of the rise in effective rates of pay has come about informally at the place of work. At both the industry level and locally, the amount of the rises has been seen to depend on much else besides the current balance of supply and demand in the labor market. This balance has certainly had its influence. In many instances employers competing for labor have taken the initiative in raising rates. More generally, the current length of order books, of which the current level of unemployment is one (inverse) indication, has affected employers' willingness to negotiate rises. But the actual rises have been different in years when the level of unemployment has been much the same; industries with substantial unemployment have raised wages no less than the others; save at the extremes, earnings in contracting and expanding industries have not diverged. Evidently the employers' willingness has not depended on the current state of activity alone. What has made them willing to accept rises in pay that raise their unit labor costs is their belief that they will be able to cover that rise by raising prices without loss of business. That belief has been reinforced by the experience of twenty years. It is also strengthened by the expectation that governments pledged to full employment will not let capacity lie idle for lack of a monetary demand sufficient to employ it at the current level of costs. But in any one bargain it acts on the employer's mind as a sense that he is only taking part in a general movement. If he puts himself under a renewed pressure to raise his prices, he will find that others are coming under the same pressure at the same time. When later he does actually raise his prices, he will bring no retribution down on his head from customers or competitors, for he will not have stuck his neck out, he will only have been moving forward with the others in "the annual round."

The annual rise has thus come to be seen as containing a conventional element. A conspicuous settlement early in the season, a hint of the government's views or the line that mediators will be taking, latterly even news of what is going on among European neighbors—such things help to form a consensus about the size of rise to be generally expected. The trade unions help to shape this consensus and extend it. Once formed, it tends to realize itself. Any one party to a negotiation feels himself no longer a free agent but impelled by all around him. No one is conscious of pushing out in front: the union is only struggling to overtake arrears, the employer cannot afford to be left behind. To resist a claim for the expected amount will be costly and ultimately futile, to grant it will prove harmless because the others will be granting it too. The same spontaneous collusion permits the subsequent price rises that enable higher costs to be borne without squeezing profit margins. A tacit combination thus develops the capacity for self-propulsion. It is to this that has been ascribed the persistent element in the actual rise of British wages year by year that statistical analysis has found uncorrelated with the balance of supply and demand in the British labor market,[3] and the cases of wages rising ahead of productivity even in the presence of quite heavy unemployment which the OEEC Committee of Six found, notably in Denmark.[4]

In sum, British governments concluded that the rise of costs sprang from more than market forces and could not be restrained by adjusting market forces alone. Its essential condition was the discretionary element in the fixing of wages and prices. Both were "administered," and they had come to be administered by a consensus of expectations that issued in a spontaneous collusion to depreciate sterling. The remedy was to appeal to those who had the discretion to exercise it more reasonably and get their expectations to cluster about a more viable norm.

Let us now consider in turn the actual application of guidelines to growth and to incomes.

II. GUIDELINES FOR GROWTH

In the interwar years proposals for economic planning had usually meant that government would take over the command of the

---

[3] L. A. Dicks-Mireaux and J. C. R. Dow, "The Determinants of Wage Inflation: United Kingdom, 1946–56," *Journal of the Royal Statistical Society,* A, 122, 2, 1959.

[4] W. Fellner *et al., The Problem of Rising Prices* (OEEC, 1961), c. V. esp. pp. 46, 48.

economy, or a sizeable sector of it that was nationalized, and would direct its operations by issuing to its subordinate executives instructions formulated in accordance with a unified and comprehensive plan. Since Jean Monnet shaped the French recovery program after the war, however, the name of planning has been given to a very different procedure. It has been called "indicative planning" to distinguish it from the old command or imperative planning, but a more descriptive title would not speak of planning at all but rather of "guidelines for growth." Procedures similar to the French have grown up in other countries of Europe, notably the Netherlands, Sweden, and the Republic of Ireland. The United Kingdom adopted them when its National Economic Development organization was set up in early 1962.

The basis of these procedures is a continued reliance on decentralized and independent decision-taking under the constraints and incentives of the market; but because the discipline of the market proves slack in places, the procedures are brought in to provide supplementary coordination and stimulus. Some of the slack in the market economy is noted in the introduction to the British National Plan of 1965.[5] Left to itself, it was pointed out, the market economy does not provide a sufficient incentive to increase British exports. "Also, the forces of competition often operate too slowly. Then again, where productive units are large and investment decisions have to be taken two to five years ahead, competing companies tend to bunch their investment, holding back and moving forward together, producing surplus or overstretched resources. There is, too, little doubt that inadequacy of investment in British industry has resulted in increasing home demand being met by a greater flow of imports than the economy could afford." There was need also to make independent decisions more consistent with one another by assembling and exchanging information. "Both Government and industry have to plan several years ahead and it is desirable to co-ordinate the forward estimates of both. Public expenditure cannot be planned realistically without some idea of the rates at which the economy can be expected to grow and of the size of other claims on resources, for example, for industrial

[5] *The National Plan* (Cmnd. 2764, Sept., 1965). The quotations are from c. 1, pars. 11, 13.

investment. . . . Similarly, industrialists should benefit, both from the collection of the plans of other industries which are their customers, and from a knowledge of the intentions of Government— by far the largest buyer in the country."

The formulation of the guidelines goes through three stages. First, management in the private and public sectors is asked to project the main dimensions of its activities over the ensuing four or five years, on the assumption of a certain rate of growth of the economy around it—how it expects its output to grow, with what inputs of resources, and what investment program. Second, a central staff assembles these projections, to see whether in the aggregate they provide a desired rate of growth, whether they are consistent with one another according to input-output analysis, and whether they will balance the three major accounts of savings and investment, foreign payments, and manpower. Inconsistencies require reference back to and discussion with the industries concerned. The revised projections should compose a course of development for the whole economy that is practicable insofar as it is free of foreseeable internal contradictions. In the third stage this course of development—perhaps with some choice of variations— is brought under discussion by the spokesmen of management and the trade unions together with the government. There is room here for the implanting of social objectives insofar as these can be sought by government action, in a housing program, for instance, or a regional development policy. But this application of public policy and the executive arm of government is something distinct from the function of the adopted and published plan as a propagation of guidelines for growth.

This function it fulfills basically by providing information. The projection of a self-consistent and attainable course of development is a means of coordinating and stimulating the decisions that continue to be taken independently by private and public agencies.

Is that means effective? What effect it has taken can hardly be disentangled from all else that has borne on the growth of the economies that have used it. French growth, it can be argued, would have gone on rapidly enough in earlier years without guidelines, and in the last two years has been checked by price stabilization despite guidelines availability. The rapid growth that has accompanied indicative planning since its adoption in the Republic of Ireland in 1956 may be ascribed to changes in government policy, or to an upsurge of energy in the business community of which the plan was a manifestation and not a cause. In the United Kingdom plans have been before the public only since 1963, and as yet their purpose is not widely understood. But it can be said that the exercise of making projections and discussing them with the planning staff has proved helpful to some of the industries concerned, and that insofar as firms undertake long-range programming of their investment and are conscious of having underestimated the expansion of their market in the past, they find the plan useful as a form of market research.

III. Guidelines for Prices and Incomes

Principles and procedures have been developed in four stages, the first and last under Labour governments, the middle two under Conservative.

When in 1947 the Labour government found it imperative to check the rise in costs, it suggested what was virtually a wages policy to the Council of the Trades Union Congress; but the Council was wary of it, and agreement could be reached only on the need to increase production "while costs and prices are held steady"[6]— nothing was said about how they could be so held. But the next year the government moved on its own. Its statement of policy[7] contained at least implicitly some formulation of guidelines—that the general level of personal incomes should not rise more than the volume of production, but that a greater rise would be justified "from a national point of view" in particular cases. The one case named was where the rise was necessary to attract labor to an undermanned industry. In accepting the statement the Trades Union Congress added other cases, and against the government's plea that customary differentials among occupations should not be upheld when the national interest called for change, it urged "the need to safeguard those wage differentials which are an essential element in the wages structure" because they are required to sus-

[6] Statement on the Economic Considerations affecting relations between Employers and Workers (Cmd. 7018, Jan., 1947), par. 21.

[7] Statement on Personal Incomes, Costs & Prices (Cmd. 7321, Feb., 1948).

tain "standards of craftsmanship, training and experience."[8] But
the main object of the government's statement was not to guide
the movements of incomes but to secure the observance of an
immediate standstill in them. I hinted that the alternative was some
"interference with the existing methods of free negotiation," it
warned that rises in costs owing to rises in pay might not be "taken
into account in settling controlled prices"; but its reliance was on
voluntary cooperation. This it received in full measure. The leadership of the Trades Union Congress stood by what came to be
known as "the wage freeze"; the employers' organizations accepted
the rule that there should be no increase in dividend distributions.

For two years these leads were followed with a remarkable fidel-
ity, but in the course of 1950 wage restraint broke down. The cause
was no rejection of principle at the national level, but the building up of pressure among the rank and file. Much of this arose
from the continuing rise in the cost of living; but probably even
more was built up by the disturbance of customary relativities.
While rates in most industries were unchanged, in a few they continued to be raised by cost-of-living sliding scales. Within industries
earnings rose unevenly over rates through "wage drift" at the place
of work. Those who were left behind saw their remedy in a wage
claim. To deny them the right to raise it was to discriminate against
them and deny them justice. Mounting pressure from the locals
had already broken through wage restraint, when the Trades Union
Congress formally rejected it in September, 1950.

The next year the Conservatives came back to office—as it
proved, for thirteen years. Their early endeavors to secure agreement on a wages policy were rebuffed, and they fell back on
exhortation, but they were more willing than the Labour government had been to use monetary and fiscal restraints. The sterling
crisis of 1957, however, showed that these had not been enough.
The Council on Prices, Productivity and Incomes that was then
set up to supplement them marks a second stage in the development of guidelines. If these were indispensable, but could not be
worked out by agreement, nor promulgated by government without
charges of interference with free negotiation, might they not be

---

[8] Recommendations of the Special Committee on the Economic Situations
as accepted by the General Council at their Special Meeting on Feb. 18, 1948.

accepted from independent hands? The appointment of a council of three, made up of a judge as chairman, an accountant, and an economist, offered a combination of impartiality and expertise. Also there was no more talk of "wages policy," with its implication of exclusive responsibility or discriminatory countermeasures: the title of the Council spoke of "incomes," and that only after prices and productivity. But the terms of reference were drawn widely— "having regard to the desirability of full employment and increasing standards of life based on expanding production and reasonable stability of prices, to keep under review changes in prices, productivity and the level of incomes (including wages, salaries and profits) and to report thereon from time to time." In fact, in its first report the Council rejected "the suggestion that a percentage figure should be announced by which average money wages could increase during a year or other period without damage to the national interest." It found the main cause of the rise in prices and incomes in high demand, and recommended "a policy of damping down the intensity of total demand" even though this meant a rise in unemployment above the existing level of 1.8 per cent—"in our opinion it is impossible that a free and flexible economic system can work efficiently without a perceptible (though emphatically not a catastrophic) margin of unemployment of this kind."[9] This last remark was especially resented by trade unionists, whose wage claims were unlikely in consequence to have been influenced by the Council, although its analysis of the recent course of events advanced the discussion of the diagnosis of inflation.

The renewed pressure on sterling in 1961 brought in the third stage in the development of policy. In part the measures of that fall did but extend earlier lines—there was to be a pay pause, as in 1948; and the need to raise production, put first in 1947, was now recognized by setting up the National Economic Development Council. But two other measures followed that were new: the government itself assumed the responsibility for laying down guidelines, and it set up a special body to watch over their observance.

"In recent years," the government stated, "national production per head has risen by about 2 to 2½ per cent a year. We ought to

---

[9] Council on Prices, Productivity & Incomes, First Report (Feb., 1958), c. VIII., par. 31; c. Vi., pars. 134, 135.

be able to do better than this but on present trends it seems likely to increase at about this rate in 1962. It is accordingly necessary that the increase of wages and salaries, as of incomes, should be kept within this figure during the next phase."[10] The statement went on to allow of bigger rises in two cases—"as part of an agreement under which those concerned made a direct contribution, by accepting more exacting work, or more onerous conditions, or by a renunciation of restrictive practices, to an increase of productivity and a reduction of costs"; and "where the building up of manpower in one industry relatively to others, or the prevention of a threatened decline, is plainly necessary." But some traditional bases for rises in pay—such as rises in the cost of living, profits, or productivity —were now no longer sufficient of themselves; and although the comparisons with the levels or changes in rates of pay in similar employments that had been accepted as guides, especially in the public services, would still be taken into account, greater regard must at the same time be paid to the considerations underlying the guidelines.

The special body set up to watch over the observance of the guidelines was the National Incomes Commission. Its composition, like that of the now dissolved Council on Prices, Productivity and Incomes, was designed to combine judicial impartiality with business experience and academic expertise. Its function was mainly to examine retrospectively particular pay settlements referred to it by the government and report on them in the light of the guidelines.[11] There was no mention of prices in its terms of reference. It was concerned with profits only insofar as it was enjoined to have regard, among other things, to profit margins and dividends when considering a pay settlement, and to report from time to time on whether restraint of pay was resulting in any undue growth of profits in the aggregate. It was to publish its findings, but was armed with no sanctions for them, nor could it in any case undo the past: its function was essentially to influence public opinion. In one significant respect, however, it could do more: in reporting on past settlements it could make recommendations for the improvement of future dealings between the parties, and within

---

[10] Incomes Policy: The Next Step (Cmnd. 1626, Feb., 1962).
[11] National Incomes Commission (Cmnd. 1844, Nov., 1962).

the public service alone it might be asked by the government, in effect, to make recommendations about current claims. The idea emerged here of an independent body charged with bringing the guidelines to bear through discussion with the parties to a negotiation.

It was a disability of the Commission from the first that the trade unions repudiated its authority and refused to appear before it. They saw it as an agency created by the government to apply rules which the government had promulgated unilaterally and for which the government alone must continue to take the responsibility: it could not escape this by setting up an independent Commission to pass judgment upon settlements. This device, moreover, was objectionable in itself: no third parties, however impartial and distinguished, had the right to prescribe to any worker the terms on which he should work; he must remain free to make his own bargain. The employers did appear before the Commission, however, and it carried out its inquiries and issued its reports until the end of the Conservative administration in 1964. Its work was valuable in several ways. It brought out the public interest in particular settlements and explored the field of fact and argument that must be covered when the guidelines are to be applied to the circumstances of those settlements in all their complexity. It made employers aware that they might be exposed to examination and publicity if they made settlements outside the guidelines. In one case—the salaries of a university staff—it pioneered the discussion with the parties to a still prospective determination of how it should be shaped in the public interest.

The return of the Labour party to office in 1964 made possible the fourth stage of development, partly because the new administration was concerned to devote far more of its energies to making incomes policy effective than its predecessors had been, but also because the leaders of the Trades Union Congress were willing to go farther to meet the government. It was this willingness that made possible a Joint Statement of Intent[12] by government, the organized employers, and the Trades Union Congress by which management and unions not only accepted the principles of keeping the rise of incomes in line with that of productivity, and stabil-

---

[12] Dec. 16, 1964.

izing the price level, but pledged themselves "to co-operate with the Government in endeavouring, in the face of practical problems, to give effective shape to the machinery that the Government intends to establish" to keep prices and incomes under review and to advise whether their behavior in particular cases "is in the national interest as defined by the Government after consultation with management and unions." This machinery consisted, first and foremost, in a National Board for Prices and Incomes; beyond that lay an early warning system for pay claims and price rises.

The National Board took the place of the National Incomes Commission. In some ways it had the same function; and the guidelines[13] it was given for pay marked no departure from the previous formulation but only a development. But in other ways the new Board was very different. It was given guidelines not only for pay but for prices, and the first case referred to it was one of prices. Its members included a national trade union leader, and the trade unions were willing to work with it. The change in their attitude was probably in part simply because of their greater willingness to meet the wishes of a Labour government, but was also made possible by a difference in the Board's approach: it did not sit to pass judgment, but entered into discussion with parties whose agreement it endeavored to influence but not to supersede. This was the most important difference, and yet, it marked only the development of one of the two sides of the old Commission. This Commission had had a judicial component and sat as a court of inquiry into past events; but it had also made recommendations designed to influence future decisions, and in one instance it had worked over the grounds of such a decision with the interested parties. The new Board dropped the first side and extended the second. Its chairman, Aubrey Jones, was not a lawyer but a director of a big engineering firm and former minister of supply in a Conservative government. In the Board's first report[14] he made it clear how he saw its task. "There are two possible causes," the introduction to the report declared, "lying behind the phenomenon of rising prices. First, demand may be too high in relation to the

---

[13] *Prices and Incomes Policy* (Cmnd. 2639, April, 1965).

[14] National Board for Prices and Incomes. *Report No. 1* (Interim), Road Haulage Rates (Cmnd. 2695, June, 1965).

capacity to meet it. Secondly, even though demand may be reasonably in line with capacity, old habits, inherited attitudes and institutional arrangement may nonetheless all still combine to exert an upward pressure on prices." Dealing with the first cause is the task of the government; with the second, that of the Board. It means changing attitudes. "Experience has shown that attitudes are not changed by a use of the fiscal and monetary weapons at the disposal of Government. Nor are they susceptible to legislation— habits are not changed by law. We see ourselves as promoting change by conducting a continuing dialogue with managements, unions and indeed Government." It is in this spirit of consultation and cooperation that the Board has dealt with the cases so far referred to it—trucking charges; wages and prices in printing; the price of bread, and bakers' wages and hours; the prices of soap and detergents; the salaries of administrative and clerical staff in electricity supply; salaries of staff in the Midland Bank; electricity and gas tariffs; pay of railroad workers; pay of the armed forces and of the higher civil service.

The provision for early warning awaits a statutory basis. Its intention is that those responsible for changes in the prices of a selected list of goods and services, and in pay, hours, or other major terms of employment, should be required to give advance notification to the government of proposed rises or improvements. If the proposal, although accepted by the Trades Union Congress, gave it some difficulty, that may be because it brings a compulsory element into the field of free negotiation; but it will also have been unwelcome because it overlaps the early warning system set up by the Congress itself.

The adoption of this system by a majority vote of the Congress meeting in September, 1965, is a salient feature of this fourth stage of development, and may prove a landmark. The affiliated unions inform the Council of the claims they are entering, and a committee of Council meets once a month to consider them. There are four courses it may follow. On some it makes no comment, although this does not imply endorsement. At the other end of the scale it may call in representatives of the union concerned and argue with them. In both the intervening courses it offers written observations: in the one it only asks the union to consider the bearing on its claim of the principles of prices and incomes policy, but in the other, and this so far has been the course most often followed, it calls the union's attention to some specific feature of its claim that seems to conflict with those principles. In the last resort, it can do no more than advise. The system remains experimental. But it is significant in expressing the philosophy according to which the unions should both accept the need for an income policy and the responsibility for carrying it through themselves, so far at least as it lies within the power of one party to the wage bargain; or, to put the same view the other way about, if the unions claim to remain masters in their own house and resist outside intervention into free negotiations, they should themselves insure that those negotiations work out consistently with the national interest. This requires a substantial internal coordination. British trade unionism is far from that as yet, but there is some movement toward it, and the example of Sweden is well known to trade union leaders.

It is too early to assess the effectiveness of recent measures. They have been applied just at the time when, under an upsurge of demand, earnings were rising at much more than the average speed of the last twenty years, in the United Kingdom as in many of its European neighbors. Allowance must be made for the braking distance of any economy that has gathered so much momentum. From the experience of the last fifteen months, it begins to appear that the braking distance for prices is shorter than that for incomes.

IV. Possible Lessons for the United States

One country's experience holds lessons for another only if it has gone farther and already resulted in success or failure for reasons that can be established. British experience has not done that. But some features of it already seem sufficiently marked and significant to deserve mention.

A first observation is that the strongest pressures against the guidelines for pay have been set up not by the determination of any group to thrust forward relatively to the others, but by the sense of injustice under which those groups smart who feel they have been left behind. This causes special difficulty when guidelines are first applied, for at any one time in the general but irregular rises of recent years there will always have been some who were lagging. But even after initial difficulties have been surmounted the disturbance of relativities will continue to give trouble wherever actual earnings move ahead of negotiated rates through "wage drift," as they have done persistently in much of British and (even more) Scandinavian industry.

This leads to the further observation that the guidelines laid down primarily for negotiated changes in pay will fail of their intended effect if the negotiations do not themselves control the subsequent course of earnings on the job, or provide a means of administering the internal proportions of the wage structure as well as the movement of the structure as a whole. The basic requirement is control of the movement of earnings on the job. The industry-wide agreements that predominate in the United Kingdom and its European neighbors do not provide this, especially when a substantial proportion of the wage earners work under systems of payment by results. The advantage appears by contrast of the detailed specification of rates in the American plant contract and the adherence to these rates during the currency of the contract.

Evidently much depends here on the attitude of management, its concern with the administration of the pay structure as a major responsibility of the general manager, and its determination, having negotiated an agreement, to hold its employees to it. British experience suggests that in the matter of guideline observance the most willing of trade union leaders cannot do better than the managers in his industry give him the chance to do. The leader of the Amalgamated Engineering Union, dealing recently with the causes of wildcat strikes, "held that the employers were largely responsible because, in the immediate postwar years, they had often conceded in the face of unofficial action what they refused to concede in negotiations. He contended that this had created an atmosphere in which pressure had become the order of the day."[15]

This matters the more because full employment brings a diminution in the trade union leader's power of leadership: the individual member depends less upon the national officers of his union for

[15] Sir William Carron, in evidence to the Royal Commission on Trade Unions and Employers' Associations, as reported in *The Times,* Feb. 16, 1966.

protection and has less to fear from repudiating their authority. Hence, the further observation that compliance with guidelines depends on their being understood not merely by a relatively limited number of leaders at the center but by their members up and down the country. The same need, only quantitatively less formidable, exists within employers' organizations. On both sides the basic resistances are at the place of work, and they are very strong. They arise from the persistence of old attitudes in new circumstances. They can be removed only as attitudes can be changed. In some forms of public policy ways of doing this have been developed—in rural betterment, for example, it is recognized that publication of improved methods worked out at the agricultural research station will do little without an extension program. Such a program is equally necessary if guidelines are to be adopted.

In the procedures that the United Kingdom has tried, there is one that serves this end among others. We saw how the National Board for Prices and Incomes has set out not to set in judgment on past changes in prices and pay but to engage in discussions with those who remain responsible for changes still to be made. This way of working has the obvious advantage of being timely. But much more important, it enables—indeed, obliges—the Board to reason with unions and management. In doing so it respects their freedom of negotiation while asking them to consider how their decisions will affect the public interest, and suggesting to them how they can take it into account. Its reports make the line it takes in this way clear to other industries. It may thus be regarded as the agency not of an enforcement but of an extension program.

One other recent British development deserves attention insofar as it marks both a change of attitude and is a means of extending that change. The procedure which the Trades Union Congress is now following for the notification of claims to its own Council would not have been thinkable even three years ago. It marks and in turn promotes a consolidation of the policies of the unions and a delegation of more authority to their national leadership. One reflection is that here, as in Sweden, the prospect of governmental intervention in the field of voluntary bargaining stimulates the parties to preserve their independence by bringing the course of bargaining under a measure of their own central control. Again, as in Sweden, it appears that the exercise of such control depends on consultation and discussion, on the two-way internal flow of information and argument. A further lesson of this development is suggested by the sheer number of claims which the Trades Union Congress has been dealing with: had systems of self-government in these matters no other merit, they would still be needed to lighten the load that must otherwise rest upon any national board.

Some of these observations have concerned features of the British experience that may be distinctive. But at the last what may be most instructive is the extent to which the United Kingdom has been following the same course as other countries. There have been striking similarities in the development of ideas. That the National Incomes Commission of 1962 and the National Board for Prices and Incomes of 1965 were designed so closely on the lines sketched by Gardner Ackley in his evidence to the Joint Committee of Congress in 1958[16] and that the criteria for price and pay behavior promulgated by the British government in 1965[17] corresponded almost textually to the "guideposts for noninflationary wage and price behavior" in the Report of the Council of Economic Advisors in 1962, may in part be the result of Washington publications being read in Whitehall; but it also shows how different men will arrive at similar conclusions under the pressure of similar circumstances.

Guidelines, indeed, have been suggested by a diagnosis of symptoms common to a number of countries. Basically this diagnosis is that the market economy leaves tolerances within which decisions on investment and on pay and prices are discretionary. The adjustments of the market are sometimes sluggish; the movement of prices, including the rate of interest, cannot always be relied upon to perform its function as a feedback in making independent choices consistent with one another. This consistency, it is held, then tends to be sought from the outset, by a spontaneous process of coordination or concertation of judgments and expectations about norms that are justified to each because adopted by others. Guideline policy offers guidance in discretionary decisions and endeavors to improve the norms around which consensus forms.

[16] U.S. Congress, Joint Economic Committee, *The Relationship of Prices to Economic Stability and Growth* (Washington, D.C.: U.S. Government Printing Office, 1958).

[17] *Prices & Incomes Policy* (Cmnd. 2639, April, 1965).

HARRY G. JOHNSON

Balance-of-Payments Controls and Guidelines for Trade and Investment

HARRY G. JOHNSON is professor of economics at the University of Chicago and editor of the Journal of Political Economy. *He believes that the voluntary restraint program has reduced the United States payments deficit. But he is also concerned with the economic and political costs of the program. Rather than pay these costs, he would prefer an international monetary system which would enable the United States to finance a much larger payments deficit and, should this not come about, a move toward flexible exchange rates.*

The problems raised by controls over international trade and capital movements, whether "voluntary" or legally imposed, should really be dealt with as a whole, since such controls have been prompted by the chronic balance-of-payments deficit of the United States over the past nine years, and the different forms of them should be conceived as a group and related to the evaluation of the deficit problem. Moreover, as the government's experts occasionally observe with unwarranted surprise, "money is fungible," so that controls over different forms of capital movement cannot be analyzed effectively in isolation from one another. For the purposes of this volume, however, a distinction has been drawn between controls on trade and direct foreign investment, which impinge on the activities of manufacturing business, and controls on indirect investment, which impinge on the activities of financial intermediaries, both bank and non-bank. This paper is concerned with controls of the former type, responsibility for the latter falling to Professor Meltzer, whose paper is also included in this volume; but some overlap is inevitable if the functions of both papers are to be served.

GUIDELINES IN PERSPECTIVE

On a superficial view, at least, the development of the guideline approach to private business transactions abroad has been an extremely recent phenomenon, dating back no more than about a year and a half, although it has evolved rapidly and changed substantially in form during that time. The guideline approach to foreign business transactions, and the use of controls, are, however, no new departure in United States foreign economic policy; what are new departures are the balance-of-payments motivation of the guidelines and the appeal to business to sacrifice profits for the sake of the national interest. Previously, guidelines and controls had been used for purposes generally approved by business, or applied to foreign producers and countries in the commercial interests of American business. The specific references here are, first, to the embargo on trade with the communist bloc in strategic items and the generally discouraging attitude of the administration toward other trade with the communists, a policy whose futility has become increasingly evident and which is in process of being reversed; second, to the use of the political power of the United States and the threat of commercial policy action to induce Japan to introduce "voluntary" restraints on exports to the United States that might disrupt the American market;[1] and third, to the "legislative history" and understandings which have prevented United States foreign aid from being used for investment in nationalized industries in the less-developed countries that would compete with American international commercial enterprises in certain activities, notably

---

[1] The United States Embassy to Japan has calculated that in 1963, 18.0 per cent by value of Japanese exports to the U.S. were under quantitative controls imposed unilaterally by Japan; this figure excludes all items subject to bilateral or multilateral agreement, of which the most important are cotton textiles under the G.A.T.T.—supervised International Arrangements for Cotton Textiles which superseded previous bilateral arrangements to control cotton textile imports from Japan.

oil exploration and refining. These policies have been as objectionable in principle as the present guidelines in substituting administrative decision and covert negotiation for the processes of open competition in the market. But with respect to them business has displayed that characteristic schizophrenia to which Milton Friedman has recently called attention.[2]

The foregoing examples concern the use of guidelines and controls affecting private trade and investment. The guidelines approach has been applied, however, in a far more sweeping way—and apparently with the full approval of business—in the international transactions of the United States government itself. The progressive tying of foreign economic assistance over the past nine years and the increasingly strenuous effort to reduce overseas defense expenditure and to match expenditures by military sales have involved the same progressive substitution of administrative decision and decree for commercially oriented choice as are entailed in the present guidelines, and the same sort of economic inefficiency in government operations as now concerns private business. This fact has, however, been concealed by the mythology of private enterprise in America, according to which increased inefficiency in government is the legitimate first resort of business against increasing competitive pressures. It should be no cause for surprise that, having been pushed so steadily down the road of increasing inefficiency by the persistence of the balance-of-payments problem, the administration should ultimately have been driven to the conclusion that it was the turn of business to bear some of the burden of inefficiency involved in coping with that problem as the country has chosen to cope with it. Nor is it surprising that many businessmen should have protested—"irresponsibly," in the administration's view—against the extension of deliberate inefficiency to their own operations from the sphere of government where by convention it properly belongs and have demanded that the burden be passed to someone else, the irresponsible free-spending tourist and the similarly adjectivally described recipients of foreign economic assistance being currently the most popular candidates.

[2] Milton Friedman, "The Schizophrenic Businessman: Friend and Enemy of Free Enterprise," address to the Young Presidents' Organization, April 27, 1966.

To complain about the new guidelines for foreign business operations on this level is indeed irresponsible and narrowly self-seeking, an attempt to evade rather than tackle the fundamental problem—the United States balance-of-payments situation. The guidelines must be assessed in the broad perspective of that problem.

THE BALANCE-OF-PAYMENTS PROBLEM

From a long-range historical point of view, the sustained balance-of-payments deficits of the United States since 1958 can be seen as the reflection of a dynamic international disequilibrium associated with the ultimate postwar economic recovery and subsequent economic growth of Western Europe and the formation on the strength of that growth of the European Economic Community. International disequilibrium reflected in balance-of-payments deficits and surpluses is the necessary consequence of dynamic disturbances of this kind occurring in a regime of fixed exchange rates, when the various countries are prepared neither to play strictly by the rules of a fixed exchange rate system and make the adjustments of domestic demand and monetary conditions required to preserve international equilibrium nor to ride out the slow working of the natural processes of international adjustment by the provision of adequate financing by surplus to deficit countries.

Broadly speaking, the run of abnormally large payments deficits the United States has incurred since 1958 can be divided into a succession of one-to-two year phases, according to the major item in the balance of payments a deterioration in which has appeared as the proximate cause of the deficit and to the correction of which the administration has directed its balance-of-payments policy. In 1958 and 1959, the problem appeared to lie in lack of United States competitiveness on merchandise trade, and policy began to be directed to export promotion on the one hand and to aid-tying and domestic military procurement on the other. In 1960–61, the problem appeared to be an abnormal outflow of short-term capital, which eventually prompted an increase in short-term interest rates. In 1962, the problem turned into an abnormal outflow of indirect long-term capital, which prompted the imposition of the Interest Equalization Tax. In 1964 the problem turned again into an abnormal outflow of capital, primarily short-term capital but also long-term indirect and direct investment. This prompted the renewal and extension of the Interest Equalization Tax and the "voluntary restraint" program of February, 1965. Since then, the problem has appeared as one of abnormally high direct investment, superimposed on the prospective adverse effects on the payments balance of rising defense expenditure in Vietnam and a booming domestic economy. This has prompted the toughening of the "voluntary restraint" program in December, 1965, and the special new program of ceilings on direct investment by non-financial corporations introduced at that time.

The fact that the apparent cause of the deficit has shifted at relatively short intervals has contributed substantially to the impression, sustained despite the longer-run evidence to the contrary, that the deficit was bound to be a short-lived phenomenon. This impression has underlaid official United States policy and encouraged the successive resort to a series of policy measures each of which was genuinely intended at the time it was introduced to be temporary, and each of which could be justified on that ground as a purely temporary departure from basic principles, but each of which has turned out in fact to have been a mere palliative that has subsequently required supplementation by still stronger measures of intervention in the market process, each justifiable on the grounds of its apparently temporary and special nature.

THE THREE PHASES OF THE DEFICIT

From a more fundamental point of view, the prolonged experience of deficit can be divided into three major phases, of which the third is just beginning.

The first was the phase in which successful European Economic Recovery, reinforced by the devaluations of 1949, made Europe competitive to the United States in world export markets for manufactures. Contributing factors were the inflationary experience of the United States during the prolonged period of postwar dollar shortage and the additional commitments to capital exports for development assistance and overseas defense expenditure that the United States had undertaken in response to its postwar leadership in the Western world.

The second was the phase in which, as a consequence of the

post-1958 convertibility of European currencies and the persistent reluctance of the United States authorities to recognize that—in consequence of the rapidly developing integration of world capital markets—the United States could not continue to pursue a low-interest rate policy dictated by purely domestic objectives, the United States became a supplier of capital to Western Europe on a scale inconsistent with its competitive capacity to generate a current account surplus. In this phase, the fungibility of capital has preserved the appearance of a problem confined to a particular section of the capital market, a problem which the administration could convince itself and the private institutions involved was caused by inordinate expansion of foreign investment by that sector, which expansion should be restrained by legislative or "voluntary" action both in the national interest and in the interest of the private institutions of the sector itself. The administration has helped by confusing the issues with the notion that the excess European demand—as it sees it—for American capital is a consequence of the relative underdevelopment of European capital markets and not of relatively low United States interest rates.[3]

The credibility of the notion that the interventions in the capital market developed in this phase were purely temporary has been sustained by two fundamental assumptions, in addition to the convenient fact that the proximate source of renewed difficulty has appeared—quite naturally and predictably—in different sectors of the capital market in successive subphases of the period. One has been the assumption that, by virtue merely of the United States holding the line on domestic wages and prices, the problem of the United States deficit would solve itself through European inflation. That assumption has been rapidly losing its validity as a consequence of the current United States economic boom, which has removed the possibility of relying on mild relative United States economic stagnation to hold down prices and forced the administration increasingly to rely on the wage-price guideposts; of the

[3] An illustration of the obfuscation resulting from this style of "structuralist" thinking is contained in the 1966 Annual Report of the Council of Economic Advisers. Page 165 contains the statement: "In part because of this better organization, interest rates and flotation costs are considerably lower in this country." Flotation costs are a genuine index of financial efficiency; interest rates are primarily the result of national monetary policy.

intensification of the war in Vietnam, which has necessitated growing overseas expenditures on defense; and of the stiffening of European resistance to the long-hoped-for European inflation that would remove the competitive underpinnings of Europe's surplus with the United States.

The domestic economic boom, in its turn, as well as the belief that European resort to the United States for supplies of capital has been "structural" in nature, has been associated with the invalidity of the second fundamental assumption. This assumption, which runs through the thinking of successive annual reports of the Council of Economic Advisers, is that monetary policy has in fact been quite restrictive in its effects in recent years. This belief is associated with the practice of judging the restrictiveness of monetary policy by the level of prevailing interest rates relative to some past level or historical norm, a practice understandable among the general public or in the banking community but somewhat inexplicable among the sophisticated advisers that the administration has at its disposal. If judged instead by the rate of expansion of the money supply that has occurred in recent years, even on the narrow definition of currency plus demand deposits but especially on the broader definition of the money supply as these plus time deposits at all commercial banks, monetary policy has been extremely expansionary, so much so as to lead some observers to attribute the boom to monetary policy rather than to the much touted tax cut of 1964. The rapid rate of monetary expansion recently could well account for the "excessive" exports of private capital that have appeared to be the cause of the continued balance-of-payments deficit and have served as justification for the new controls on private foreign investment.

These considerations introduce the nascent third phase of the balance-of-payments problem of the United States. It appears probable that, owing to the rising cost of the war in Vietnam, the effects of the domestic boom on the balance of payments (including especially a rapidly rising demand for imports, but also the threat of rising prices to exports), and European economic and policy developments, the balance of payments is extremely unlikely to improve further and very likely to deteriorate. The assumption that guidelines for domestic and foreign private economic behavior are purely temporary departures from the basic principles of American economic organization can no longer be maintained. The question naturally arises, in what direction will, or should, this branch of economic policy move now?

THE HISTORY AND NATURE OF THE GUIDELINES

Before approaching that question, it is necessary to review in more detail the history and nature of present guidelines on foreign trade and investment. It is convenient to begin with the Interest Equalization Tax, which, although not itself a guideline but rather a cleverly designed discriminatory tax on new security issues by other advanced industrial countries in the American market (from which Canada was exempted by special arrangement), which introduced the policy of discrimination against foreign demanders of American capital. That tax, as many observers predicted at the time, had its major effect on such issues during the period between the proposal of it and the time when its terms, which were to apply retroactively, became clarified; that effect was to induce the postponement of many such new issues, particularly by Canadian borrowers. In addition, and also as predicted by some commentators, the tax induced substantial substitution of long-term borrowing from banks for new issues, an effect which led to the extension of the tax to such borrowing as part of the balance-of-payments program of February, 1965 (together with its renewal for two more years). The history of the tax therefore illustrates one of the main economic defects of such efforts to discriminate in the capital market, the inducement to substitution of other forms of finance for the one discriminated against and the need to extend discrimination progressively through the capital market.

The balance-of-payments program of February, 1965, was, as mentioned, introduced in response to the rapidly rising outflows of capital in the form of long-term bank loans, direct investment, and especially short-term lending. The program had two aspects. One, administered by the Federal Reserve System, was the setting of "guidelines" for banks and non-bank financial intermediaries, restricting the increase in their claims on foreigners to a small percentage of the amounts outstanding at the end of 1964, which is discussed in Professor Meltzer's paper. The other, administered by the Department of Commerce, involved asking between five and six hundred large non-financial corporations engaged in international trade and investment to make a maximum effort to expand the net balance of their exports of goods and services plus their repatriation of earnings from the developed countries, less their capital outflows to such countries, and also to repatriate their liquid funds.

For the business community program, in contrast to the financial community programs, no explicit guidelines were set for the individual participating companies. The March, 1965, statement of the Secretary of the Department of Commerce on the program referred instead in general terms to "an average improvement in balance of payments terms, in 1965 of 15–20 per cent over the 1964 results," leaving leeway for variations associated with the special problems of individual companies, to be negotiated individually with the Secretary. These private confidential negotiations, together with the stress laid on the personal responsibility of the company presidents for their companies' programs, constitute in their way a significant new departure in the relationship of government and business in this country, toward the political concept of the corporate state. The program also required the reporting of some past statistics, and the inauguration of quarterly reports by the companies to the Department of Commerce.

The willingness of the participating companies to cooperate in the program was undoubtedly greatly strengthened by the widespread and deeply felt resentment of the policies of General de Gaulle, engendered by his public pronouncements around the time the program was initiated, a resentment which expressed itself in a desire to back up the President's balance-of-payments policy. The program was remarkably effective in achieving its objectives, especially in view of the widespread doubts expressed at the time about whether it could be made to work. Naturally, however, it was not as effective as the Council of Economic Advisers and the Department of Commerce have since claimed.

A preliminary tabulation of results for 233 companies (out of the over five hundred participants[4]), assumed to be a representative

---

[4] Cited by Andrew H. Brimmer, assistant secretary of the Department of Commerce for Economic Affairs, in an address before the Toronto Board Traders Association, Toronto, March 2, 1966.

sample, showed that these companies had more than fulfilled their original expectations under the 1965 program, the actual improvement on their credit balance on the selected balance-of-payments transactions being 13.3 per cent (nearly $1 billion) as compared with an expected 10.6 per cent.[5] The 13.3 per cent falls substantially short, however, of the 15–20 per cent range mentioned by the Secretary in his March statement; but it would perhaps be fairest to conclude that it represents a mutually satisfactory compromise between target and promised achievements adopted as bargaining positions, rather than as real goals. The form of the new guidelines for direct investment—averaging 1965 and 1966 outflows—also implies that the companies varied considerably in their degree of compliance with the voluntary program in 1965.

While the voluntary restraint program for international corporations thus appears to have worked in the aggregate more or less as intended, it appeared to the administration by the autumn of 1965, first, that some more intensive efforts yet would be required to remedy the balance-of-payments deficit, and that there was "disquieting evidence that plans for direct investment in 1966 remained at a high level."[6] The focus of the guideline policy for private external transactions thus shifted to direct investment, and the 1965 programs were renewed and strengthened. In the business community program, the estimated overall improvement of $1.3 billion on selected balance-of-payments transactions in 1965 over 1964 became a target improvement of $3.4 billion, while companies were requested to reduce the foreign short-term assets held by themselves and their foreign affiliates to the end-1963 level. Specific guidelines ("targets") in addition were set for direct investment, to apply to each individual company: direct investment, defined to include both capital outflows and investment of retained earn-

<hr>

[5] On this basis, Assistant Secretary Brimmer concluded that "we will almost certainly achieve the overall improvement goal of $1.3 billion for the more than 500 participants." A goal in dollar figures was' not mentioned in the Secretary's March, 1965, statement, and the figure of $1.3 billion is referred to in his December, 1966, statement only as an estimate of the improvement in the net contribution of the business community to the balance of payments in 1965 as compared with 1964. Accuracy of a late estimate of the results of a program can scarcely be accepted as equivalent to fulfillment of its initially stated goals.

[6] 1966 Report of the Council of Economic Advisers, p. 166.

ings of foreign affiliates, during the two-year period 1965–66 combined should be limited to 90 per cent of the amount during the three-year period 1962–64, permitting an average for the two years 35 per cent above the base average but actually entailing a reduction in 1966 as compared with 1965. (This formula was designed to provide equity between companies complying or over-complying with the 1965 program and those undercomplying or not previously included and also to forestall the repetition of the experience of the February guidelines, the anticipation of which prompted substantial anticipatory outflows of capital.) The number of companies included was expanded by about four hundred—all those with direct investments abroad of $2 million or more at the end of 1964. The list of countries operations which are to be included in the reckoning was extended to include Canada—direct investment in Canada had increased in 1965, whereas direct investments elsewhere had been reduced—and a number of less developed countries with large American direct investments. Requirements for past statistics and current quarterly reporting were greatly extended; and again, great stress was placed on the personal responsibilities of company presidents both for the quarterly reporting and to the program.

EVALUATION OF THE GUIDELINES

In the early 1950's, the late Sir Dennis Robertson coined the phrase "ear-stroking" to describe the techniques then being used by the British economic authorities—techniques which in British terms closely resembled guidelines—to supplement the traditional means of guiding the donkey of private enterprise by the carrot of prospective profits and the stick of prospective losses. It is clear that the administration has moved rapidly from the ear-stroking to the ear-twisting stage of the exercise, if it is not actually grasping for more sensitive parts of the animal. What can be said about the experience of guidelines in the foreign trade and investment field so far, and what can be said about the prospects for the future?

Unfortunately, the experience has been too short to say much more than that, by and large, these guidelines have worked. They have worked in two senses: They have been broadly effective in achieving their balance-of-payments objectives, and they have been operated—thus far—so as to secure a substantial degree of cooperation and active participation from private business. As against this consideration, it must be recalled that this cooperation derived much of its initial stimulus from the galling of the United States by De Gaulle and that it was founded on the expectation that the program of voluntary restraint would be temporary—not over two years, as Secretary Henry H. Fowler promised. The fading of irritation with De Gaulle, the disappearance of the expectation of an early termination of the program, and the sharp tightening of its restrictiveness in December, 1965, all imply that the "voluntary" character of the program will wear increasingly thin, and that it will either lose its effectiveness as the participating companies become more restive and less honor-bound about compliance or have to be replaced by more and more overt directives from the Secretary of the Department of Commerce to the companies involved in foreign operations and more and more policing by the Department of the detailed operations of these companies.[7]

The latter is by far the more likely course of development, given the present balance-of-payments situation of the United States, the specific rapid evolution of the guidelines policy for foreign trade and investment, and the general evolution of guidelines policy as applied both to the foreign economic transactions of the United States government and private domestic business. The result will inevitably be a radical change in the character of American capitalism. The obvious threat lies in the economic inefficiency associated with the replacement of the market forces of competi-

---

[7] New information which became available between the time this paper was prepared and went to press indicates that this crossroads has already been reached. A Commerce Department report issued May 10, based on information from 618 leading corporations which account for the bulk of the transactions covered by the voluntary program, estimated a contribution toward reducing the balance-of-payments deficit by only $919 million, as compared with the target of $3.4 billion. The main reason for the difference, it appears, is that in fixing the direct investment guidelines for 1966, the Commerce Department greatly overestimated the amount of direct foreign investment that actually occurred in 1965 and therefore the reduction that would occur in 1966. (This is yet another of the defects of the guidelines approach—the difficulty of fixing targets so as to achieve the desired result.) See Edwin L. Dale, "Payments Goal is Found Lagging," *The New York Times,* May 11, 1966, p. 63, col. 1.

tion by government decision and control, whatever the facade of voluntary cooperation thrown up to disguise the transformation. The more subtle danger, however, lies in the elevation of the presidents of American domiciled international corporations into informal and intimate political colleagues of the administration, responsible for the execution of policies of government control and direction of the country's international economic activities through their leadership of their corporations. Responsibility of this kind inevitably becomes reciprocal—if the great corporations sacrifice their economic interests for political and public goodwill, the government for which they do so incurs an obligation to render compensating services to the corporations. Responsibility commands obligation and favors offered in secret private negotiations command favors obtained the same way. That way lies the corporate state. It can, of course, be argued that from this point of view the December guidelines, which apply equally to all individual companies, are preferable to the private treaty technique of the earlier February guidelines. But the December guidelines are not binding legal requirements, and the door has been left open for negotiation over the special circumstances of individual companies.

The foregoing remarks refer to the domestic implications of the intensification of the guidelines approach. But the foreign repercussions are also important, as sharp political controversy in Canada over the impact of the new guidelines has clearly shown. Some eminent Canadians have seen in the guidelines an attempt to foist onto their economy the costs of coping with the United States deficit, an attempt which they regard as an infringement of Canadian sovereignty. They emphasize that the guideline pressures for more exports will induce purchases by affiliates of American companies of higher cost American components and parts instead of lower-cost domestic products, that the pressures for repatriation of short-term funds and for local financing will raise the costs both of these affiliates and of Canadian-owned businesses, and that the restriction of direct investment in Canada will impede Canadian growth without helping the United States balance of payments, because the money will be found instead through new securities issues in New York allowed by Canada's exemption for the Interest Equalization Tax. The *quid pro quo* for this exemption is a Canadian guarantee not to use United States capital to build up Canada's international reserves.[8] The implementation of that guarantee, incidentally, illustrates the international infectiousness of the guidelines approach: in order to prevent it from being broken by unexpectedly large receipts from sales of wheat to Russia, the Canadian finance minister was led last autumn to request the Canadian securities dealers to withhold new issues from the New York market until after the New Year. Concern over the impact of the United States investment guidelines on the operations of American affiliates in Canada, also, is undoubtedly partly responsible for the recent issuance by the Canadian Department of Commerce of a set of guidelines for foreign-owned enterprises operating in Canada.[9]

ARGUMENTS FOR THE GUIDELINES

In defending the guidelines, the administration has used three main types of arguments. The first appeals to the fact that it is the private capital outflow, rather than government overseas expenditure, that has grown rapidly since 1960. The implication is that the private sector is responsible for the current deficit and in equity must bear the burden of remedying it. This argument is essentially specious; the fact that a deficit can be associated at a particular point of time with an abnormal volume of certain types of transactions establishes neither that the cause of the deficit is to be found in those particular transactions nor, even if this were true, that the proper remedy is to curtail those transactions.

The second defense stresses the "expansive" nature of the guidelines in the context of international relations. One variant of

[8] For a strong and superficially well-documented statement of this Canadian reaction, see "The Economic Effects of the Guidelines," address by the Honorable Eric W. Kierans, Minister of Health of the Province of Quebec to the Toronto Society of Financial Analysts, February 1, 1966. A more moderate and reasoned discussion of the impact on Canada of U.S. balance-of-payments policy with respect to capital movements is contained in the statement of the Honorable Mitchell Sharp, Minister of Finance, on Canadian-American Financial Relations, delivered in the House of Commons, January 27, 1966.

[9] It should be recorded that the implementation of the domestic guidelines also has had foreign repercussions: Canada has been unhappy about the holding down of the price of aluminum, an important export, while Chile in particular has balked at cooperating in holding down the price of copper.

this defense stresses that direct investment is after all being allowed to run at 35 per cent above the 1962–64 rate in 1965–66; thus is restriction of profit opportunities made to appear as almost immodest license. Another stresses that expansion of exports but not contraction of imports gains credit in guideline terms. But expansion of exports by what may in effect be forced subsidization at the private expense of the international corporations is not necessarily socially beneficial; and if, as the Canadians referred to above have charged, the subsidy is at the expense of reduced efficiency of production in foreign countries, the beneficiality of the exercise to the world economy is still more problematical. Moreover, it is very questionable how long the administration will be able to avoid giving credit for import reduction, when it is obvious that a dollar reduction of imports is as effective as a dollar more of exports or a dollar less of foreign direct investment from a strictly balance-of-payments point of view, and may well be far less costly in terms of the company's private profit-maximizing objectives.

The third defense approaches the economic heart of the matter, by contrasting the guidelines favorably with the alternative means of restricting capital outflows, an increase in the level of United States interest rates. The 1966 Report of the Council of Economic Advisers argues: "Compared with reliance solely on restrictive general monetary measures that might conceivably hold down capital flows to the same extent, the selective credit techniques have the obvious advantage of allowing monetary policy to respond to the needs for domestic credit, as well as to affect the 5–10 per cent of total credit that flows abroad" (p. 168). The phrasing of the last part of this sentence is typically opaque, but the message is clear: the guidelines are the price that has to be paid for the freedom to hold down domestic interest rates when otherwise they would have to be raised to keep international capital flows under control.[10]

---

[10] The Report attempts to buttress this argument with various arguments to the effect that "the selective approach is consistent with an appropriate composition of the private capital outflow." Some of these arguments beg the question of what is really appropriate. The most questionable on theoretical grounds is the contention that "The guidelines approach of the voluntary programs tends to permit the business firms and banks themselves to select the most attractive investment opportunities: the investments foregone

The Alternative to Guidelines

This is the crucial issue, at least in the context of the present balance-of-payments situation: between low interest rates and the necessity of guidelines on the one hand, and higher interest rates without the need for guidelines on the other. The belief in the necessity of low interest rates to the prosperity of the country, however, is under contemporary circumstances a belief in a myth, the joint product of a deep-rooted historical suspicion of the "Money Trust" and the "Eastern financiers" in the American popular mind and of the vulgar Keynesian identification of full employment policy with cheap money policy. The more sophisticated Keynesian theory that has informed the thinking of the Council of Economic Advisers in recent years and that motivated the 1964 tax cut indicates that full employment is compatible with tight money policy provided that fiscal policy is expansionary enough. Unfortunately, vulgar Keynesianism has continued to influence policy via the identification of tight money with interest rates higher than depression levels, and the mistaken corollary implication that monetary policy in this country has already become dangerously restrictive, from the point of view of full employment policy, has in fact reached the limits of its powers and usefulness in that direction.

Within the context of the present balance-of-payments problem, then, the issue is between tighter guidelines and tighter money; this is also, not surprisingly, the issue in domestic economic policy. But in both contexts, the issue is posed fundamentally by the adherence of the United States to the modern version of the gold standard system of international monetary organization, and the consequent ineluctable pressures on the United States to play by the rules of the modern gold standard game as these have been progressively modified by the more successful European players. The modifications consist precisely in the substitution of guidelines policies,

would yield a smaller return than the average for all new foreign investments."

There is no reason to expect that the returns on marginal investments will be equalized as between business firms and/or banks, and therefore little reason to expect that the investments foregone by some would not have yielded a higher return than the investments allowed to others.

applied domestically to prices and wages and internationally to capital movements, for the traditional monetary mechanisms of international adjustment. In a fundamental sense, the choice for the United States is between practicing playing the guidelines game of the present system of fixed exchange rates and insisting on a change in the game itself, before it becomes too late. Such a change could be forced by unilateral United States action. Either a refusal to convert dollars into gold any further for the central banks of other countries, or more boldly a refusal to guarantee repurchase on demand of gold once sold, would force the European countries to choose between themselves assuming responsibility for financing United States balance-of-payments deficits at the current fixed exchange rate and allowing the exchange value of the dollar to adjust freely to its equilibrium level.

ALLAN H. MELTZER

The Regulation of Bank Credits Abroad: Another Failure for the Government's Balance-of-Payments Programs?

ALLAN H. MELTZER is professor of economics at the Graduate School of Industrial Administration, Carnegie Institute of Technology. He asserts that the voluntary restraint programs laid on United States banks and other financial institutions have increased the outflow of gold from the United States, although the programs have reduced the United States payments deficit. In the years preceding the adoption of the programs, he observes, foreigners acquired a substantial volume of liquid dollar assets, especially claims on United States banks. He argues that the voluntary program has reduced the ability of foreigners to borrow dollars in the United States, and that, consequently, they have reduced their holdings of dollars.

The United States's balance-of-payments programs have failed. Although the government's program has achieved some of its other aims—for example, raising income and reducing unemployment—it has not succeeded in balancing our international accounts without a gold outflow. The magnitude of the failure is impressive. Between 1957 and 1965, we used $9 billion of gold—

40 per cent of the stock of gold held in 1957—to settle our accounts with foreign countries. In 1965 the gold outflow amounted to 11 per cent of the gold stock held at the end of 1964 and was the largest percentage reduction in any year since 1958. There is no other period during the last ninety years in which the percentage reduction of the gold stock has been as large as it has been in the past eight years.

The increasing reliance placed on informal controls, guidelines, and threats is evidence of the failure of prior policies to achieve simultaneously the goals of price stability, increased use of domestic resources, and equilibrium in the balance of payments. When faced with a choice, United States policymakers followed the unfortunate tradition set by many foreign governments, imposing exchange controls or other restrictions on the use of resources and threatening to impose additional controls if present controls fail to stop the gold outflow.

Controls on international capital movements and other restrictions have been justified on the ground that there is a conflict between the domestic and international aims of policy. The way in which the conflict has been resolved suggests that domestic economic goals have been given the highest priority and the avoidance of controls a much lower priority. Choosing higher employment levels in preference to a larger gold stock can be defended on both social and economic grounds; the preference for a larger gold stock, purchased at a cost measured in units of freedom, is much harder to defend. But stating the issue in this way focuses too much attention on differences of opinion about the ranking of social priorities and too little attention on the economic consequences and on the success or failure of the exchange control program. Moreover, conflicts between long-term policy goals or objectives have been discussed frequently. Much less attention is paid to the costs of seeking short-term improvements at the expense of long-term adjustment. Informal controls and "jawbone" techniques are one manifestation of the importance policymakers attach to short-term gains.

This paper discusses one set of informal controls—the Federal Reserve's guidelines for international lending. Since these guidelines are part of a program designed to achieve a variety of domestic and international goals, I will, first, list some recent policy goals and discuss some of the conflicts among them that led to the use of controls. I will then argue that controls on foreign loans and investments (1) reveal a preference for short-term gains at the expense of longer-term gains, (2) conflict with the aims of United States policy, (3) have failed to achieve any significant, short-run improvement in the balance-of-payments position, and (4) have delayed the long-run adjustment. Finally, I will suggest an alternative approach, designed to achieve most of the goals of United States policy without the use of exchange controls or other restrictive practices.

Policy Goals and Achievements

Among the stated goals that policymakers have reaffirmed periodically, the following are most relevant to the present discussion:

1. wages should be tied to productivity;
2. domestic inflation should be prevented;
3. the outflow of gold should be stopped;
4. the dollar price of gold and the exchange rate should be maintained;
5. unemployment should be reduced;
6. the European Common Market should be strengthened;
7. tariffs should be reduced and world trade liberalized and expanded;
8. the growth rate of output should be maintained at a high level.

The list is long and could be made longer by adding the desire to change the distribution of income, to aid less developed countries, to maintain military commitments, or to keep the dollar as a reserve currency. There is little point in embarking on a lengthy discussion to establish that policymakers have multiple goals, some of which conflict with other goals. Choices among goals, or ends, are inevitable in a world of limited resources. Moreover, there is little point in debating here about the goals that have been chosen or the priorities that have been assigned.

It is instructive, however, to consider how many of the stated aims have been achieved and to ask whether more would have been accomplished if different priorities had been assigned or if different means had been used to achieve the chosen ends of policy. First, I will discuss the achievements and failures of recent policy and outline the analysis that formed the basis of the choices that have been made. I will then suggest an alternative policy which would have been more successful in achieving some of the stated ends of the policymakers.

There are two clear successes and one apparent success during the past five years: the real growth rate of the economy has increased and unemployment has been reduced. While the dollar price of gold has been kept at $35 an ounce and the official exchange rate has been maintained, the exchange rate policy has been only partly successful. The United States is not the first country that claimed to maintain fixed and uniform exchange rates while introducing a number of restrictions that increased the cost of particular foreign exchange transactions. The so-called interest equilization tax and the restrictions on loans and investments abroad are de facto changes in the exchange rate for particular commodities.

Policy has failed to achieve the other five goals on the list. Although the wholesale price index rose less in 1961–64 than in the middle or late 1950's, the increase during the last eighteen months has eliminated most or all of the improvement in price stability. Trade and capital restrictions have been increased, not reduced. Wages have increased faster than the Council of Economic Advisers' measure of average productivity.

The Kennedy administration inherited a balance-of-payments deficit, an economy in which substantial parts of the labor force and capital stock were unemployed, and commitments to fixed exchange rates, to strengthen the Common Market and to expand world trade. Their first attempts to deal with these problems were based on four main propositions: one, the domestic economy could be stimulated by a tax cut or an increase in the government's deficit; two, the balance of payments could be improved by the use of restrictive monetary policy; three, long-term interest rates could be reduced to promote domestic investment while short-term interest rates were raised to attract an inflow of short-term capital; four, tariff negotiations could be used to reduce barriers and restrictions against exports from the United States and other countries to Common Market countries and, thereby, contribute to an improvement in the United States's balance of payments, the growth of world trade, and the development of underdeveloped countries.

Some of these proposals offered short-term programs to expand the economy and to temporarily slow or stop the gold outflow. Others were steps toward a long-term adjustment of prices in the United States, relative to prices abroad, that were expected to produce a long-run adjustment of the balance of payments. Of the latter, one of the more important proposals was for negotiations leading to lower tariff barriers and liberalized trading arrangements, the so-called Kennedy round of tariff negotiations.

Unfortunately, the trade negotiations produced scarcely any result. This means that, with fixed exchange rates, United States exports could be increased only to the extent that export prices were low enough to offset the disadvantage of foreign trade restrictions. Many companies attempted to circumvent the trade restrictions by building or buying plants within the protected area. As businessmen are fond of noting, a large part of our increase in exports and our improved trade balance is owing to an increase of exports of machinery and materials to branch plants and new subsidiaries in Common Market countries.[1]

Thus the failure of trade negotiations to liberalize trade contributed to an increase in capital investment in Europe. Since long-term interest rates in the United States were lower than long-term interest rates abroad, non-financial corporations borrowed in the United States to finance foreign capital outlays. Financial corporations also attempted to benefit from the difference in interest rates between the United States and Europe or Japan, so that in some (but not all) recent years, the banking sector contributed to the balance-of-payments deficit.

The policy of encouraging domestic investment by reducing long-relative to short-term interest rates conflicted with the policymakers' desire to bring the balance-of-payments problem to an early end. A continuation of borrowing in the United States and investing abroad would, eventually, have eliminated the substantial differences in long-term interest rates between the United States and foreign countries that existed in 1961. The increased demand in

---

[1] For example, see the statement of Richard Fenton, president of Pfizer International, to the National Industrial Conference Board, February 17, 1966. Some of the relevant data is given in the *Survey of Current Business*, December, 1965.

the United States raised long-term rates in the United States relative to rates in major trading countries abroad; the increase in the growth rate of the domestic economy raised the expected return to investment in the United States in absolute terms and relative to the rate of return on investment in foreign countries. Some evidence that part of the adjustment of long-term interest rates had occurred by 1964 is shown by the changes in these rates between 1961 and 1964. United States long-term rates rose relative to those in Canada, the United Kingdom, France, and Japan.[2] The reduction of the difference between interest rates and expected returns at home and abroad was in the direction of long-run adjustment of the payments imbalance.

A widely discussed part of the government's program was based on the proposition that the domestic economy could be stimulated by a tax cut while the balance of payments was improved, temporarily, by the use of restrictive monetary policy. Three points should be noted, however. First, most of the gain from this policy was expected to come from a reduction in short-term capital movements as a result of higher short-term interest rates. This short-run gain could be expected to last only as long as differences between United States and foreign short-term interest rates remained sufficiently small. Balances that flow in to obtain more favorable yields flow out just as quickly when yields fall. Second, the longer-term effect of monetary restriction came through the reduction in United States prices relative to the prices in foreign markets. Relative price deflation offset some of the trade restrictions imposed by Common Market countries. Third, the policy of monetary restrictions was not maintained. Instead, the Federal Reserve increased the money supply by approximately $20 billion during the three years ending in December, 1965, one of the largest and longest periods of monetary expansion in peacetime history.

The increased rate of monetary expansion stimulated the economy. Later, the 1964 tax cut supplemented the stimulus provided by expansive monetary policy. For a time, short-term interest rates were maintained at an almost constant level by a combination of

[2] Based on long-term government bond yields for the United States, Canada, the United Kingdom, and France, local government bond yields for Germany, and the bank lending rate for Japan.

increases in the money supply and in the government's outstanding stock of interest-bearing debt issued to finance budget deficits.[3] Later, the expansion of output and the continued expansion of money spilled over to prices, and the price level began to rise.

On this interpretation, there was one major conflict between goals in the initial phase of policy. Long-term adjustment of the balance of payments would have been achieved sooner if productivity increases had been used to reduce prices rather than to maintain wages, or if long-term interest rates had increased more and employment had increased less. Prices and interest rates in the United States, relative to foreign prices and interest rates, however, moved in the direction appropriate for the long-run adjustment of the balance of payments.

The more important conflict was between the desire to stop the outflow of gold and the desire to maintain a fixed dollar price of gold. Had we chosen to abandon fixed exchange rates and the fixed $35 per ounce price of gold in 1961, it is unlikely that we would have lost more gold than we have in the past five years.[4] The balance-of-payments adjustment would have been completed. Instead, the government became impatient with the slow rate of adjustment and started the second phase of the program. A number of ad hoc measures were introduced, appeals to patriotism became more frequent, but most of the adjustment toward balance-of-payments equilibrium was cancelled.

The second phase of the government's program began with the introduction of a restriction on capital movements—the interest equalization tax—in the summer of 1963. The movement toward controls on capital gathered momentum in 1965 with the introduction of "guidelines" for lending and investing.

---

[3] The policy from 1962 to 1965 can be viewed as a mirror image of the policy during 1946–51 when interest rates were pegged by the Federal Reserve. During much of the pegging period, Treasury debt retirement kept interest rates low, and thereby reduced the quantity of money that the Federal Reserve had to issue to maintain the peg. For further discussion see K. Brunner and A. H. Meltzer, "A Credit Market Theory of the Money Supply and the Explanation of Two Puzzles in Monetary Policy," *Essays in Honor of Marco Fanno* (forthcoming).

[4] Liquid liabilities held by foreigners were approximately $22 billion at the end of 1960, and the monetary gold stock was approximately $17.5 billion. Even if foreigners had been frightened into converting ¼ of their holdings, we would not have lost more gold.

Conflicts between the goals of United States policy increased during the second phase. Further reductions in the unemployment rate were obtained by maintaining and later increasing the rate of monetary expansion. Prices rose, and part of the earlier adjustments of domestic to foreign price levels was cancelled. The conflict between fixed exchange rates and other policy goals remained. A new conflict arose between short-term reduction in gold outflow and long-term balance-of-payments policies equilibrium. I will consider the last problem below, after discussing the Federal Reserve's guidelines for foreign lending in more detail.

THE FAILURE OF THE GUIDELINE POLICY

President Johnson's balance-of-payments message of February, 1965, called upon the Federal Reserve to take a major responsibility for improving the United States balance-of-payments position. As Chairman Martin said: "For the second time in less than two years, a national program to reduce and eventually eliminate a large international payments deficit has been launched. Our first program, begun with President Kennedy's message to Congress of July 18, 1963, met for a time with a measure of success, but in the course of last year, signs of fresh deterioration appeared."[5]

The new program, introduced in March, 1965, consisted of "voluntary" restrictions on foreign loans by banks and non-bank financial institutions and on investments by United States corporations abroad. Foreign loans had risen approximately 20 per cent in 1964 and were continuing to rise in early 1965. Banks were requested to limit their increase in foreign loans to 5 per cent of their 1964 year-end totals. Non-bank financial institutions had also increased their holdings of Euro-dollars and foreign loans in 1964. They were asked to limit short-term balances and investments abroad to the 1964 year-end total and to take steps toward gradually reducing such balances to the 1963 year-end total. Longer-term investments of non-bank financial institutions were permitted to increase no more than 5 per cent above the amount held at the end of 1964.

---

[5] Statement of William McC. Martin, Jr., before the Subcommittee on International Finance of the Senate Committee on Banking and Currency, March 10, 1965, reprinted in the *Federal Reserve Bulletin* 51 (March, 1965): 399–404.

Later, adjustments in the "voluntary guidelines" were introduced to eliminate some of the opportunities for avoiding or evading the March guidelines, to permit banks with foreign loans of less than $5 million in the base period to increase foreign loans by more than 5 per cent, and in December, to extend and revise the guidelines for 1966. The 1966 guidelines permit banks to increase foreign loans by an additional 4 per cent of their 1964 base, at the rate of 1 per cent per quarter. Non-bank financial institutions are requested to increase long-term investments abroad by no more than 4 per cent of the 1964 base and to restrict short-term investments to the September, 1965, total. Foreign branches and subsidiaries, including Edge Act Corporations, are included in the program.

In making loans under the guidelines, banks and other financial institutions are requested to give first priority to loans that finance exports. Second priority is given to loans made to less developed countries, and to Japan, Canada, and the United Kingdom. Loans made by the government's Export-Import Bank, and commercial banks' participation in loans guaranteed or insured by the Export-Import Bank or the Federal Credit Insurance Association, are exempt from the guidelines and are not included in the ceiling applicable to a particular bank.

The broad purpose of this program is to "defend the dollar," a vague phrase which, when defined, usually includes the maintenance of the dollar as a reserve currency. One effect of the guidelines has been contrary to this frequently stated aim of United States policy. By assigning priorities that reduce the volume of loans to finance trade between third countries, non-export loans to developed countries and local-currency expenditures outside the United States, the guidelines work to reduce the use of the dollar as a reserve currency, as I will show more fully below.

This feature of the guideline policy is typical of the government's approach to the balance-of-payments problem. Another inconsistency becomes apparent, if we consider the relation of the guidelines to the goal of maintaining fixed exchange rates. Fixed exchange rates are often defended on the grounds that they remove uncertainty and thereby promote world trade. A program that gives priority to United States exports and restricts loans to finance trade between third countries has a much less lofty purpose. The statement of priorities in the guidelines suggests that the goal of increasing world trade has been replaced by a program of not hampering United States exports. In any case, it is difficult to find merit in the argument that world trade should be increased by restricting capital movements.

There has been little attempt, however, to justify the program in terms of world trade or world economic welfare. The original announcement of the guidelines makes clear that the purpose is to promote the administration's interpretation of the national interest. The announcement states: "Decisions on specific loan transactions must be made primarily with an eye to the national interest rather than profits. The achievement of the President's goal will be in the long-term interest not only of the nation, but also of the individual institutions which are being called upon to forego immediate advantage or gain."[6]

The last quotation raises the questions about the content of words such as "the national interest" and "the President's goal." I will consider this subject below. Before doing so, let me discuss the reasons for choosing a voluntary program and some of the results achieved to date.

The government chose to present its program as "voluntary" and informal, rather than mandatory and formal, for pragmatic reasons. Chairman Martin's candid statement to the Senate Banking and Currency Committee makes clear that the government considered taxes on bank loans, akin to the interest equilization tax, and formal exchange controls. These more formal methods were rejected not only because exchange controls are "repugnant to the principles of our economic system," but also because they were likely to be less effective. A "tax statute can hardly avoid some opportunities for legal escape," and "experience everywhere has shown that exchange regulations, if couched in general terms, can be avoided as easily as a special tax; and if elaborated in great detail, can become so oppressive that they also hamper business activities beneficial to our payments situation."[7]

[6] "Guidelines for Banks and Non-Bank Financial Institutions," *ibid.,* p. 371.

[7] *Federal Reserve Bulletin* 51 (March, 1965), see especially pp. 402–3. Note that the emphasis is placed on the United States balance of payments and not on the dollar as a reserve currency.

The desire to avoid exchange controls while restricting foreign loans meant that the meaning of "voluntary" had to be twisted. Detailed prescriptions and proscriptions are given, reports are expected, and, as already indicated, priorities are established for certain types of loans and for particular countries. Nevertheless a substantial effort has been made to present the program as a voluntary effort by bankers. Three reasons for choosing to present the program as "voluntary" are of interest.

First, it is unlikely that the program could have been introduced as quickly if it had been submitted to Congress. The program clearly discriminates in favor of banks that have been making foreign loans for some time and against new entrants, particularly banks in inland cities and non-bank financial institutions. Congress —particularly the Chairman of the House Banking Committee before whom such legislation would come—generally prefers a more uniform distribution among the states than was provided by the guidelines and might have delayed passage while awaiting the testimony of bankers in the hinterland, the managers of non-bank financial institutions, or perhaps until "more equitable" controls were designed. The administration would have been hard-pressed to defend the provision under which loans made under commitments entered into during the first two months of 1965 counted against an individual bank quota and, if in excess of the yearly quota, were to be reduced by the end of 1965. This provision was particularly offensive to the inland banks, many of whom entered the market for foreign loans in 1964. No doubt it would have been equally difficult to defend a provision discriminating against non-banks, under which non-bank institutions were told to reduce liquid and short-term assets to the 1963 or 1964 year-end total, whichever was lower, and banks were asked to refrain from increasing such assets.

Second, by making the program appear "voluntary," the Federal Reserve was able to impose controls on non-bank financial institutions. The cooperating institutions range from commercial and mutual savings banks through investment, finance, and insurance companies, to mutual funds, pension funds, college endowments, charitable foundations, and state retirement funds. Congress has been reluctant in the past to extend Federal Reserve authority to non-member commercial banks, so there is reason to believe that it might have refused to grant authority under which the Federal Reserve could regulate all financial institutions. Moreover, the Federal Reserve had no clear idea in March, 1965, of the precise regulations that it wished to apply to the non-bank institutions. The guidelines for non-banks remained "tentative" from early March to late June, 1965, while information on the foreign asset holdings of such institutions was collected and processed.

I want to emphasize the way in which the controls on non-bank financial institutions were introduced. There is no other case to my knowledge in which controls were applied by an agency that had no authority to regulate, without a clear idea of the regulations that were to be applied and without information about the magnitude[8] of the problem they sought to control. I hope I am correct in assuming that Congress would have been reluctant to grant authority to the Federal Reserve under these circumstances.

The administration was convinced, however, that control of commercial bank lending would prove ineffective without similar or more stringent controls on non-banks. Commercial banks had approximately $10 billion of loans outstanding at the end of 1964 and had increased foreign loans by 18 to 20 per cent during the year. The data eventually collected from the non-banks showed that these institutions held $9.7 billion in foreign assets and had increased their foreign assets by $1 billion (11 per cent) in 1964. The failure of the interest equalization tax taught the administration that one form of loan is a substitute for another. Unless the more obvious substitutes were regulated, controls on commercial banks could be expected, at most, to reduce the capital outflow for a short time. After a few months, substitution of non-bank loans for bank loans would have renewed the outflow of credit to foreign countries.

A third reason for making the program appear voluntary is implicit in much of what I have said above. A minimum amount of explanation to Congress and of congressional action was required if the program could be presented as a voluntary program. The

[8] See Robert L. Sammons, "Voluntary Restraint by Financial Institutions," "The Balance of Payments Problem," Management Bulletin No. 68, American Management Association, 1965, pp. 17–21. Mr. Sammons is Adviser, Division of International Finance, Board of Governors of the Federal Reserve System.

only formal action I have found that Congress was asked to take as part of the voluntary program was contained in a bill that exempted banks and other financial institutions from prosecution under the anti-trust laws for discussing or entering into agreements. This legislation came before the Judiciary Committees of the Senate and House, rather than the Banking Committees, and focused attention on the broad purposes of the program, while avoiding discussion of the details of the financial controls. Chairman Martin made clear that the administration hoped to avoid establishing a cartel, or some NRA-type arrangement, under which bankers would be given authority to allocate a given amount of foreign loans among themselves. To date, they have been successful.[9]

In fact, the program has been an overwhelming success when judged by the aggregate measures that have been presented by spokesmen for the Federal Reserve and the administration. Table 1 summarizes some of the information provided by the government to support their position. The table shows that, through September, 1965, banks and non-banks alike remained well within the guidelines. Preliminary data for 1965 as a whole (not shown) suggests a similar conclusion. Banks acquired no more than one-third of the $500 million in additional foreign assets that they were permitted to acquire under the program.

TABLE 1

Guidelines for and Results of the Regulation
of Foreign Assets
(in billions of dollars)

Holder of Foreign Assets	Amount Outstanding		Ceiling
	12/31/64	9/30/65	12/31/66
Commercial banks	9.49	9.48	10.44
Non-bank financial institutions*..	3.39	3.10	3.25
Total	12.88	12.58	13.69

* Ceiling on assets over ten years applies only to assets in developed countries other than Canada and Japan.

Source: *Survey of Current Business,* January, 1966, p. 16.

[9] Chairman Martin's statement is reprinted in *Federal Reserve Bulletin* 51 (March, 1965).

A subsidiary goal of the program was to give priority in non-export loans to underdeveloped countries, to Canada, and to Japan. The data in Table 2 suggest that this part of the program was only moderately successful. Claims against Europeans declined about 5 per cent and claims against Japan increased about 5 per cent. But loans to Latin America increased much more slowly than in the previous year, and claims against Canadians decreased most rapidly. The totals, however, do not permit any judgment to be reached about changes in the quantity of loans demanded by firms or residents in the various countries. We know that banks could have made more loans to foreigners while remaining within the guidelines, and we know that the growth rate of output declined in Europe. But the growth rate of output declined in Japan also, without a similar reduction in United States loans to Japan. Moreover, opportunities for making profitable loans within the United States were much greater in 1965, so some inland banks may have found the guidelines a convenient reason for withdrawing from the foreign loan market.

The data in Tables 1 and 2, therefore, do not permit a firm conclusion to be drawn about the success of the guidelines. All that can be said is that claims against foreigners increased much less rapidly in 1965 than in 1964. More convincing evidence that the

TABLE 2

SHORT- AND LONG-TERM BANKING CLAIMS BY REGION
END OF YEARS FIGURES, 1963–65

(in billions of dollars)

Region	Volume of Claims		
	1963	1964	1965 *
Europe....................	2.05	2.95	2.80
Canada	.93	1.33	.94
Latin America..............	2.76	3.51	3.59
Asia†	2.94	3.97	4.17
Other.....................	.32	.47	.64
Total...............	9.00	12.23	12.14

* Preliminary.
† Mainly Japan.
SOURCE: *Treasury Bulletin,* February, 1966, pp. 98–99.

guidelines reduced foreign lending by banks and financial institutions can be obtained, however, by considering data for a longer period. The outflow of dollars resulting from loans and investments abroad was considerably smaller in 1965 than in any year since 1956. One would have to argue that a fortuitous decline in the rate of increase of the demand for United States bank loans in 1965 just happened to coincide with the government's program and reduced the outflow of dollars, attributable to the action of the financial system, to the lowest level in recent years. This argument is implausible.

These findings suggest that the guidelines have been effective. But they are a peculiar way in which to judge the effect of the policy. The reason is that there are two sides to a bank's balance sheet. When we look at what happened to the liabilities to foreigners of the United States banking system, it is much less clear that the guidelines contributed significantly—if at all—to achieve the aims of the United States balance-of-payments program in 1965.

Table 3 shows changes in assets and liabilities of the financial system during the past fifteen years. While these data have been collected in different ways at different times, the information is sufficiently accurate to give a reasonable summary of the contributions to the balance of payments by the financial sector. A minus sign in the table indicates an outflow of dollars that must be offset by some inflow or by a loss of gold.

During 1965, foreigners reduced their deposits in United States banks for the first time in fifteen years. The reduction was partly offset by purchases of United States securities. Column 2 of Table 3 shows, however, that net liabilities to foreigners decreased and contributed more than $200 million toward enlarging the outflow of gold. In 1964, the increase in liabilities to foreigners contributed more than $2.5 billion toward financing the balance-of-payments deficit. Since the deficit was not reduced by an equal amount, the net effect of the one year reduction in liabilities meant that part of the $2.8 billion had to be paid in gold. Column 3 shows that claims against foreigners—loans and investments by the banking system abroad—contributed toward a reduction of the balance-of-payments deficit. In 1964, the rise in loans and investments abroad added $3.16 billion to the balance-of-payments deficit. This amount fell to less than $1 billion in 1965, a balance-of-payments "gain" of more than $2 billion. The gain from reducing the rate of increase in foreign loans was not sufficient, however, to offset the loss of gold resulting from a decline in foreign deposits in United States banks, shown by the net movement in column one.

On balance, the banking sector contributed more to the outflow of gold in 1965 than in any postwar year, almost twice as much as in 1964, the last full year without controls. Viewed in terms of their effects on both assets and liabilities of the banking system, the guidelines appear to hinder the government's attempt to stop the gold outflow. This interpretation may be extreme. All of the reduction in deposit balances may not be the result of guidelines or controls. Large changes in the rate of growth of deposits have occurred in prior years, as the table clearly shows. Moreover,

TABLE 3

Net Movements of Banking Funds and Transactions in Long-Term Securities with Foreigners, 1951–65

(in billions of dollars)

Negative figures indicate a net outflow of dollars from the United States

Year	Net Movement (1)	Changes in Liabilities to Foreigners (2)	Changes in Claims on Foreigners (3)
1951......	− .39	.07	− .46
1952......	1.22	1.56	− .33
1953......	1.28	1.09	.19
1954......	.52	1.42	− .90
1955......	.94	1.37	− .42
1956......	.42	1.49	−1.08
1957......	− .94	.37	−1.31
1958......	− .90	.99	−1.89
1959......	3.34	4.35	−1.01
1960......	.48	2.27	−1.79
1961......	− .40	1.91	−2.31
1962......	.30	1.82	−1.52
1963......	− .84	1.89	−2.72
1964......	− .52	2.64	−3.16
1965......	−1.05	− .21	− .76

Detail may not add to total owing to rounding.
Source: *Treasury Bulletin,* March, 1966, p. 86.

foreigners—particularly those in Germany and France—may have withdrawn deposit balances because of differences in interest rates only partly the result of the guidelines policy, or for reasons completely unrelated to the guidelines.[10] For many of the same reasons that all of the reduction in the growth of foreign loans cannot be attributed to the guidelines, the total reduction in liabilities cannot be attributed to the guidelines either. The most that we can say without much more detailed analysis is that the United States increased its deposit liabilities to the rest of the world each year prior to 1965 and that the guidelines contributed to the 1965 reduction in deposit liabilities.

The guidelines may have given a little assistance to the balance of payments in 1965, or they may have done a little harm. They are far from the overwhelming success that the proponents of the guidelines claim. By pointing to only one side of the ledger, the Federal Reserve and the administration have given a distorted picture of the effectiveness of their "voluntary" form of exchange control.

LONG-TERM EFFECTS ON THE BALANCE OF PAYMENTS

Economic theory implies that welfare is increased when individual decision units take prices and profits as their guide in allocating resources. The Federal Reserve's program of restricting foreign loans proposes a different standard, and makes explicit that the framework just described is no longer regarded as useful. Priority is now given to achieving the President's goals, since, we are told, these goals are in the long-term interest of the nation and of financial institutions.[11]

It is not uncommon for governments to justify restrictions by asserting that the aims of national policy are of overriding importance, and it is not impossible to find or to conceive of cases in which the governments' argument can be justified. Government control of the money supply is a case in point. Much harm can be,

---

[10] One common explanation of the increased loss of gold attributes the outflow in 1965 to the policies of the French government. The gold loss, net of shipment to France, however, was larger in 1965 than in other recent years.

[11] *Federal Reserve Bulletin* 51 (March, 1965): 371.

and has been done, however, in the name of the public interest.

One of the tasks of economists is to analyze the effect of government programs and to see whether the programs are likely to achieve their stated goals without considerable interference with other aims of public and private policy. More often than not, the government's longer-term goal is not stated explicitly, and the economists' task is to discover which part of "the public interest" is being promoted by the proposed restriction. The case at hand is an example of the latter. In this section I discuss the effects that the program of loan restrictions is likely to have on the ends or goals that appear to be equated with the national interest for this purpose.

The discussion in the previous section suggests that the program has not yet contributed to the short-run adjustment of the balance of payments. Moreover, the data suggested that the control program does not contribute to longer-term goals, including the desire to maintain the dollar as a reserve currency and the United States as a world banking center. Foreigners have found other banking centers in which to keep their deposits and make loans. There is no reason to expect that the position of New York as a world financial center will be restored until the controls are removed or made less severe. The goal of keeping the United States as a world banker cannot be the goal that is being equated with the national interest.

How well does the program serve the goal of achieving long-run balance-of-payments adjustment? The answer is, not well at all. I have already indicated that if the gold outflow is to be stopped while the exchange rate is maintained, balance-of-payments equilibrium can be restored only by adjustments of prices and interest rates. United States prices must fall relative to foreign prices and interest rates in the United States must rise relative to foreign rates. The exchange control, or loan restriction, program works in the opposite direction. It diverts loan demand from the United States to foreign countries and requires United States corporations to finance foreign investments abroad, raising interest rates abroad relative to interest rates in the United States. These effects are in the direction opposite to the changes required for long-run adjustment.

Furthermore, investments and loans are made abroad in the

expectation of profits. Profits on foreign investment produce a return flow of dollars to the United States. Foreign investments stimulate exports to subsidiaries and open new markets to trade, thereby reducing the balance-of-payments deficit. Behrman estimates that an outflow of dollars for foreign investment produces a *net* contribution to the United States balance of payments in about three years.[12] Repayments of bank loans presumably cancel the balance of payments "drain" caused by the loan, and interest received on the loans "improves" our balances-of-payments position. It is by no means clear, therefore, that action taken in response to the profit motive is inimical to the "national interest."

These considerations suggest that our policy is short-sighted, a conclusion that would receive support if it gave the United States a short-term advantage. About the only advantage I can find is that the proportion of foreign loans held by the United States banking system is reduced, and the proportion of domestic loans is increased, per dollar of new base money issued. The program might have been defended on these grounds a few years ago, if analysis could be developed to show that domestic employment was being harmed by the diversion of bank credit to Europe. It is doubtful that this conclusion can be supported, or even that it is supportable, and in any case, the argument is quite irrelevant at the present time. Our present problem is that the rate of growth of both the money supply and bank credit contribute to domestic inflation.

In short, I can find no long-run advantage in the program. The most that can be said for the restrictions is that they might help to maintain fixed exchange rates and temporarily reduce the gold drain. Although the restrictions did not do this in the first year— and probably did the opposite—policymakers may expect that in the second or subsequent years loans to foreigners will increase less than deposits to foreigners decrease. There is no reason to expect this result. The policy raises foreign interest rates relative to United States interest rates and thus makes foreign markets more attractive places in which to keep interest-bearing deposits and in which to buy earning assets. Moreover, the United States is inflating faster relative to foreign countries than in the past, further

[12] J. N. Behrman, "Private Foreign Investment," *Journal of World Business,* 1965.

increasing the cost of foreigners of holding dollar deposits.

Even if the restrictions manage to bring about a reduction in the gold outflow, the program cannot be regarded as successful until it achieves balance-of-payments equilibrium without controls. Here the long-run results of the program are contrary to any short-run benefits. Since the spread between foreign and domestic interest rates is increased, any gains made as a result of the controls will be lost once the controls are removed. There might be some hope of removing controls in a period of recession in Europe on the argument that interest rates abroad will fall at such times. During recession, however, prices in Europe are likely to fall, or rise less rapidly than in the past. A peculiar piece of good fortune is required to get the combination of relative interest rates and prices that permit controls to be removed.

Many countries have attempted in the past to adjust to a balance-of-payments deficit by imposing a few "temporary" controls. Generally, the first set of controls becomes permanent, and new "temporary" controls are introduced. Most experience of this kind suggests that the resolution of the problem has been found in devaluation. The United States has much greater resources than other countries which can be used to make the adjustment, but so far the resources have not been used to bring about an adjustment.

Many of the failures of administration policy appear to result from a belief that balance-of-payments equilibrium will be achieved in the near future and can be hastened by introducing ad hoc measures and controls. Cagan's recent study suggests that the opposite is true.[13] He found that adjustments of prices and interest rates to restore balance-of-payments equilibrium, at times, required decades.

Among Cagan's results for the eighty-year period 1875–1955, one is particularly intriguing. His data show that the ratio of the monetary base (bank reserves plus currency) to the gold stock has fluctuated widely but has frequently returned to approximately two. Broad swings in the ratio, and/or in the gold stock, correspond to long-run changes in the purchasing power of gold. When the

---

[13] Phillip Cagan, *Determinants and Effects of Changes in the Stock of Money, 1875–1960* (New York: Columbia University Press for the National Bureau of Economic Research, 1965), pp. 52–67.

index of the commodity value of gold rises, gold flows in, and the money supply and the domestic price level rise, unless offset by changes in other sources of the monetary base. The rise in the domestic price level lowers the commodity value of gold and induces a gold outflow. If domestic monetary expansion is too large relative to changes in the gold stock, domestic prices rise more rapidly, the commodity value of gold declines, and gold flows out sooner. This reduces the stock of money, unless offset by other monetary policies, for example, open market operations that increase the monetary base and hence increase the ratio.

TABLE 4

THE RATIO OF THE MONETARY BASE TO GOLD AND AN INDEX OF
THE COMMODITY VALUE OF GOLD, 1956–65

Year	Ratio of the Monetary Base* to Gold	Index of the Commodity Value of Gold†
1956........	2.17	98
1957........	2.23	93
1958........	2.31	91
1959........	2.44	91
1960........	2.75	90
1961........	2.97	90
1962........	3.19	90
1963........	3.43	90
1964........	3.66	90
1965........	4.32	88

* The monetary base is the sum of bank reserves plus currency.
† The (approximate) ratio of the current dollar price of gold ($35.00) to the price of gold in 1926 ($20.67), 1.7, divided by the index of wholesale prices base 1926 = 100.

If we interpret a value of two as the approximate long-run equilibrium value of the ratio, we can judge the extent to which recent monetary policy has moved away from equilibrium. Table 4 extends Cagan's data for the ratio and for the index of the commodity value of gold to 1965. These data show that the commodity value of gold has declined as the monetary base has risen relative to the gold stock. The decline in the commodity value of gold is a result of the increase in the wholesale price level brought about by the relatively high rate of increase of the monetary base and the money supply. Further increases in the domestic price level and further decline in the commodity value of gold are to be expected if the rate of growth of the monetary base continues.

The table gives no indication of price changes in other countries. Sufficient inflation abroad will, of course, drive gold back to the United States. A recent issue of the *Review* of the St. Louis Federal Reserve Bank, however, gives estimates of the growth rate of the money supply and the increase in prices for six foreign countries.[14] In France, Germany, and Japan, the money supply has grown more slowly in the last year or two than in previous years, while in Italy, Belgium, and the Netherlands, the rate of monetary growth has increased. But none of these countries show a rate of price change larger than our recent increases, so these data also suggest that the gold outflow will continue.

One source of long-run adjustment is usually dismissed without much consideration—the increase in the world's stock of gold owing to increased gold production resulting from the discovery of new mines or from an increase in the purchasing power of gold. The Soviet Union has recently discovered a new source of gold that can be mined profitably at current prices. Cagan found that, on several occasions in the past, new gold production contributed to an expansion of world trade and to maintaining fixed parities. Without some increase in the world's stock of gold, it is difficult to see how the United States could restore the ratio of the monetary base to gold to two, at the present price of gold, without a major change in the current goals of policy, a severe decline in the stock of money, and increased unemployment.

CONCLUSION: AN ALTERNATIVE APPROACH

United States's balance-of-payments policy has been based on the notion that a price of $35 per ounce of gold is a constant to which all policies—domestic and foreign—must adjust. For some, any conflict among increased use of domestic resources, price inflation, and a fixed dollar price of gold should be resolved by choosing

[14] *Review,* Federal Reserve Bank of St. Louis, March, 1966.

policies that maintain the price of gold. The European restrictions against United States exports are recognized as one feature of the international economy that delays or prevents adjustment that is unlikely to be removed. Federal Reserve controls on foreign loans and other autarkic devices are justified as necessary to reduce the United States balance-of-payments deficit and the gold outflow.

The difficulty with this line of argument is that it is based on a false premise. If the analysis in this paper is valid, Federal Reserve policy—both controls and recent excessive increases in the money supply—make the balance-of-payments deficit and the gold outflow larger and delay a return to equilibrium. Other voluntary controls, guidelines, and restrictions increase our problems. One example will be cited. In 1964 the administration prevented banks from increasing prime loan rates on the grounds that higher interest rates were not in the interest of the public. Had the increase taken place, banks in the United States would have closed an additional part of the gap between foreign and domestic rates and thereby lowered the demand for loans by foreigners. Instead, the increase was prevented, loans to foreigners increased, and restrictions were imposed to reduce foreign loans.

At present, the money supply is growing at a rate of more than 6 per cent per annum. This rate of monetary growth has caused increase in the domestic price level. Continued inflation will increase the gold outflow, delay the balance-of-payment adjustment, and encourage the administration to add some of the controls they have threatened to those that they have already imposed.

It is not difficult to outline an alternative approach to the current policy problem that avoids controls, prevents inflation, maintains employment of domestic resources, and eliminates the problems posed by the continued balance-of-payments deficit. Three steps are required: First, the controls on foreign transactions should be removed; second, the growth rate of the money supply should be reduced; third, the dollar price of gold should be left to the determination of the market.

These proposals call on the government to recognize that its balance-of-payments program has failed, and that recent inflation and controls on foreign loans have offset most of the adjustment toward long-run equilibrium made during the period ending in 1964. Recent price increases generate expectations of further increases. The larger the expected increase in prices, the smaller is the rate of growth of the money supply that prevents prices from rising. The longer price increases are permitted to continue, the larger is the likely reduction in domestic employment required to restore price stability.

Policymakers are fond of quoting an old saw to the effect that policy must always be made in the short run. The statement is either a truism or a mistake. The Federal Reserve's policy of domestic inflation and restrictions on foreign loans moves us away from our long-term goals and does not achieve short-term objectives. Balance-of-payments adjustment is a long-run problem; an appropriate solution is to recognize past history as it affects the dollar price of gold and to let the market make the appropriate adjustment in the exchange rate.

PART III

Guidelines, Legal Issues, and the Governmental Process

PHILIP B. KURLAND

Guidelines and the Constitution: Some Random Observations on Presidential Power to Control Prices and Wages

PHILIP B. KURLAND is professor of law at The University of Chicago and editor of the Supreme Court Review. *He discusses the constitutional aspects of interventions by government in wage and price setting and finds no constitutional problem of a general nature.*

Once upon a time, a little shepherd boy was engaged in the task of tending sheep for some farmers while they tilled their land nearby. One day when he saw the wolf approaching the flock, the boy cried out loudly: "Wolf! Wolf!" The farmers, hearing the cries, dropped their work and rushed to protect the flock. The wolf, seeing the farmers approaching, retreated to the woods. When the farmers arrived, there was no wolf to be seen and they admonished the boy not to call them needlessly from their farm work. This sequence was repeated a half-dozen times. The next time the boy cried "Wolf!" the farmers, busy working their farms, refused to answer the call. And the wolf killed the entire flock.

Adapted from an ancient fable

In general terms the Presidency at the beginning of the 1960's is easily described: It is the focus of both the American gov-

> *ernmental system and the free world coalition, an office of*
> *great authority and commensurate responsibility. Resting*
> *firmly on the twin supports of democratic election and the*
> *necessities of a critical era, it is now a permanently strong*
> *office, an institutionalized version of the "crisis presidencies"*
> *of Lincoln, Wilson, Roosevelt, and Truman. And like the*
> *regimes from which it stems, the outstanding feature of the*
> *executive office today is power.*
>
> Hirschfield, *The Powers of the Contemporary Presi-*
> *dency,* 14 PARLIAMENTARY AFFAIRS 353 (1961)

Lawyers have so long been bemused by Charles Evans Hughes's proposition that the Constitution is what the Supreme Court says it is that they have come to believe it. It is for this reason that most lawyers asked about the constitutional questions implicit in the executive price-wage guidelines will quickly tell you that there are no such issues. For one thing, none of the questions that this procedure raises is likely to come before the courts so as properly to be denominated a "constitutional question." For another, American lawyers fail to recognize that, in large measure, the Court has not created most of the major constitutional changes that have occurred in this country's history: it has merely acquiesced, sooner or later, in the fundamental shifts of governmental power that constitutional revision means. It would have been better, therefore, had this background paper been undertaken by an English constitutional lawyer, a modern Bryce, or even a Laski. They, lacking the alleged benefits of judicial review in their own country, understand better than we do the essence of constitutional change. For what we are concerned with here is not an isolated phenomenon of presidential authority but an aspect of the shift of power to the executive branch of the national government. Even regarded more narrowly, we are talking about a constitutional change, for, as Andrew Shonfield, writing of the Kennedy steel fight of 1962, recently pointed out:[1] ". . . the American business community as a whole, for all the protests against Kennedy's 'interference,' was in no doubt that what had been done was not just an odd deviation by a President who was thought to be anti-business, but the expression of a new and abiding relationship be-

[1] SHONFIELD, MODERN CAPITALISM 367 (1965).

tween private and public authority in decisions about the price of anything which was deemed to be a key product—whatever that meant." Whether Shonfield was right about the opinion of the American business community, I submit that he was right about the conclusion that he attributed to them.

Handicapped by my own training as an American constitutional lawyer, I can offer only the myopic evaluation that relies on opinions of the Supreme Court which, as I have said, tend to record rather than create fundamental constitutional changes, especially in this area of economics. I find some solace in the fact that I perpetrate no fraud: The sponsors of the symposium, strong believers in the doctrine of *caveat emptor,* were warned about my inadequacies before I accepted their commission. With little promise of any substantial return, I propose then to draw from the Supreme Court decisions some relevant criteria on which to base judgment of the constitutional propriety of the present wage-price guidelines. The result will necessarily be that this "background" paper may be so far in the background as to be out of the picture.

The power of government to regulate prices and wages is typical of the changes in constitutional doctrine that are reflected in judicial opinions rather than created by them. In order to understand the shifts of power that I shall recall here, it should be remembered that a division of functions between state and national authority—that is, a concept of federalism—premised the development of the country. This history, too, demonstrates a reflection in government structure of changing needs and interests, but suffice it for our purposes to report that throughout the nineteenth century and into the twentieth, the assumption was that the federal government was limited to the powers granted to it by the Constitution while all other governmental authority was left with the states.

I. State Power to Control Prices and Wages

DECLINE AND FALL

The theory of constitutional limitations on the power of the states to fix prices and wages must begin with the case of *Munn v. Illinois,*[2] the major *Granger Case* of 1877. There, in what pur-

[2] 94 U.S. 113 (1877).

ported to be a magnificent victory for the populist forces battling the capitalists and their railroads, the Court sowed the seeds of what was to be a bitter harvest for the prevailing forces. For, although the Court gave the victory to the states in their assertion of power to fix rates for railroads and warehouses, it inverted the common-law principles by making such price-fixing power the exception rather than the rule when in fact it had been the rule rather than the exception.[3] Here was born the judicial notion that only businesses "affected with a public interest" were subject to governmental authority to fix prices. The majority opinion went on to hold that the question of the adequacy of the prices fixed was singularly of legislative and not of judicial concern. Typically,[4] the Court got itself off on the wrong track by an abuse of history: a misconstruction of an esoteric seventeenth-century document by Lord Hale.[5]

It should be conceded, however, that there were stronger forces at work than the opinion of the Court in limiting the power of government to control prices and wages. As McAllister said in 1930, when the power was at its nadir:[6] "The exercise of this power has been checked, but not by the judicial interpretation of Lord Hale's phrase. It has been checked because, in the words of Mr. Justice Holmes, people have come to think that way. And it was a man named Adam Smith who first led them to think that way." In short, Holmes was wrong—for his time—in suggesting that Spencer's *Social Statics*[7] was not a part of the Constitution.

[3] See Hamilton, Affectation with a Public Interest, 39 YALE L.J. 1089 (1930).

[4] See Kelly, *Clio and the Court: An Illicit Love Affair,* [1965] SUPREME COURT REVIEW 119.

[5] See McAllister, *Lord Hale and Businesses Affected with a Public Interest,* 43 HARV. L. REV. 759 (1930); MAGRATH, MORRISON B. WAITE: THE TRIUMPH OF CHARACTER ch. 10 (1963).

[6] 43 HARV. L. REV. at 767.

[7] "The Fourteenth Amendment does not enact Mr. Herbert Spencer's *Social Statics.* . . . a constitution is not intended to embody a particular economic theory, whether of paternalism and the organic relation of the citizen to the State or of laissez faire. It is made for a people of fundamentally differing views, and the accident of our finding certain opinions natural and familiar or novel and even shocking ought not to conclude our judgment upon the question whether statutes embodying them conflict with the Constitution of the United States." Lochner v. New York, 198 U.S. 54, 75–76 (1905).

It was exactly because Spencer was a part of the American Constitution for the seventy years following the Civil War that Supreme Court opinions during this period treated the power to control prices of commodities and services as an exception to the general rule. It was for this reason, too, that Mr. Justice Field took exception to the majority opinion in *Munn v. Illinois:*[8]

> The public is interested in the manufacture of cotton, woollen, and silken fabrics, in the construction of machinery, in the printing and publication of books and periodicals, and in the making of utensils of every variety, useful and ornamental; indeed, there is hardly an enterprise or business engaging the attention and labor of any considerable portion of the community, in which the public has not an interest in the sense in which that term is used by the court in its opinion; and the doctrine which allows the legislature to interfere with and regulate the charges which the owners of property thus employed shall make for its use, that is, the rates at which all these different kinds of business shall be carried on, has never before been asserted, so far as I am aware, by any judicial tribunal in the United States.

Mr. Justice Field need not have worried. For the time being, at least, the *Zeitgeist* was on his side. Except in the situations where the state had conferred a monopoly on a business, the Court was most reluctant to find that any business was "affected with a public interest." In *Wolff Co. v. Industrial Court,*[9] of particular interest because it equated wages of labor with prices of commodities as enjoying the same exemption from governmental control, Mr. Chief Justice Taft set forth what has come to be considered the classic standard of the Court's position at the time:[10]

> Businesses said to be clothed with a public interest justifying some public regulation may be divided into three classes:
> (1) Those which are carried on under the authority of a public grant of privileges which either expressly or impliedly imposes the affirmative duty of rendering a public service demanded by any member of the public. Such are the railroads, other common carriers and public utilities.
> (2) Certain occupations, regarded as exceptional, the pub-

[8] 94 U.S. at 141.
[9] 262 U.S. 522 (1923).
[10] *Id.* at 535.

lic interest attaching to which, recognized from the earliest times, has survived the period of arbitrary laws by Parliament or Colonial legislatures for regulating all trades and callings. Such are those of the keepers of inns, cabs and grist mills. . . .

(3) Businesses which though not public at their inception may be fairly said to have risen to be such and have become subject in consequence to some governmental regulation. They have come to hold such a peculiar relation to the public that this is superimposed upon them. . . .

The third category was, of course, the amorphous one. But the Court, with the ultimate decision in its hands, made clear that it meant something special:[11] "The expression 'clothed with a public interest,' . . . means more than that the public welfare is affected by continuity or by the price at which a commodity is sold or a service rendered." And, as Mr. Justice Sutherland later pointed out:[12] "A business is not affected with a public interest merely because it is large or because the public are warranted in having a feeling of concern in respect of its maintenance."

Of course, during this time, most of the decisions were by divided courts, with Justices Holmes, Brandeis, and Stone contesting the authority of the Court to tell the states that they could not set prices or fix wages.

If the dissents sound more persuasive than the majority opinions—and to me they certainly do—they remained minority views despite their intrinsic merit. What brought about the change was not the logic or reasoning of the dissenters, but the fall from grace of the market as the primary if not the sole standard for determining prices and wages. It was the facts, not the law, that brought about the change, the facts that were detailed by Mr. Justice Brandeis in his dissent from one of the last gasps of laissez faire economics as constitutional doctrine. Writing in 1932, in *New Ice Co. v. Liebmann,* he said:[13]

The people of the United States are now confronted with an emergency more serious than war. Misery is wide-spread, in a time, not of scarcity, but of over-abundance. The long-continued depression has brought unprecedented unemployment,

[11] *Id.* at 536.
[12] Tyson & Brother v. Banton, 273 U.S. 418, 430 (1927).
[13] 285 U.S. 282, 306, 311 (1932).

a catastrophic fall in commodity prices and a volume of economic losses which threatens our financial institutions. . . .

. . . There must be power in the States and the Nation to remold, through experimentation, our economic practices and institutions to meet changing social and economic needs. . . .

REVIVAL

If nothing succeeds like the appearance of success, it is probably also true that nothing fails like the appearance of failure. There are many who would attribute the change in the course of Supreme Court opinions on state power in the area of economic regulation to the change in judicial personnel that followed Roosevelt's court-packing plan. But, in fact, there was no change in personnel between the *New Ice* case and *Nebbia v. New York*,[14] which shattered the earlier precedents. The only change in personnel that made a difference between *Tyson*[15] and *Nebbia* was the substitution of Hughes for Taft. And *Nebbia* came long before the 1936 election made possible Roosevelt's attempt to restaff the high tribunal. The fundamental change was in the public respect for laissez faire theory as constitutional principle. Classical economics was dethroned largely because of its apparent failure to solve the problems of the Great Depression. And when this change of attitude was reflected in Supreme Court doctrine, Mr. Justice Roberts was prepared to state for the majority the position that Stone and Holmes and Brandeis had been putting forth in dissent for some years. Writing for a five-man majority, Roberts disposed of seventy years of precedents with a vengeance:[16]

> We may as well say at once that the dairy industry is not, in the accepted sense of the phrase, a public utility. We think the appellant is also right in asserting that there is in this case no suggestion of any monopoly or monopolistic practice. It goes without saying that those engaged in the business are in no way dependent upon public grants or franchises for the privilege of conducting their activities. But if, as must be conceded, the industry is subject to regulation in the public interest, what constitutional principle bars the state from correct-

---

[14] 291 U.S. 502 (1934).
[15] See note 12 *supra*.
[16] 291 U.S. at 531–32.

ing maladjustments by legislation touching prices? We think there is no such principle. The due process clause makes no mention of sales or of prices any more than it speaks of business or contracts or buildings or other incidents of property. The thought seems nevertheless to have persisted that there is something peculiarly sacrosanct about the price one may charge for what he makes or sells, and that, however able to regulate other elements of manufacture or trade, with incidental effect upon price, the state is incapable of directly controlling the price itself. This view was negatived many years ago. *Munn v. Illinois.* . . .

Mr. Justice Field's fears about the majority opinion in *Munn* became realities at last. How he must have shaken his tomb when Roberts announced further:[17]

If the law-making body within its sphere of government concludes that the conditions or practices in an industry make unrestricted competition an inadequate safeguard of the consumer's interests, produce waste harmful to the public, threaten ultimately to cut off the supply of a commodity needed by the public, or portend the destruction of the industry itself, appropriate statutes passed in an honest effort to correct the threatened consequences may not be set aside because the regulation adopted fixes prices reasonably deemed by the legislature to be fair to those engaged in the industry and to the consuming public. And this is especially so where, as here, the economic maladjustment is one of price, which threatens harm to the producer at one end of the series and the consumer at the other. The Constitution does not secure to anyone liberty to conduct his business in such fashion as to inflict injury upon the public at large, or upon any substantial group of the people. Price control, like any other form of regulation, is unconstitutional only if arbitrary, discriminatory, or demonstrably irrelevant to the policy the legislature is free to adopt, and hence an unnecessary and unwarranted interference with individual liberty.

The shackles were off. The issue over price controls was returned to the state legislatures for resolution. For the time being at least, no single economic ideology was equated with constitutional mandate. *Nebbia* was not the coup de grace. That didn't come until 1941 in *Olsen v. Nebraska*,[18] when the five-to-four majority of

[17] *Id.* at 538–39.
[18] 313 U.S. 236 (1941).

Nebbia was converted into a unanimous judgment, an achievement that the earlier doctrine seldom achieved.[19]

CONTINUING LIMITATIONS

The states are still not absolutely free to engage in price-fixing at whim. There is still a remnant of state constitutional limitations that looks like the older economic due process decisions.[20] There remain the standards suggested in Roberts' opinion quoted above that have to be met.[21] Such controls may not be "arbitrary, discriminatory, or demonstrably irrelevant." The Court has retained the power that Waite tried to throw away in *Munn v. Illinois:* the power to pass on the reasonableness of the rates fixed. It is no longer a stringent limitation.[22] But the Court has retained one real power of restraint over state price-control powers: the commerce clause.

A year after the New York milk price-control statute was sustained against attack under the due process clause of the Fourteenth Amendment, its application was enjoined as a violation of the commerce clause in *Baldwin v. Seelig.*[23] As the Court has recently said,[24] however, this does not mean that such price-fixing is itself an infringement of the powers of the national government,[25] even where it is applied to the purchase within the state for processing and sale outside the state.[26] It does mean that where the effect of the price-fixing is such as unreasonably to burden the traffic in interstate commerce—a standard as variable as the shifting majorities of the Supreme Court can possibly make it[27]—it

---

[19] The *Wolff* case, *supra* note 9, was decided unanimously.

[20] See Hoskins & Katz, *Substantive Due Process in the States Revisited,* 18 OHIO ST. L.J. 384 (1952).

[21] See text at note 17 *supra.* The possibility of revival of "economic due process" in the near future is rather slim. See McCloskey, *Economic Due Process and the Supreme Court: An Exhumation and Reburial,* in KURLAND (ed.), THE SUPREME COURT AND THE CONSTITUTION 158 (1965).

[22] See, e.g., Power Commission v. Hope National Gas Co., 320 U.S. 591 (1944).

[23] 294 U.S. 511 (1935).

[24] Polar Co. v. Andrews, 375 U.S. 361 (1964).

[25] Highland Farms Dairy v. Agnew, 300 U.S. 608 (1937).

[26] Milk Control Board v. Eisenberg Farm Products, 306 U.S. 346 (1939).

[27] See POWELL, VAGARIES AND VARIETIES IN CONSTITUTIONAL INTERPRETATION 142–79 (1956).

will be stricken as invalid. For all practical purposes, the commerce clause, unlike the old due process clause, leaves the states free to fix prices whenever a legislative majority determine it appropriate unless the Court determines that the national interest is adversely affected by such action.[28]

II. National Power to Control Prices and Wages

SUBSTANTIVE DUE PROCESS

The foregoing excursus into state price-fixing is not as irrelevant to the subject of national authority that is our immediate concern as might appear.

State governments have, as earlier indicated, a reservoir of authority not taken from them by the provisions of the national Constitution.[29] Generally, this capacity has been designated as the "police power." That term was probably best described by Mr. Justice Holmes in his dissent in the *Tyson* case,[30] where the Court struck down a state's attempt to fix prices for markups on theater tickets. Holmes's definition and his thesis about it clearly anticipated the future direction that the Court would take, even if those decisions were to come too late to preserve state governments as viable parts of our national system:[31]

> . . . police power often is used in a wide sense to cover and, as I said, to apologize for the general power of the legislature to make a part of the community uncomfortable by a change.
>
> I do not believe in such apologies. I think the proper course is to recognize that a state legislature can do whatever it sees fit to do unless it is restrained by some express prohibition in the Constitution of the United States or of the State, and that Courts should be careful not to extend such prohibitions beyond their obvious meaning by reading into them conceptions of public policy that the particular Court may happen to entertain.

[28] See Townsend v. Yeomans, 301 U.S. 441 (1937); Cities Service Co. v. Peerless Co., 340 U.S. 179 (1950).

[29] This was formalized in the language of the now moribund Tenth Amendment: "The powers not delegated to the United States by the Constitution, nor prohibited by it to the States, are reserved to the States respectively, or to the people."

[30] See note 12 *supra*.

[31] 273 U.S. at 446.

Whether within Holmes's notion or not—and it was not—the Fourteenth Amendment's due process clause was read by the Court to be that "express prohibition in the Constitution of the United States" that precluded the extension of the police power to fixing prices, except in those businesses "affected with a public interest."

The federal government has no general equivalent of the "police power," except perhaps in the District of Columbia.[32] Insofar as it engages in the practice of price-fixing, it must rely on specific grants of authority from the Constitution, to wit, the commerce clause and the war power. But just as the police power of the states is confined by the due process clause of the Fourteenth Amendment, so, too, are the powers of the national government confined by the due process clause of the Fifth Amendment. Although the Court had fewer opportunities to indulge itself in limiting national action because it violated the principles of Spencer's *Social Statics*—in large measure because the national legislature had also adopted Adam Smith—it made it quite clear that the economic principles imported into the Fourteenth Amendment were also a portion of the Fifth.[33] It was to be expected, therefore, that the lifting of these restrictions against the states would be quickly followed by reassessment of the meaning of the Fifth Amendment. And so it was. And it is here that the connection between the state cases and the federal power is made clear.

Just as in the state cases, so too with regard to the federal government, the issue was resolved in a case involving the fixing of milk prices. In *United States v. Rock Royal Co-op.*,[34] the Supreme Court held in reliance on *Nebbia v. New York*:[35]

> Since *Munn* v. *Illinois,* this Court has had occasion repeatedly to give consideration to the action of states in regulating prices. Recently, upon a re-examination of the grounds of state power over prices, that power was phrased by this Court to mean that "upon proper occasion and by appropriate measures the state may regulate a business in any of its as-

[32] See Block v. Hirsch, 256 U.S. 135 (1921).
[33] See, e.g., Adair v. United States, 208 U.S. 161 (1908); Adkins v. Children's Hospital, 261 U.S. 525 (1923).
[34] 307 U.S. 533, 570–71 (1939).
[35] See text at note 23 *supra*.

pects, including the prices to be charged for the products or commodities it sells."

The power of a state to fix the price of milk has been adjudicated by this Court. . . . The power enjoyed by the states to regulate the prices for handling and selling commodities within their internal commerce rests with the Congress in the commerce between the states.

The removal of the straitjacket of classical economic theory from price-control legislation was quickly extended to wages as well in *United States v. Darby:*[36]

> *Validity of the wage and hour provisions under the Fifth Amendment.* Both provisions are minimum wage requirements compelling the payment of a minimum standard wage with a prescribed increased wage for overtime of "not less than one and one-half times the regular rate" at which the worker is employed. Since our decision in *West Coast Hotel Co.* v. *Parrish,* 300 U.S. 379, it is no longer open to question that the fixing of a minimum wage is within the legislative power and that the bare fact of its exercise is not a denial of due process under the Fifth more than under the Fourteenth Amendment. Nor is it any longer open to question that it is within the legislative power to fix maximum hours. . . .

The *Darby* opinion had more important effects on federalism. As Mr. Justice Roberts, who was a member of the unanimous Court that decided the case, later said:[37]

> Of course, the effect of sustaining the Act was to place the whole matter of wages and hours of persons employed throughout the United States, with slight exceptions [most of which have since been removed], under a single federal regulatory scheme and in this way completely superseded state exercise of the police power in this field.

THE WAR POWER

As indicated earlier, one of the two constitutional bases on which the national government power to impose price controls must rest is the "war power." One will look long before discovering the "war power" in the interstices of the Constitution, except

[36] 312 U.S. 100, 125 (1941).
[37] ROBERTS, THE COURT AND THE CONSTITUTION 56 (1951).

insofar as that document authorizes Congress to "declare" war, certainly an obsolescent notion at best. It should not be surprising therefore that the "war power" is an amorphous concept. Mr. Justice Jackson described it as "vague, undefined and undefinable."[38] But it is clear from our experience in two world wars that whatever else it includes, it authorizes the national legislature to provide for the most far-reaching controls on prices, wages, and rents.

Even before the demise of substantive due process, the Court sustained the power of Congress to legislate price controls in time of war. In 1917, pursuant to authorization from Congress, the President fixed the prices that could be charged for coal. The Court found this within the exercise of the war power, but retained for itself the authority to pass on the reasonableness of the prices so fixed.[39] To a large degree, price controls imposed under the war power are free of many restraints that might be imposed on similar controls asserted by the national legislature under different authority. For example, the procedural requirements dictated by the Fifth Amendment may be considerably foreshortened, as they were during World War II.[40] These controls might be retroactively applied.[41] Contract prices might be renegotiated long after the event.[42] And the undefinable scope of the war power is matched by the undefinable period during which it might be utilized; for "the war power includes the power 'to remedy the evils which have arisen from its rise and progress' and continues for the duration of that emergency."[43]

"But even the war power does not remove constitutional limitations safeguarding essential liberties."[44] The right to contest the validity of the controls imposed must be made available, even if the machinery is more summary and streamlined than would be considered adequate in time of peace.[45] And the procedural re-

---

[38] Woods v. Miller Co., 333 U.S. 138, 146 (1948).

[39] Highland v. Russell Car Co., 279 U.S. 253 (1929).

[40] See Yakus v. United States, 321 U.S. 414 (1944); Bowles v. Willingham, 321 U.S. 503 (1944); Lockerty v. Phillips, 319 U.S. 182 (1943).

[41] Woods v. Stone, 333 U.S. 472 (1948); cf. Fleming v. Rhodes, 331 U.S. 100 (1947).

[42] Lichter v. United States, 334 U.S. 742 (1948).

[43] Woods v. Miller Co., 333 U.S. 138, 141 (1948).

[44] Home Bldg. & Loan Assn. v. Blaisdell, 290 U.S. 398, 427 (1934).

[45] See cases cited in note 40 supra.

quirements of the Fifth and Sixth Amendments must be preserved if criminal sanctions are to be invoked by way of enforcement.[46] If the war power is the broader and more menacing basis for the imposition of price and wage controls, it is nonetheless still subject to judicial screening to assure the minimal decencies that procedural due process demands.

THE COMMERCE POWER

As already indicated, the national power to regulate prices and wages was quickly established after the Court's decision in *Nebbia*. The Court has never withdrawn from the proposition as stated, for example, in *Power Comm'n v. Pipeline Co.*:[47]

> It is no objection to the exercise of the power of Congress that it is attended by the same incidents which attend the exercise of the police power of a State. The authority of Congress to regulate the prices of commodities in interstate commerce is at least as great under the Fifth Amendment as is that of the States under the Fourteenth to regulate the prices of commodities in intrastate commerce.

There remained the requirement that the rates fixed were to be subject to judicial scrutiny, but the standard was not a difficult one to meet:[48] "By long standing usage in the field of rate regulation, the 'lowest reasonable rate' is one which is not confiscatory in the constitutional sense." There was still also the requirement that due process be met by affording "a fair hearing" and requiring that the administrative agency's conclusion be based "upon findings of fact supported by substantial evidence."[49] And it is here that war-power price controls are more extensive than those exercised under the commerce power. For under the war power, there need not be hearings preceding the price-fixing but only an opportunity for judicial review after the fact.[50]

There remained only the necessity, in order for the federal price-control power to become plenary, to extend the scope of the

---

[46] United States v. Cohen Grocery Co., 255 U.S. 81 (1921).
[47] 315 U.S. 575, 582 (1942).
[48] *Id.* at 585.
[49] See *id.* at 599.
[50] See cases cited in note 40 *supra*.

interstate commerce power to the most local incidents of that commerce. And this authority, too, was soon legitimized by the Court. In *Wickard v. Filburn,* the Court said:[51] ". . . even if [the regulated] activity be local and though it may not be regarded as commerce, it may still, whatever its nature, be reached by Congress if it exerts a substantial economic effect on interstate commerce, and this irrespective of what might at some earlier time have been defined as 'direct' or 'indirect.' " And only a little over a year ago, in sustaining the validity of the Civil Rights Act of 1964 "legislating," as the Court said, "against moral wrongs,"[52] the Court defined congressional power thus:[53]

> . . . the power of Congress to promote interstate commerce also includes the power to regulate the local incidents thereof, including local activities in both the States of origin and destination, which might have a substantial and harmful effect upon that commerce.

The Court's conclusion should put to rest any question about the scope of the congressional authority:[54]

> It may be argued that Congress could have pursued other methods to eliminate the obstructions it found to interstate commerce. . . . But that is a matter of policy that rests entirely with Congress not with the courts. How obstructions in commerce may be removed—what means are to be employed—is within the sound and exclusive discretion of the Congress. It is subject only to one caveat—that the means chosen by it must be reasonably adapted to the end permitted by the Constitution. We cannot say that its choice here was not so adapted. The Constitution requires no more.

III. PRESIDENTIAL AUTHORITY TO CONTROL PRICES AND WAGES

THE CHANGING SCOPE OF EXECUTIVE POWER

The plethora of quotations from the cases demonstrating the broad power of state and national governments to impose price and wage controls have another function. For it should be noted that in none of the cases does the Court consider any branch of

[51] 317 U.S. 111, 125 (1942).
[52] Atlanta Motel v. United States, 379 U.S. 241, 257 (1964).
[53] *Id.* at 258.
[54] *Id.* at 261–62.

the government except the legislative branch as the one to which that power has been entrusted either under the "police power" or the "war power" or the "commerce power." The executive branch can, of course, be entrusted with the authority to fix prices and wages pursuant to legislative action.[55] But the Court has never sustained the authority of the executive to engage in this function absent such authority. That is not to say that it has denied the right of the executive to do so. It simply has not had such a question before it. One may draw inferences from the absence of examples of the exercise of that function by the executive. For, as Mr. Justice Frankfurter once said:[56] ". . . a consistent and unexplained failure to exercise power not obviously conferred . . . may be equally persuasive that the power claimed was never conferred." But in a time of expanding presidential authority this is a rather tenuous basis for such a conclusion.

Unlike the enumerated legislative powers granted to Congress by Article I of the Constitution and the specification of jurisdiction of the federal courts in Article III, the creation of the presidential office in Article II is comparatively barren of specific assignments. There are some scholars who have derived from this difference an intention on the part of the Founding Fathers to give an exceptionally broad range of authority to the President. Thus, Lawrence H. Chamberlain, one of the more recent exponents of this notion, offers these propositions:[57]

> The framers feared legislative tyranny more than executive tyranny, so they set about erecting a system that would impede excessive legislative enthusiasm while encouraging executive action. One has only to compare Article I, the legislative article, with Article II, the executive article, to see how clearly this conscious intent is incorporated in the language. Article I begins: "All legislative powers herein granted shall be vested in a Congress of the United States"; whereas Article II declares: "The executive power shall be vested in a President of the United States of America."
>
> In the one case, the grant is partial, limited; in the other,

[55] See, e.g., United States v. Rock Royal Co-op., 307 U.S. 533 (1939).

[56] United States v. American Union Transport, 327 U.S. 437, 459 (1945) (dissenting).

[57] Chamberlain (ed.), *The Congress and the Presidency,* in THEORY AND PRACTICE IN AMERICAN POLITICS 43–44 (1964).

completely unqualified. Following the enumeration of things Congress can do, there is another enumeration of things it shall not do; the President's broad general grant of power is not circumscribed by a single prohibition, express or implied. . . . The framers had two objectives: they wished to impede and inhibit precipitous legislative action; they also sought to free and protect the executive from legislative control. . . .

As I read this, I tend to think that Mr. Chamberlain's wish is father to his thought. As we shall see, the relevant Supreme Court decisions read history differently. Certainly logic might also suggest that, having given little power to the executive, there was no need to suggest inhibitions on that authority. For the substantive duties specified in Article II were primarily "to execute" the laws and to serve as "Commander-in-Chief" of the armed forces. One thing that is clear, however, is that Chamberlain is reflecting the opinion of our time, or at least the opinion of those who have taken to writing about the office of the presidency, especially after their love affair with the "dynamism" of the Kennedy administration.

The conflict of opinion about the role of the President in American government is not a novel one. Two vocal holders of the office expressed the opposing ideologies in what have become standard terms. President Theodore Roosevelt, as might be expected, asserted:[58]

The most important factor in getting the right spirit in my Administration, next to the insistence upon courage, honesty, and a genuine democracy of desire to serve the plain people, was my insistence upon the theory that the executive power was limited only by specific restrictions and prohibitions appearing in the Constitution or imposed by Congress under its Constitutional powers. My view was that every executive officer, and above all every executive officer in high position, was a steward of the people, and not to content himself with the negative merit of keeping his talent undamaged in a napkin. I declined to adopt the view that what was imperatively necessary for the Nation could not be done by the President unless he had some specific authorization to do it. My belief was that it was not only his right but his duty to do anything that the needs of the Nation demanded unless such action was forbidden by the Constitution or by the laws.

[85] T. R. ROOSEVELT, AUTOBIOGRAPHY 388–89 (1926).

Under this interpretation of executive power I did and caused to be done many things not previously done by the President and the heads of the Departments. I did not usurp power, but I did greatly broaden the use of executive power. In other words, I acted for the public welfare, I acted for the common well-being of all our people, whenever and in whatever manner was necessary, unless prevented by direct constitutional or legislative prohibition. I did not care a rap for the mere form and show of power; I cared immensely for the use that could be made of the substance.

His successor in office, also as might be expected, took a different view of his function:[59]

The true view of the executive function is, as I conceive it, that the President can exercise no power which cannot be fairly and reasonably traced to some specific grant of power or justly implied and included within such grant as proper and necessary.

The publicists of today, whether they be Arthur Krock in *The New York Times,* or those making their views known from the halls of ivy, have come down heavily on the side of "T.R." and against Taft.

Not untypical of this literature announcing the demise of congressional government and the transfer of governmental power to the executive is Professor Burns's recent book bearing the significant title *Presidential Government.* It is in fact a plea for extended executive power as well as a description of the assumption of that power by Kennedy and Johnson in what Burns would have us believe was the tradition of great Presidents. He reads the 1964 election as a validation of this concentration of political authority in the White House.[60] "More than ever the White House is a command post for economic, political, diplomatic, and military combat."[61] And the objective of this power is "freedom through equality."[62] The spirit of his thesis is to be found in these words:[63]

A committee of Congress, appointed in 1789 to consider the proper form of title for the President, recommended that he

[59] TAFT, OUR CHIEF MAGISTRATE AND HIS POWERS 139–40 (1916).
[60] BURNS, PRESIDENTIAL GOVERNMENT 276–77, 309–10 (1966).
[61] *Id.* at 313.
[62] *Id.* at 248–60, 321, 322.
[63] *Id.* at 288.

be addressed as "His Highness, the President of the United States of America, and Protector of Their Liberties." This long and somewhat royal title was not very popular, but recent Presidents, through the "essential genius of the Presidency," have given that title to themselves and to their office.

Another astute observer of the political scene, Professor Koenig, finds the same trends and also approves of them.[64] Touching on matters closer to the immediate subject of this paper, he finds, however, a growing "gap between the President's authority and his responsibilities concerning the economy. . . . The *President* will be expected to hold down inflation and to jog up economic growth. . . . *He* must maintain a high degree of industrial peace, and at the very least avoid repetitions of anything like the long steel strike of 1959–1960."[65] Koenig urges legislative authorization for broader powers in the area of economic controls, but:[66]

> In the absence of adequate statutory authority, the President will need to rely all the more upon executive means to forward his economic policies. He and his aides can use the conference method more widely to spread information and to help form opinion as, for example, among industry and union leaders on issues of price and wage stability. The government contract and the manipulation of government spending, the several pressures that Kennedy employed in the 1962 steel price crisis—all these and more constitute richly varied executive means to further the President's policy and the public interest.

Writings like those of Koenig and Burns—and they are representative of a far larger body of expression—are not constitutional doctrine. But to the extent that they do accurately reflect the general attitude of the community, they are the stuff of which constitutional doctrine will be made. Significantly, both Koenig and Burns anticipate the alliance of the Supreme Court with the President in the expansion of the executive powers. As Koenig phrased it:[67]

> The full dimensions of the executive power clause are yet to be explored, and, by creative interpretations, they could become a great boon for strengthening the President as adminis-

[64] KOENIG, THE CHIEF EXECUTIVE (1964).
[65] *Id.* at 292–93. (Emphasis added.)
[66] *Id.* at 294.
[67] *Id.* at 406.

trative chief. The United States Supreme Court, in its civil rights ruling and its requirement of a wholesale revision of the districts of the House of Representatives, has clearly befriended the cause of the continuously strong Presidency. The Court, altogether logically, could take up the executive power clause with results equally favorable to the Presidency.

This may be accurate forecasting of where the Supreme Court is going to go. For, as Burns has said:[68] "Perhaps the most extraordinary but least remarked expansion of presidential government lies in the extension of its influence to the Supreme Court." But it does not represent the attitude that the Court has expressed in the past.

SOME JUDICIAL VIEWS OF THE EXECUTIVE POWER

It is true that in the area of foreign affairs, the Court has been more than generous in interpreting presidential authority.[69] But it did not purport to find this authority in the grant of executive authority in Article II but rather by way of succession of the presidency to the foreign affairs powers of George III.[70] So, too, the powers of the President as commander-in-chief of the armed forces in time of war have generally but not uniformally been construed broadly.[71]

There have been relatively few judgments announced by the Court on the powers of the President over domestic affairs. Even the presidential removal of a presidentially appointed executive official, however, was first grudgingly approved[72] and then all but rescinded.[73] Justices Holmes and Brandeis dissented from allowing

---

[68] BURNS, PRESIDENTIAL GOVERNMENT 315–16 (1966).

[69] E.g., United States v. Curtiss-Wright Corp., 299 U.S. 304 (1936); United States v. Belmont, 301 U.S. 324 (1937); United States v. Pink, 315 U.S. 203 (1942); Chicago & S. Airlines v. Waterman Corp., 333 U.S. 103 (1948).

[70] United States v. Curtiss-Wright Corp., 299 U.S. 304 (1936).

[71] See, e.g., the Japanese Exclusion Cases, Hirabayashi v. United States, 320 U.S. 81 (1953); Korematsu v. United States, 323 U.S. 214 (1944). But in these cases congressional sanction was forthcoming. See also The Prize Cases, 2 Bl. 635 (1863); United States v. Chemical Foundation, 272 U.S. 1 (1926); Steuart & Bro. v. Bowles, 322 U.S. 398 (1944). But see Ex parte Milligan, 4 Wall. 2 (1866); Duncan v. Kahanamoku, 327 U.S. 304 (1946).

[72] Meyers v. United States, 272 U.S. 52 (1926).

[73] Humphrey's Executor v. United States, 295 U.S. 602 (1935); Wiener v. United States, 357 U.S. 349 (1958).

the President to exercise the power of removal contrary to the wishes of Congress. Holmes wrote:[74]

> The arguments drawn from the executive power of the President, and from his duty to appoint officers of the United States (when Congress does not vest the appointment elsewhere), to take care that the laws be faithfully executed, and to commission all officers of the United States seem to me to be spider's web inadequate to control the dominant facts. . . . The duty of the President to see that the laws be executed is a duty that does not go beyond the laws or require him to achieve more than Congress sees fit to leave within his power.

And Brandeis concluded his dissent thus:[75]

> In America, as in England, the conviction prevailed then [at the time of the framing of the Constitution] that the people must look to representative assemblies for the protection of their liberties. And protection of the individual, even if he be an official, from the arbitrary or capricious exercise of power was then believed to be an essential of free government.

THE YOUNGSTOWN CASE

All in all, in the area of domestic affairs, the Court in the past has tended to side more with the legislature than the executive. And this is particularly clearly revealed in the one case that may have some relevance to the subject under discussion. That case, *Youngstown Sheet & Tube Co. v. Sawyer,*[76] arose out of a situation in which the wage-price structure was under elaborate controls established by the President pursuant to the mandate of Congress. It is interesting to note that it was the steel industry that originated the challenge to presidential authority in 1952, just as it was that industry that did so in 1962. The major difference, of course, is that "steel" prevailed in 1952. And that difference, in itself, may be a signal of the different climate of opinion today that might be the cause for a different constitutional construction. It is also relevant that, in 1952, the President met the challenge by direct confrontation, although other alternatives were available

[74] 272 U.S. at 177.
[75] *Id.* at 294–95.
[76] 343 U.S. 579 (1952). See WESTIN, THE ANATOMY OF A CONSTITUTIONAL LAW CASE (1958).

to him.[77] In 1962 and since, the President has chosen more devious means to effect his powers, suggesting, perhaps, a less certain attitude about his constitutional authority.

The *Youngstown* case arose, it will be recalled, in the middle of the Korean conflict, a time not too different from the present insofar as commitment of American armed forces abroad is concerned. In order to prevent a strike in the steel industry, President Truman issued an executive order authorizing the Secretary of the Department of Commerce to seize and operate most of the steel mills in the country. The order relied solely on the powers conferred on the President by the Constitution. Congress received two messages from the President informing it of the action taken and, in effect, inviting them to act either in derogation of his actions or in support thereof. Congress remained silent. The steel companies successfully secured an injunction against the seizure; the injunction was stayed by the Court of Appeals; and the Supreme Court quickly asserted its jurisdiction. By a vote of six to three, the Court held that the President was without power to seize the mills. There were seven opinions covering 132 pages.

The opinion of the Court was written by Mr. Justice Black. It was comparatively short and, to the ears of the steel companies, quite sweet:[78]

> The President's power, if any, to issue the order must stem either from an act of Congress or from the Constitution itself. There is no statute that expressly authorizes the President to take possession of property as he did here. Nor is there any act of Congress to which our attention has been directed from which such a power can fairly be implied. . . .
>
> The order cannot properly be sustained as an exercise of the President's military power as Commander in Chief of the Armed Forces. . . .
>
> Nor can the seizure order be sustained because of the several constitutional provisions that grant executive power to the President. . . . The Constitution limits his functions in the lawmaking process to the recommending of laws he thinks wise and the vetoing of laws he thinks bad. And the Constitution is neither silent nor equivocal about who shall make laws which the President is to execute. . . .

[77] See Freund, *The Year of the Steel Case*, 66 HARV. L. REV. 89 (1952).
[78] 343 U.S. at 585, 587, 588–89.

It is said that other Presidents without congressional authority have taken possession of private business enterprises
in order to settle labor disputes. But even if this be true, Congress has not thereby lost its exclusive constitutional authority
to make laws necessary and proper to carry out the powers
vested by the Constitution "in the Government of the United
States, or any Department or Officer thereof."

The Founders of this Nation entrusted the lawmaking
power to the Congress alone in both good and bad times. It
would do no good to recall the historical events, the fears of
power and the hopes of freedom that lay behind their choice.
Such a review would but confirm our holding that this seizure
order cannot stand.

Mr. Justice Frankfurter, who joined the Black opinion, nevertheless did not appear willing to go to the limits suggested therein.
For him, as usual, the problem was not quite so simple. For him,
our governmental structure was complicated. He found it "absurd
to see a dictator in a representative product of the sturdy demo-
cratic traditions of the Mississippi Valley. The accretion of dangerous power does not come in a day. It does come, however slowly,
from the generative force of unchecked disregard of the restrictions
that fence in even the most disinterested assertion of authority."[79]

The powers of the President are not as particularized as are
those of Congress. But unenumerated powers do not mean
undefined powers. The separation of powers built into our
Constitution gives essential content to undefined provisions in
the frame of our government.[80]

The essence of the Frankfurter position was that because the
question of presidential authority to effect seizures under such circumstances had been debated by Congress before it adopted the
Taft-Hartley Act, Congress had decided to refuse that authority
to the President. The congressional decision precluded the exercise
of presidential power.

Douglas, like Frankfurter, joined the Court's opinion. He conceded that executive action under the circumstances would be
more efficient than the invocation of "the ponderous machinery"
of the legislature.[81] But the Constitution commands the use of the

[79] *Id.* at 593–94.
[80] *Id.* at 610.
[81] *Id.* at 629.

less efficient. "The Framers with memories of the tyrannies produced by a blending of executive and legislative power rejected that political arrangement."[82] "Today a kindly President uses the seizure power to effect a wage increase and to keep the steel furnaces in production. Yet tomorrow another President might use the same power to prevent a wage increase, to curb trade-unionists, to regiment labor as oppressively as industry thinks it has been regimented by this seizure."[83]

Jackson came to the question embarrassed, perhaps, by an earlier opinion that he had rendered as attorney general for President Franklin Roosevelt, when that President seized the North American Aviation Company during World War II. Attorney General Jackson had then said:[84]

> The Presidential proclamation rests upon the aggregate of the Presidential powers derived from the Constitution itself and from statutes enacted by the Congress. The Constitution lays upon the President the duty to "take care that the laws be faithfully executed." Among the laws which he is required to find means to execute are those which direct him to equip an enlarged army, to provide for a strengthened navy, to protect Government property, to protect those who are engaged in carrying out the business of Government, and to carry out the provisions of the Lend-Lease Act. For the faithful execution of such laws the President has back of him not only general law-enforcement power conferred by the various acts of Congress but the aggregate of all such laws plus that wide discretion as to method vested in him by the Constitution for the purpose of executing the laws.

Jackson disposed of the embarrassment early in his opinion:[85]

> That comprehensive and undefined presidential powers hold both practical advantages and grave dangers for the country will impress anyone who has served as legal adviser to a President in time of transition and public anxiety. While an interval of detached reflection may temper teaching of that experience, they probably have a more realistic influence on my views than the conventional materials of judicial decision which seem unduly to accentuate doctrine and legal fiction.

[82] *Id.* at 633.
[83] *Id.* at 633–34.
[84] 89 Cong. Rec. 3992 (1943).
[85] 343 U.S. at 634.

But as we approach the question of presidential power, we half overcome mental hazards by recognizing them. The opinions of judges, no less than executives and publicists, often suffer the infirmity of confusing the issue of a power's validity with the cause it is invoked to promote, of confounding the permanent executive office with its temporary occupant. The tendency is strong to emphasize transient results upon policies—such as wages or stabilization—and lose sight of enduring consequences upon the balanced power structure of our Republic.

For Jackson as for Frankfurter the answer wasn't easily derived from the language of the Constitution. "Presidential powers are not fixed but fluctuate, depending upon their disjunction or conjunction with those of Congress."[86] And, with this in mind, the seizure must be held invalid, because:[87] "When the President takes measures incompatible with the express or implied will of Congress, his power is at its lowest ebb, for then he can rely only upon his own constitutional powers minus any constitutional powers of Congress over the matter."

Certainly the solicitor general's claim for unlimited power in the presidency had to be rejected:[88]

> The example of such unlimited executive power that must have most impressed the forefathers was the prerogative exercised by George III, and the description of its evils in the Declaration of Independence leads me to doubt that they were creating their new Executive in his image. Continental European examples were no more appealing. And if we seek instruction from our own times, we can match it only from the executive powers in those governments we disparagingly describe as totalitarian. I cannot accept the view that this clause is a grant in bulk of all conceivable executive power but regard it as an allocation to the presidential office of the generic powers thereafter stated.

Neither the President's power as commander-in-chief, nor any other power specified in Article II, nor the argument for powers *"ex necessitate* to meet an emergency,"[89] authorizes the President to act in this realm that belongs to Congress and in a way that con-

[86] *Id*. at 635.
[87] *Id*. at 637.
[88] *Id*. at 641.
[89] *Id*. at 649.

travenes congressional unwillingness to invest the power in the President.

> With all its defects, delays and inconveniences, men have dis-
> covered no technique for long preserving free government
> except that the Executive be under the law, and that the law
> be made by parliamentary deliberations.
>
> Such institutions may be destined to pass away. But it is
> the duty of the Court to be last, not first, to give them up.[90]

Mr. Justice Burton, who was the fifth of the justices to join in the opinion of the Court, also relied on the specifics of congressional action:[91]

> The controlling fact here is that Congress, within its con-
> stitutionally delegated power, has prescribed for the President
> specific procedures, exclusive of seizure, for his use in meet-
> ing the present type of emergency. Congress has reserved to
> itself the right to determine where and when to authorize the
> seizure of property in meeting such an emergency. Under
> these circumstances, the President's order of April 8 invaded
> the jurisdiction of Congress. It violated the essence of the
> principle of the separation of governmental powers. . . .

Mr. Justice Clark, who joined only in the judgment and not in the Black opinion, offered but a variation on the Frankfurter-Jackson-Burton theme. It must be said for him that he seemed to see what these others were unwilling to see, that Black's broad pronouncement was inconsistent with the more limited inhibitions on the executive power that they would impose.

> I conclude that where Congress has laid down specific
> procedures to deal with the type of crisis confronting the
> President, he must follow those procedures in meeting the
> crisis; but that in the absence of such actions by Congress, the
> President's independent power to act depends upon the grav-
> ity of the situation confronting the nation. I cannot sustain
> the seizure in question because here . . . Congress had pre-
> scribed the methods to be followed by the President in meet-
> ing the emergency at hand.[92]

The dissenting justices were, at least, able to join forces in a single opinion, written by the chief justice. Vinson was joined by

[90] *Id.* at 655.
[91] *Id.* at 660.
[92] *Id.* at 662.

Reed and Minton. He found a plethora of reasons to support the seizure, almost all of which, however, derived from the proposition that if the President was exerting "extraordinary powers [we] should be mindful that these are extraordinary times. A world not yet recovered from the devastation of World War II has been forced to face the threat of another and more terrifying global conflict."[93] Hindsight reveals and foresight suggests that the extraordinary has become the commonplace and is likely to remain so for the indefinite future. Under the circumstances existing, however, Vinson found authority for the presidential seizure in his duty to carry on this country's foreign affairs, in his duty to effectuate the congressional defense program, in congressional inaction after the President indicated the course he was taking, in the national power of eminent domain, in the very large number of occasions on which similar power has been exerted in the past.[94]

> The President immediately informed Congress of his action and clearly stated his intention to abide by the legislative will. No basis for claims of arbitrary action, unlimited powers or dictatorial usurpation of congressional power appears from the facts of this case. On the contrary, judicial, legislative and executive precedents throughout our history demonstrate that in this case the President acted in full conformity with his duties under the Constitution.[95]
>
> History bears out the genius of the Founding Fathers, who created a Government subject to law but not left subject to inertia when vigor and initiative are required.[96]

Those who tend to oversimplify their analysis of Supreme Court decisions might ponder these facts: Of the six-man majority, two were former senators; two were former attorneys general; one was a law professor whose governmental experience was largely with the executive branch; and one was a former chairman of an administrative agency. Of the dissenters, one was a former secretary of the treasury and "assistant President"; one was a former solicitor general; and one was a former senator. Truman had appointed

---

[93] *Id.* at 668.

[94] Frankfurter's opinion contained a lengthy appendix setting forth presidential seizures, some with and some without congressional authorization. *Id.* at 615–28.

[95] *Id.* at 710.

[96] *Id.* at 700.

two of the majority to their Supreme Court posts. He had also appointed two members of the minority to their high judicial offices. All five of the others were appointed by Franklin Roosevelt, not known for his reticence in exercising the powers of his office.

IMPLICATIONS OF YOUNGSTOWN

Are there lessons to be derived from the *Youngstown* case that have relevance to the presidential "price-wage guidelines"? The answer would be more certain if *stare decisis* were a more vigorous doctrine in the Supreme Court[97] and if there were any certain means of bringing the issues before that tribunal for adjudication. But there is little likelihood that the issues will be subjected to judicial review. For, as John W. Davis once said, not when he was counsel to the steel companies in the *Youngstown* case, but when he was solicitor general successfully defending the President's unilateral action withdrawing certain lands from public entry in contradiction of congressional mandate:[98]

> . . . in ways short of making laws or disobeying them, the Executive may be under a grave constitutional duty to act for the national protection in situations not covered by the acts of Congress, and in which, even, it may not be said that his action is the direct expression of any particular one of the independent powers which are granted him specifically by the Constitution. Instances wherein the President has felt and fulfilled such a duty have not been rare in our history, though, being for the public benefit and approved by all, *his acts have seldom been challenged in the courts.*

He might have added that there are all sorts of reasons other than public acquiescence why the challenge may not be made in the courts.

One can only speculate, then, about what the logical derivations of *Youngstown* are for the problem of presidential wage and price controls, without any assurance whatsoever that they provide guidelines to the problem of guidelines.

[97] See Israel, *Gideon v. Wainwright: The Art of Overruling,* in KURLAND (ed.), THE SUPREME COURT AND THE CONSTITUTION 263 (1965).

[98] Brief for the United States, in United States v. Midwest Oil Co., 236 U.S. 459 (1915), quoted by Vinson in the Youngstown case. 343 U.S. at 691.

Whatever else may be unclear about the constitutional problem, the one thing that is clear is that the subject of price and wage controls is properly within the province of Congress. It is not so clear that the present practices can be said to amount to the imposition of such controls by the President. If no more is involved in the executive guidelines than a presidential appeal to public opinion, there can be little doubt that this is an appropriate function of the executive office.[99]

So, too, if the action taken in response to the President's demand can be said to be "voluntary," there can be little or no question about the constitutionality of the activities engaged in by the President to secure restraints on rising markets. But the Supreme Court has become rather sophisticated—some would say oversophisticated—about what action in response to government pressure can be denominated "voluntary."[100] And certainly if the standards the Court has adopted with reference to criminal proceedings are also applicable here, there can be little doubt that the response, in many instances at least, has been coerced and not "voluntary." Compliance resulting from the threat of withdrawal of government contracts, or from the threat of depressing the market through the sale of stockpiled goods—stockpiled on the theory of the exigencies of public defense, or at least those from the threat of withholding allocations from public construction programs can hardly be said to be voluntary. These sanctions—if not that of threat of public infamy—must be said to amount to compulsion.

Does the use of sanctions such as these bring the presidential price-control program within the ban of the *Youngstown* case? Again the answer is less than certain. For there are major differences between *Youngstown* and the immediate issue. Perhaps if we look no further than the "opinion of the Court" in that case, the answer is that the presidential guidelines are unconstitutional. For it would have to be said here, as it was said there, that presidential action finds neither specific nor implied authorization in any act of Congress or in the language of the Constitution itself.[101]

---

[99] See KOENIG, THE CHIEF EXECUTIVE 186 (1964).

[100] See *Developments in the Law—Confessions,* 79 HARV. L. REV. 935, 954 (1966).

[101] See text *supra* at note 78.

On the other hand, it is clear that the judicial majority in that case did not really rest on so simple a proposition.

In *Youngstown,* much reliance was placed on the refusal of Congress to give the President the sanction which he attempted to use. Here we have nothing but congressional silence, which might even be construed as acquiescence. And there is a bigger difference which might, depending on one's point of view, be placed on one side of the scale or the other. In *Youngstown,* Congress had specified the objectives of stabilization and the President had attempted to use what the Congress said was an improper means for attaining that objective. In the guidelines situation almost the reverse is true. Congress has not authorized wage and price controls. On the other hand, the means by which they are attained—some of which are indicated above—have been placed in the hands of the President by congressional delegation and appropriation. In short, the question here may be said to be one of ends not means. In *Youngstown,* the problem was rather of means than ends.

It may be said with more certainty that the legislature could not authorize the effectuation of price and wage controls in the manner in which it is sought to be accomplished under the present system. For there is provision neither for hearings on which to base the price and wage limits sought to be imposed, nor is there provision for judicial review, an aspect of due process that could not be dispensed with even in time of war. There is an arbitrary selection of those who are subjected to controls which is, to some extent, the necessary result of the limited form of sanctions available. But to some extent it is the result of a choice based on what seem to be different considerations. Koenig illustrates, in a slightly different context, what I have in mind:[102]

> For all of Kennedy's invocations of a labor-management duty to heed national interest, his own conduct was not always free from the taint of expediency. Indeed a double track was sometimes discernible in the Kennedy administration's approach to labor-management relations. Two labor disputes of 1962 illuminate the contrast. In the first, strikes loomed at North American, Ryan, General Dynamics, and Lockheed, manufacturers of missiles and aircraft. A special Presidential board recommended union-shop elections to resolve the dis-

[102] KOENIG, THE CHIEF EXECUTIVE 291–92 (1964).

pute. The two powerful unions involved—the United Automobile Workers and the International Association of Machinists—welcomed the board's recommendation, but the employers cold-shouldered it. Kennedy backed up the board in a strong statement holding that if the employers rejected the peace plan, the country should blame them for the ensuing trouble.

In a second dispute, where labor rather than management rejected a Presidential Board's findings, Kennedy's course was altogether different. A strike of the Chicago and North Western Railway, which inflicted severe economic injury upon nine midwestern states, commenced when the Order of Railroad Telegraphers rejected a Presidential board's recommendation that the union abandon its demand for a veto over job reductions caused by new technology and other factors. The Presidential board proposed a formula to cushion lay-offs through liberalized unemployment, retraining, and severance benefits. Kennedy, departing from his accustomed procedure, pronounced no words of personal endorsement of the board's report, nor censure for the union. Wholly ignoring the railroad's readiness to negotiate a contract reflecting the board's proposals, the President entreated "both sides" to make "sufficient concessions" to find accord.

IV. INCONCLUSIVE CONCLUSIONS

Would that my data afforded me the certitude for pronouncing judgment that their data seems to afford students of economics. I fear that all I can say on the issue is that the present means of imposing wage and price controls is constitutionally suspect. I am sure, however, that there are members of my profession who could answer the issue in no uncertain terms. Some on one side and others on the opposite side. Perhaps I could, too, if my predilections were more deeply involved.

There is a clearly constitutional, probably effective, but politically difficult method for the national government to impose price and wage controls: by congressional legislation. There is a constitutionally dubious, probably ineffectual, but politically feasible method for imposing wage and price controls: by presidential fiat. The latter is the present choice. It will probably not be the constitutional doubts but rather the ineffectiveness of this choice that will bring about a change, if there is a change.

There is a way to resolve the constitutional issues. But it is not likely to be taken. For it would require handling of this political hot potato by the national legislature, which has been described by one of its more prominent members as "Congress: The Sapless Branch."[103]

Congress could, if it would, clarify the constitutionality of the wage-price guidelines simply by taking up the question whether it wishes to authorize wage-price controls and, if so, how. Should it enact appropriate legislation, as it did with Taft-Hartley, presumably the executive office would be confined to the utilization of those means for attaining the ends that Congress prescribes.[104] If it should reject the idea of price-wage controls, it would also bring the presidential action within the ban of the *Youngstown* decision. There are, of course, two big "ifs" involved in this conclusion. The first "if" relates to congressional willingness to treat the subject. The second "if" concerns the willingness of the Court to adhere to principles that it has earlier announced.

In the course of this century, the states have surrendered their role as meaningful components in our system of government by failing to recognize that the necessary concomitant of power is responsibility. In the words of Patrick Henry, Congress may profit from their example. Seven hundred and fifty years ago, at Runnymede, began a chain of events that eventually resulted in the supremacy of legislative over executive power in Anglo-American government.[105] Somewhere in the recent past, perhaps with the Great Depression, perhaps at Pearl Harbor, perhaps at Los Alamos, the United States crossed the watershed and started moving toward a restoration of the supremacy of the executive power. How far we have traveled is hard to say. The success or failure of presidential price and wage controls may give us some basis for judgment. For myself, I would join Mr. Justice Jackson, when he said in *Youngstown*:[106]

> . . . emergency powers are consistent with free government only when their control is lodged elsewhere than in the Execu-

[103] CLARK, CONGRESS: THE SAPLESS BRANCH (rev. ed., 1965).
[104] Little v. Bareme, 2 Cranch 170 (1804).
[105] See HOLT, MAGNA CARTA (1965); THORNE, DUNHAM, KURLAND, & JENNINGS, THE GREAT CHARTER (1965).
[106] 343 U.S. at 652–53.

tive who exercises them. That is the safeguard that would be nullified by our adoption of the "inherent powers" formula. Nothing in my experience convinces me that such risks are warranted by any real necessity, although such powers would, of course, be an executive convenience.

In the practical working of our Government we already have evolved a technique within the framework of the Constitution by which normal executive powers may be considerably expanded to meet an emergency. Congress may and has granted extraordinary authorities which lie dormant in normal times but may be called into play by the Executive in war or upon proclamation of a national emergency. . . . Under this procedure we retain Government by law—special, temporary law, perhaps, but law nonetheless. The public may know the extent and limitations of the powers that can be asserted, and persons affected may be informed from the statute of their rights and duties.

In view of the ease, expedition and safety with which Congress can grant and has granted large emergency powers, certainly ample to embrace this crisis, I am quite unimpressed with the argument that we should affirm possession of them without statute. Such power either has no beginning or it has no end. If it exists, it need submit to no legal restraint. I am not alarmed that it would plunge us straightway into dictatorship, but it is at least a step in that wrong direction.

PHILIP B. KURLAND

Comments

Thus far I have two observations to make about this conference. The first is that the shorter the speech, the more popular the speaker. And I aim for popularity. The second observation is that economists are divided into two groups. I hadn't known this before. But now I know that there are *macro*-economists and *micro*-economists. Macro-economists are those who are concerned with theory and have no interest in the facts, and for micro-economists, it's the other way around. I intend to put that knowledge to good use—if not here, then just down the street a little.

One thing that seemed to impress itself on me during the course of the discussion is that we are certainly not here to praise Caesar. Indeed, we are here to bury him. The sole question is whether Antony, who seeks to replace Caesar with a tripartite sort of organization formulating similar kinds of rules, or Brutus, who is seeking a free market economy, is going to succeed to the throne. I make no predictions. But I'm sorry Mr. Ackley isn't here to participate in the burial ceremonies.

According to the classification that I previously suggested to you, if I were a macro-lawyer, I should be extensively concerned here with the shift of power or the assumption of power in our country by the Executive branch of the government. That's a large and philosophical theme which requires no facts and, as a matter of fact, not much theory. If I were a micro-lawyer, I would be concerned with dealing with the law cases and decisions in great detail. The only trouble is that there aren't any cases on this subject, so I am in a position of being capable of dealing with the topic neither as a macro-lawyer nor as a micro-lawyer. You are the ones who suffer as a result.

The paper that I presented at the behest of George Shultz and George Stigler—and I mean to shift the responsibility to them—contains a few obvious points and not much more. The bulk of the paper is concerned with proof of a fact that probably doesn't need proving any more, that there is no longer any constitutional question about the power of the national government to assert control over prices and wages and rents, not to speak of federal control over foreign exchange and the other fiscal powers which it has always enjoyed. If it wasn't true seventy-five years ago, I don't think there are many constitutional lawyers who'll argue the proposition that, as of today, either by reason of the war power or by reason of the commerce clause, it is quite clear that the national government does have the authority to fix prices, wages, rents, and foreign exchange. The problem that we have here, if we are going to find a constitutional problem, is not essentially a problem for the judiciary to answer. And this is especially true in the absence of the normal type of sanctions in government regulation, that is, those utilizing the courts as enforcement agencies. In the absence of such sanctions, the judiciary is not likely to be a source of information about the constitutional power that we are concerned with this evening.

I point out, too, in my paper, that there is no constitutional problem if these price and wage guidelines and guideposts—and I must confess my ignorance in not understanding the essential difference between guideposts and guidelines—are purely hortatory. There is no constitutional issue if the response to them is a totally voluntary response. Certainly, there can be no question that the Executive branch of the government can attempt to bring out the best elements of the business and labor communities and ask them not to ask what the country can do for them and so on and so forth.

I think I'm right, however, in my assumption that there is really some sanction involved—that the response, to the extent that any response is secured, is not entirely a voluntary one. And—again from today's session—I seem to glean the fact that where there are no sanctions there is no response, and where there is a sanction there is a response. Now, given this notion that the price fixing, the wage setting, is more than a voluntary effort upon the part of business and labor the question is: Does the President have the authority to impose the sanctions in this area?

I suggested earlier that I have very little to guide me and therefore very little to offer you in terms of how to reach an answer to that question. I suggested earlier that I had no cases, but in fact I do have one case—the case with which you are all familiar. It involved the seizure of the steel mills by President Truman in the course of the Korean War. But the *Youngstown Steel* case, which is my case, is certainly somewhat less than decisive of the problem that we have here, although there are similarities. In both the *Youngstown Steel* situation and in the present activities of the Executive branch of the government, we find an absence of congressional authorization. If there is that similarity, however, there is also an essential difference—and, I think, a major difference— between the *Youngstown* case and the present one. And that difference is that the congressional silence of the moment, which is somewhat deafening, is ambiguous. The congressional silence at the time of the *Youngstown* case was not ambiguous. The Executive authority at that time had sought from Congress the authorization and the power to engage in seizure in the event it was necessary to help the President enforce the wage and price controls. Congress had quite clearly refused to give him that power and a large majority of the Court rested, I think, essentially on the proposition that what Congress had specifically refused, the President could not assume he had been granted.

The problem that remains, assuming that the power is in the presidency—which is a doubtful assumption—is: Does he meet the constitutional standards that would be demanded of Executive action had it been authorized by Congress? And this is exactly the problem that Mr. Meltzer has already expressed to you. It's the question whether due process and equal protection are being afforded those persons who are being regulated by the existing price and wage controls.

We have seen that in earlier times, if the power of the national government was exercised pursuant to the war power—a power which I point out is hard to discover in the Constitution but which everybody now agrees exists—there were certain powers which the government could exercise. The stringencies of the due process clause are not quite so great in time of war as they would be otherwise. But even so, the Court has made it clear that there must be an opportunity, at least, for judicial review. This was afforded even during the crises of the Second World War but it certainly is, I suggest, absent under the existing circumstances.

What's more, to the extent that the power is now exercised pursuant to the commerce power of the national government, a good deal more protection has to be made available to those parties who are subject to such controls. They can be summarized very quickly in terms of the necessity for notice, the necessity for specification of standards, the necessity for an opportunity to be heard, in addition to the obligation to provide some form of judicial review to make a determination as to the arbitrariness of the governmental action. These due process requirements, I submit, are not to be found under the existing system. And I heard a good deal of complaint, I think, in the discussions today about their absence—even if those complaints were not framed in constitutional language.

The other proposition that Mr. Meltzer has already suggested to you is the necessity for conforming with standards of equal protection. I was going to say with the equal protection clause, but the fact of the matter is, of course, that there is no equal protection clause applicable to the national government. But, in a quick reversal of the ordinary position, which my lawyer colleagues will understand if no one else does, it seems that the equal protection clause of the Fourteenth Amendment is applicable to the national government by way of the due process clause of the Fifth Amendment. In any event, arbitrary discrimination—an unjustified discrimination in the application of a national law—would seem to be as unconstitutional under the due process clause if effected by the national government as it would be under the equal protection clause if imposed by the state government. And what you have here, on the slight record that has been made, is a selection of victims—if I may use that word—which indicates no basis for classification, no reasoned basis for distinguishing those on whom sanctions have been imposed from those on whom sanctions have not been imposed, even though both engaged in exactly the same behavior.

As I suggested earlier, the sole basis for action seems to be based on whether there is a whip available or perhaps a carrot, or even the deprivation of the carrot, to single out a particular industry or a particular labor organization for the kind of sanctions that the Executive branch wishes to impose. If there is, the restraints can and will be effective, otherwise they will be ignored.

I have overrun my time. In conclusion, I should say that when I was asked to write this paper, I began to feel a bit like Alice in Wonderland. That feeling has not been dissipated by reason of writing the paper. It has not been dissipated by reason of my participation in the conference today. And I look forward to enjoying Alice's adventures further in the future course of this conference.

BENJAMIN AARON

Comments

I must say that I feel like an imposter in this gathering. I'm not a constitutional lawyer and, as for my knowledge of economics, I think the kindest thing I can say in my defense is that I'm a functional illiterate. As a matter of fact, I feel very much like that unfortunate unemployed West Virginian who confessed that he could read numbers but he could not read the alphabet, so that when he was traveling on the highway looking for a job and he saw a sign indicating what he assumed to be the next town, he said, "I can tell how fer, but not whar to." And that's very much the way I feel in this group. But I am comforted by the moral of a fable by James Thurber to the effect that fools rush in where angels fear to tread. But the angels are all in heaven and few of the fools are dead. So I'm going to just go ahead.

Like Mr. Kurland, I find that my predilections are not deeply involved in the question treated in his paper. Perhaps this is because I believe that the efforts of the Executive branch to control wages and prices have not thus far impermissibly encroached on constitutional liberties and are not likely to do so in the future.

I should say at once that I do not share what I take to be Mr. Kurland's view: that the sanctions used by the government to compel unions and employers to adhere to wage and price guideposts amount to *improper* "compulsion." The adjective is mine,

Benjamin Aaron is professor of law and director of the Institute of Industrial Relations, University of California at Los Angeles, and a past president of the National Academy of Arbitrators.

not his, but I think the word "compulsion," used without a modifier, is meaningless in this context. The compulsion is primarily economic, and to me at least, it is similar to that exerted by unions and employers against each other in collective bargaining. Many an employer and many a union has had to comply with the dictates of its adversary—to yield to compulsion, if you will—simply because the latter had superior economic power. And this use of economic power by the Executive branch against private parties—no matter how overbearing or distasteful it may be to some—seems to me to be of a completely different order than the use of coercive police power to extract a confession from one accused of a crime.

Now, I fully agree with Mr. Kurland that none of the questions raised by the guidepost procedure is likely to come before the Court so as properly to be denominated a constitutional question. The Executive branch must and does have a wide discretion in withdrawing government contracts, selling stockpiled goods, withholding allocations from public construction programs—to use the examples that he mentioned. The problem arises when that discretion is exercised for an allegedly ulterior and unlawful purpose.

But how can the Court isolate and weigh such a motive? It may be instructive in this regard to consider the analagous problem of protecting First Amendment rights of witnesses before congressional committees. The congressional power to investigate and to compel testimony during investigations, although not stated in the Constitution, is implied when appropriate to an exercise of Congress' recognized functions.

Until a few weeks ago, I would have felt reasonably safe in saying that the general rule—except perhaps where the NAACP is involved—is that where the subject being investigated is one which Congress may validly legislate, a proper legislative purpose will be presumed. And, on that assumption, some legislative committees have been able, as we all know, to carry on investigations which in fact have been directed primarily to exposure of witnesses to public infamy—to use another of Mr. Kurland's terms—even though the courts have never accepted the view, urged by Woodrow Wilson in his book, *Congressional Government,* that "the informing function of Congress should be preferred to its legislative function." The Supreme Court's recent decision in *DeGregory vs. Attorney General of New Hampshire* makes the foregoing generalization a little shakier perhaps, but I think it may still hold good for the limited purpose for which I am using it here.

Now, in exercising the economic powers mentioned by Mr. Kurland, the Executive branch may be assumed—for purposes of this discussion—to be acting out of mixed motives, just as congressional committees frequently do. But I submit that the Supreme Court's reluctance to protect claimed First Amendment rights of an unwilling witness before a congressional committee, solely on the ground that there is strong evidence that the committee's principal aim is to expose the witness to public infamy, presages an even greater disinclination on the Court's part to prohibit the use by the Executive branch of economic pressure which, although arguably punitive, can be justified on another ground.

The point is that there are no ready standards that the Court can apply. As Mr. McCloskey's essay, cited by Mr. Kurland, so persuasively demonstrates, the Court's renunciation of judicial review of statutory economic regulation, through the application of "economic due process" standards is virtually absolute.

Even if the Court could be induced to consider the constitutionality of economic or social compulsion exerted by the Executive branch to compel adherence to the guideposts, I think it most unlikely that the decision would be against the government. The federal stick-and-carrot technique was sustained against constitutional attack in *Steward Machine Company vs. Davis* involving Title IX of the Social Security Act. There, too, the challenge, as summarized by Mr. Justice Cardozo for the Court, was "that an ulterior aim is wrought into the very structure of the act and . . . that the aim is not only ulterior, but essentially unlawful." But a majority of the Court in that case drew a line between duress and inducement and held that Title IX of the Social Security Act fell on the right side. In his dissent, Mr. Justice Butler said: "The terms of the measure make it clear that the tax and credit device was intended to enable federal officers virtually to control the exertion of powers of the states in a field in which they alone have jurisdiction and from which the United States is by the Constitution excluded."

Now let me paraphrase that statement. The steps taken by the administration make it clear that the guidelines policy was intended to enable federal officers virtually to control the economic decisions of private citizens in a field in which they are free to act, absent regulatory legislation, and from which the President is by the Consitution excluded. That still sounds like a dissenting opinion to me.

Before moving on to the non-constitutional aspect of this problem, I should like to return briefly, and by way of summary, to two analogies suggested by Mr. Kurland.

In the matter of the involuntary confessions the case for judicial intervention is strong because governmental powers are being used to deprive private citizens of rights to which they are entitled under the Constitution. In the steel seizure case, as Mr. Kurland points out—and I'm entirely in agreement with him—the Court was willing to intervene, because the President was purporting to exercise a power not granted him by the Constitution and specifically denied him by the Congress.

But the guidepost case, it seems to me, is substantially different from the other two. Here, the Executive branch is exercising powers that it undeniably has and the private citizens involved have no constitutional immunity from the economic pressures to which they are being subjected. At the most, we have an exercise of Executive power that is distasteful. I wouldn't go so far as Mr. Kurland in saying that it is constitutionally suspect. I would say it is *morally* suspect.

And now I understand that, according to the guideposts as announced by our chairman, I'm entitled to go off on a frolic and detour of my own. I would like to indicate another reason for my lack of concern about the legality of the administration's efforts to secure adherence to its guideline and guidepost policy.

It is clear, I think, that strong Executive intervention—if resorted to repeatedly—will *not* achieve its purpose and will prove to be extremely dangerous politically. Presidential arm-twisting—or, to use the happier metaphor suggested by Mr. Johnson, with all its delicate implications, presidential ear-twisting—loses its force in direct proportion to the frequency of its use.

In 1949, President Truman caught the U.S. Steel Corporation off balance when he promptly denominated the report of his fact-finding board "fair and reasonable" and strongly implied that, if the corporation rejected the board's recommendations, it would be foolish, unreasonable, and solely responsible for any consequential strike. The corporation did reject the board's recommendations and the strike was called, but public opinion was substantially on the side of the union, and the strike settlement, as I recall it, was largely in the union's favor—all this notwithstanding the President's assurance to both parties at the time he created the board that its findings and recommendations would not be binding on either of them.

In 1952, the President's equally strong endorsement of the Wage Stabilization Board's recommendations in the steel dispute had no similar effect, as some of us well remember. The strike was called, the companies stood firm, the seizure attempt was foiled by the Supreme Court, and the President's prestige was severely damaged.

Of course, in national emergencies the Chief Executive will do whatever he thinks the situation requires—no matter how dubious his constitutional authority may be. My former boss, Mr. William H. Davis, chairman of the National War Labor Board, used to remark that in times of national crisis, the President does what is necessary to save the country. And sometimes, after the emergency is over, the Supreme Court holds that he acted unconstitutionally —thereby saving the Constitution.

To me, at least, it is apparent that the important problems raised by the guidepost policies are, first, whether it makes sense economically and, second, whether it can be made to work. I am not qualified to discuss the first problem and my comments on the second —based on personal experience and observation—are, I'm afraid, rather negative. Wage and price stabilization policies have not been notably successful in the past. Neither presidential exhortation nor economic pressures applied by the Executive branch have brought about the national consensus that is necessary to make stabilization measures viable over an extended period. Indeed, as our wartime experience demonstrates, even legislative restrictions retain their practical effectiveness for only a short time. Our tendency is to seek consensus through tripartite participation in policy making and administration, as we did during World War II and in the Korean conflict. Perhaps the device might work in the same imperfect way again, but we must be realistic in our expectations. Tripartism means an abandonment of precise and consistent formulas and the substitution therefore of collective bargaining, a process once described by Dexter Keezer—with the air of the unbelieving farmer after his first look at a giraffe—as that "excessively praised process of fumbling, bluffing, and bulldozing toward an adjustment that should be made with hairbreadth precision." Dexter was reacting to what must have been to him a traumatic experience as a public member of the National War Labor Board, but his comment about collective bargaining is the familiar reflex of a good man troubled by the imperfections of this world. As Mr. Dunlop has emphasized in his paper, we have not adequately explored the various alternatives that lie between the opposite poles of adherence to the present guidepost policy and its complete abandonment.

My conclusion is, however, that no policy will long endure that does not draw its strength—and its weakness—from collective bargaining. For better or for worse, that appears to be the American way.

FREDERICK R. LIVINGSTON

Comments

I think the title for this session might more appropriately be "legal basis for guidelines, if any."

This young audience might still remember Rodgers and Hammerstein's hit show *Oklahoma*. I looked up the record album yesterday, and it was originally produced on Broadway in 1943. You may remember that it had a song sung by Ado Annie entitled, "I Cain't Say No." Ado Annie's plaint was that if she said "yes," her chastity might be placed in jeopardy. There are many businessmen around the country today who feel they can't say "no" to L.B.J. There might be a parallel here. I leave it to you.

As a lawyer, I have been concerned about the changing character of the guidelines, which started as a *guide* and have now been transformed into an *edict*. If you make a comparison of the 1962 Report, in which the guidelines were originally published, and the 1966 Report, you will find a significant change in emphasis.

The 1962 Report said, and I quote: "An informed public, aware of the significance of major wage bargains and price decisions, and equipped to judge for itself their compatibility with the national interest, can help to create an atmosphere in which the parties to such decisions will exercise their powers responsibly." It then stated that the guideposts are "aids to public understanding."[1]

Frederick R. Livingston is a senior partner in the law firm of Kaye, Scholer, Fierman, Hayes & Handler and a widely experienced negotiator of union-management agreements.

[1] Report of Council of Economic Advisers, 1962, pp. 185–86.

And *no* specific figure was given as to the standard by which wage increases should be measured.

The 1966 Report stated on the other hand, and I quote: "These actions (alluding to the steel wage negotiations and the rollback of price increases in steel and aluminum) and many others clearly reaffirmed the Administration's strong commitment to the guideposts as an essential pillar for price stability."[2] That's sure an aid to public understanding! It goes on to say, "For 1966, the Council specifically recommends that the general guidepost for wages of 3.2% a year be continued."[3]

Increasingly, the administration has "enforced" the guidelines by such measures as overwhelming publicity, personal appeals by the President and members of the Council, threatening the sale of stockpiled materials, threatening antitrust actions, threatening IRS actions, threatening the loss of government business, and threatening reduction in federal grants under various programs such as highway construction.

These and other enforcement measures have been extensively detailed in the public media. A typical example was recorded in the November 12, 1965, *Wall Street Journal.* The *Journal* reported that aluminum prices were rolled back, not simply because of the threat to sell off part of the federal stockpile, but also because of the pressure of the following threats:

> A review of antitrust actions against Alcoa and possibly other members of the industry; a review of rates on electric power sales to the industry by Federal generating plants such as the big Bonneville project in the West; substitution of other material for aluminum wherever possible in defense and Agency for International Development projects; and Internal Revenue reviews of income taxes of the aluminum companies.[4]

The administration of the guidelines has been troublesome, not so much on constitutional grounds—I agree with Mr. Kurland that there are not any constitutional problems per se—but in its lack of

[2] Report of Council of Economic Advisers, 1966, p. 89.
[3] *Ibid.,* p. 92.
[4] There are similar reports by other responsible newspapers and magazines. For example, the *Washington Post* (January 8, 1966, by Joseph Kraft, and January 3, 1966, editorial and article by Harvey Segal) and the *Wall Street Journal* (January 13, 1966, by Alan Otten).

fair dealing. I do not think lawyers have a monopoly on the concept of fair dealing, but as lawyers we are trained in certain basic concepts of fair dealing. There are three main areas that I find troublesome: (1) There is no procedure for hearings to establish the appropriate guideline in the first instance; (2) the administration of the guidelines has been highly selective and is contrary to the spirit of the constitutional provision for equal protection of laws; and (3) their administration in the selected cases lacks due process.

I would like to discuss these seriatim.

With respect to establishing the guidelines, there has been no method for hearing labor or management or representatives of the public as to what are the appropriate standards to be maintained. I realize these are highly technical problems, but this does not mean that interested parties cannot be heard. Instead of that, the Council announces the guidelines *ex cathedra* and the result is that they don't have public acceptance. In its 1966 Report, the Council unilaterally changed the basis for formulating the guidelines, which it had used for the past five years, and this resulted in wide public criticism by the AFL-CIO and by many others. No wonder. Certainly, due process for the people concerned with this issue called for some form of hearing, some form of consultation, for setting a figure instead of announcing it as a decree from on high as a magic number that the Council, in its infinite wisdom, thought was appropriate.

Let's look at the administration of these guidelines and whether or not they provide equal protection. From my observation, they have been enforced in an arbitrary, unfair way. Pressure has been applied to some industries and not to others without any rational standards of demarcation. It has resulted in uncertainty whether or not, when you go to the bargaining table, you may be watched, whether or not your collective bargaining negotiations may be subject to challenge or the price adjustments that may arise out of them may be subject to adjustment.

The government activities have been described in a variety of ways: government by edict, government by arm-twisting, government by threat, government by presidential muscle. You name it. If it's vitriolic, it's been used.

One of the other things that bothers me is that the Presidential exhortation hasn't been in equal volume. To revert to musical terms, sometimes it's sotto voce and sometimes it's forte. Let me just cite a few examples, and in citing them, I'm not passing judgment on whether or not these particular instances were justified or not. I am merely calling to your attention some actions taken by the administration.

The UAW settlement with the Big Three auto companies was well above the guidelines. There is dispute whether it was 4 per cent or 4.7 per cent, but I think that's quite irrelevant. It is generally agreed that it exceeded the magic number 3.2.

President Johnson stated at the time that he was pleased by statements of the parties that "this settlement takes full account of both the public and private interest, that it will mean jobs, and that it will be noninflationary." And then, after the G.M. and Ford settlements, he said that he hoped other industries would "not use the auto settlement as a pattern."

In the Longshore dispute in 1963, Senator Morse headed up a fact-finding board that recommended a settlement that amounted to approximately 5.25 per cent. Walter Heller, then chairman of the Council of Economic Advisers, said: "Well, the guidelines don't suggest a flat three or any other percentage figure. Nevertheless, this was a very special situation. It is not one which we would like to see followed as a precedent." He went on to say that there were special factors present, particularly work rules.

On the other hand, in that fair city that I live in that sometimes has water and sometimes has air conditioning, we had a transit strike in 1966. When the strike was settled—and frankly I don't think it was a very good settlement myself—the President said, "I don't believe that any settlement that violates the guideposts to this extent is in the national interest."

And Gardner Ackley said, "I deeply regret that the strike had to be settled on terms that far exceed the government's wage guideposts." It may be a strange coincidence that the new mayor of New York City happened to be a Republican.

We all remember the loud and clear messages that came out in late 1965 at the time of the steel increase: Roger Blough took a few steps backward, there was the aluminum rollback and the threats on stockpiles. Those messages were very loud.

The most recent public pronouncement, and one that I find

rather disturbing, came in relation to the *New Jersey Operating Engineers* case. First, Mr. Peter Weber, president of the New Jersey Operating Engineers Union, was called down to Washington to meet with the Council of Economic Advisers. Whether it was a wise procedure I think leaves some very serious question. Mr. Weber didn't. He rebuffed them. Now, ultimately, they resolved that dispute—at least that's what I read in the papers—by resorting to arbitration with joint arbitrators, the Secretary of Labor, Bill Wirtz, and Raymond Male, the New Jersey Commissioner of Labor and Industry. I happen to have very warm personal regard for Bill Wirtz. I think he is one of the most wonderful people that has ever been in public office, but I seriously question whether he should be sitting as arbitrator under these circumstances. I think questions can be raised whether he is in a position to approach this problem with an open mind. Frankly, I think that the administration makes a very serious mistake when it places a cabinet officer, who has such a well-deserved reputation for integrity, in a position that can cast even the slightest doubt upon that reputation. This is a terribly high price to pay for trying to fit things within some preconceived notions of magic figures. And I think it is most unfortunate the secretary has been placed in that position.

I cited these illustrations to point up what seems to me a case of vigorous enforcement that's predicated primarily on vulnerability. This does not conform to any concept we have of equal protection of the laws.

I'd like to pass now to the due process concept. Even the guidelines, as enunciated, recognize that there might be exceptions to the magic 3.2 figure. Certainly, parties publicly accused of violation are entitled to a hearing before they are condemned. No such procedure exists today. No procedures are established for determining whether any particular price or wage increase is within the guidelines or an exception to the guidelines. There are no provisions for hearings or for an affected union or company to present its side of the story to an impartial fact finder. What happens is that the administration unilaterally decides that a particular wage or price increase is beyond the guidelines and not within the exceptions and then exerts various pressures for a cutback.

After preparing my notes over the weekend for this session, I had the privilege of reading John Dunlop's perceptive paper that came into my office on Monday. John Dunlop is one of those economists without benefit of a law degree who delineates issues with the kind of precision we lawyers like to feel we have. He put flesh on a skeletal idea relating to due process that I was seeking to crystallize. John did it much better than I, and I am taking the liberty of quoting from his paper:

> I am always impressed with how different a case may look after it has been presented in a forum which permits full review of the facts and contending arguments as compared to the reports of government or academic experts. The judgment that a wage or price increase in our economy is violative of the public interest is a serious conclusion that should warrant dispassionate review with full opportunity for the presentation of contesting views. The present policy does not afford this elementary right.

As a lawyer, I doff my cap to that good economist, John Dunlop.

Perhaps even more serious is the undermining of the integrity of the Council of Economic Advisers by transforming it into an enforcement agency. It was never established for that purpose. I think for the CEA to cast itself in this role or to be cast in this role by the President—take your choice—is a distortion of its basic purpose.

FUTURE PUBLIC POLICY

So far I have pointed up difficulties with the program as I see it. I would like to suggest for future consideration of public policy that, while lawyers specializing in labor relations may be pseudo-economists, pseudo-psychologists, and sometimes lawyers, I don't profess to have the economic answer to the need for continuing the guidelines. I can say, from my own experience at the bargaining table—and I have reviewed this with people on my staff—that the guidelines have not been a factor at the bargaining table so far as we can see. Some of the economists in our workshop tell us that the settlements over the past few years show a parallel. Frankly, I think this is pure coincidence. I have not seen any really serious discussion of the guidelines in bargaining sessions. That they are used as a bargaining ploy on occasion, I concede, but that they are the real factor in the ultimate bargaining, I deny. I still think that market factors and economic power—which are some-

what synonymous—are the factors that decide what happens at
the collective bargaining table.

In any event, it would seem to me the time has come for public
debate—the kind of debate that we're having here today—to
determine whether or not the guidelines should be continued. Mr.
Dunlop suggests that some form of guidelines should be continued
and suggests that the necessary consensus of business and labor
can best be developed through the reconstituted President's Committee on Labor-Management Policy. This may be a desirable first
step, but I would go a step further. I would say the second step
should be that, after the Labor-Management Committee has a recommendation, it should be considered in depth by the Joint Economic Committee of Congress, and, Step 3, if the public debate
there reveals a consensus in favor of continuation, there should be
a legislative base for such guidelines. As pointed out by Mr. Kurland, there must be a statutory base for wage-price control even
under the war powers. And I submit that if they're going to have
real public acceptance, they ought to have a legislative base. This
does not mean that Congress should set the guidelines; it means
that Congress should confirm or deny by debate and vote whether
there is public consensus for the Council to continue setting the
guidelines. It also means that Congress could establish procedural
standards for the formulation and administration of the guidelines
and provide any funds and staff necessary to carry out these
procedures.

If the guidelines are continued, they should meet—in my judgment—three basic standards: (1) There should be a procedure for
public hearings to determine the appropriate guideline or the range
of such guidelines; (2) there should be legal safeguards to assure
equal standards for application and equal protection of the laws;
and (3) there should be procedures for hearings with appropriate
due process safeguards.

Since I have little sympathy for the overall guideline policy, it is
somewhat difficult for me to elaborate these basic standards and
suggest an improved procedure if the guidelines are to be continued. Some procedural reforms are evident, however.

The Council seems to be the logical body to determine the
guidelines in the first instance. The Council, however, should be
required to hold public hearings before guidelines are adopted, at

which interested persons and public figures could present their views. The Council should also be encouraged to consult informally in advance with those to whom the guidelines will be applicable and, of course, the guidelines themselves should make a clear and reasoned demarcation as to whom they apply.

Under no circumstances should the Council have a role in the administration of the guideline principles. This would debase the integrity of the Council and limit its effectiveness in its important functions as economic adviser to the President. Furthermore, experience has shown that the Council does not have the staff nor the close working relationship with labor and management necessary for effective administration.

One possibility might be an interdepartmental committee established by the Secretaries of Commerce and Labor to administer the guidelines. Such a committee should develop procedures to insure that those accused of violating the guidelines have a fair opportunity to present their case in a public forum. The committee could itself, or through appointed panels, hold hearings and issue reports in the nature of fact-finding recommendations. Fact-finding has proved a successful method for resolving difficult labor disputes in the past by throwing the spotlight of public attention upon a controversy and appealing to the moral suasion of public opinion. A similar procedure is worthy of consideration here.

Finally the question arises: What sanction should be available to enforce the guidelines? Sanctions are inconsistent with voluntarism. Therefore, I would give the simple answer that there should be no sanctions. Guidelines are supposed to be, and will work best as, a method of focusing public attention and opinion on wage and price decisions that significantly affect the public. In this context it is not only legitimate but desirable for the administration to publicize its position, predicated upon the recommendations of the fact-finding board.

CONCLUSION

In summing up, I would state:

1. The guidelines have not been effective at the collective bargaining table.

2. Administration of the guidelines does not meet the basic safeguards for due process and equal protection of the laws.

3. If the guidelines are to be continued, they should be reformulated to represent the consensus of labor and industry so that they will have a greater receptivity.

4. If reformulated, they should be given a legislative base with appropriate safeguards to assure due process.

RALPH HELSTEIN

Comments

I find myself in the position of the vocalist who turned to her accompanist and said, "You don't seem to like my singing." And his response was, "Well, you know I play the white keys and I play the black keys, but you sing in the cracks." I'm very much afraid that I'm going to be singing in the cracks if there are any.

It is perfectly permissible in the law to start your observations with complete disavowals, as I noticed Ben Aaron did. I am not an economist. I am no longer a lawyer. I know very little about either the legal issues involved here or the economics.

I am persuaded by Mr. Kurland's analogy to Marc Antony. We're not here to praise guidelines. Although I'm not sure yet whether we're ready to bury them, I'm perfectly willing to pick up a shovel and start digging.

I think that I share the views expressed by Mr. Kurland with reference to constitutional questions and also—performing my function of mediating between these two views—I share Ben Aaron's views that the guidelines won't work unless they reflect the wishes of the parties who are to be affected, which, in the final analysis, I would suggest might very well involve the public interest that they were designed to protect initially.

I think, however, that there is warrant in making just a couple of observations in connection with what seems to me, at least, to be some basic legal questions that have been touched on already,

Ralph Helstein is president of United Packinghouse, Food and Allied Workers, AFL-CIO, and a member of the Executive Council, AFL-CIO.

but which I think can well be emphasized.

There is, I believe, *a complete denial of due process,* not only of the methods used in enforcement, which, as Ben Aaron has suggested, may well be moral rather than legal, but clearly also in the formulation of the guidelines in the first instance. There is no participation in the formulation of these guidelines on the part of the people who would be most directly affected. And I find particularly offensive in this kind of an operation the proposition that we start dealing with what we assume, for whatever reason, that the only sources of the kinds of pressures that we're trying to control rests in the relationship between *wages* and *prices.* It seems to me that we might apply equal energy and perhaps come up with much better solutions if we worried about *supply* and made certain that there would *not* be *excessive demand.* I suggest that it is almost a contradiction of terms to speak of excessive demand in a nation that currently has thirty-five million people living in poverty or below the accepted governmental lines of poverty.

Secondly, it seems to me that we deny the very substance of Anglo-Saxon notions of equity when we start with the proposition that the *only* way we can provide our people with a bigger piece of pie is by making that total pie greater, without dealing at all with such equitable considerations as to whether or not the distribution in the first instance is satisfactory or fair.

It seems to me the guidelines fail entirely to deal with this. And I think that so long as they continue to do so, they will and should meet with resistance.

PART IV

Reports of Workshop Discussions

DOUGLASS V. BROWN

Report

In trying to summarize what we've talked about in the last two days, it seems to me that I can dogmatically make two points without fear of contradiction from any member of our group. The first is that we ranged over a very wide range of subjects. The second is, unless I had fallen asleep at one point or other, I heard nobody express violent enthusiasm either for the guidelines or the guideposts.

One of the interesting things that came out in the course of yesterday's discussion was that if you look separately at the guidelines—those having to do with international affairs—and the guideposts—those having to do with wages and prices—they seem to have differed quite substantially: first, with respect to the degree of *impact* they have had and, secondly, and more particularly, with respect to the amount of *resentment* they have generated.

It may be interesting to try to identify the reasons for these differences. As for resentment, there seems to have been relatively little with respect to the guidelines. As we all know, there seems to have been a great deal with respect to the guideposts.

As I try to distill what was said, it seems to me that the lesser degree of resentment with respect to the guidelines stems perhaps from two factors: (1) a greater degree of participation on the part of those affected in the development of the guidelines and (2) a crasser reason, that the guidelines don't seem to threaten harm to

Douglass V. Brown is Alfred P. Sloan Professor of Management at the Massachusetts Institute of Technology and a noted economist and arbitrator.

many people or at least don't seem to threaten a great deal of harm to very many people.

With respect to the guideposts, there was not this advance consultation and at least potentially—and perhaps in some instances, actually—there is the possibility of harm to people affected.

On the impact angle, it seems reasonably clear that the guidelines have had more traceable impact than the guideposts. And it seems that perhaps the reason for the greater impact of the guidelines is that hovering in the background of these informal voluntary controls is a whole host of controls which just could conceivably be turned loose if there is noncompliance.

With respect to the guideposts, there is much more limited possibility of control and, perhaps, in the case of wages, none at all. I should say, because it ties into the point I'm going to make later, that with respect to the guidelines, there was a slogan that commanded a greater loyalty than any similar slogan that could be found in the guidepost area; namely, "You gotta save the dollar."

The comments I have made so far have to do with the *impact,* if you will, of the guidelines and the guideposts. I turn now to the question of the *merits* of the guidelines and the guideposts.

With respect to guidelines, there was a marked feeling among many members of our group that they were not really necessary. There was concern expressed about their impact on other countries. There was concern expressed lest the United States guidelines would lead to a multiplication of controls elsewhere, and a more general concern that the introduction and application of the guidelines was an impedance to a desirable trend that had been going on toward freer world markets.

With respect to the guideposts, there was a pretty general feeling that they were impractical to enforce except in a very small proportion of cases, that because of these difficulties any attempt at enforcement or application was replete with inequities, and that because of these administrative problems and the apparent—small results—and not necessarily in the right direction at that—a dim view should be taken of the guideposts.

Interestingly, however, I think there was some feeling that if the guideposts or something like them did not exist, it would be necessary *for political reasons* to invent them.

I think there was a general feeling that it would be more profitable, rather than to focus attention on guidelines and guideposts, to focus attention on somewhat broader, more fundamental problems. Here I will mention three areas specifically: first, the whole question of variable exchange rates and the price of the dollar; secondly, the whole area of monetary policy; and, finally, certain structural, institutional features of the economy. These three areas, it was suggested, might better be the focus for study.

ROBBEN W. FLEMING

Report

I made my apologies in advance to my group for what a wayward lawyer with a basic 1-A course in economics might say about their views as a result of these discussions.

In any event, we started out our discussion with an effort to bridge the gap between those who had a labor-economics approach and were primarily interested in the wage-price problems and those whose experience and expertise were more nearly in the foreign investment and balance-of-payments areas. We did this by talking about the mechanism for control, and the extent to which one could say that the lessons in one area might have application in another area. We very shortly found that, with respect to foreign investments on the part of the individual companies, we had no one in our group who had particular interest and experience in this area.

We then talked about federal reserve policies and the banks, and we agreed that this was not the same kind of problem which one had in the wage-price area. The constituencies were quite different, as were the rules of the game. The banks were used to receiving guidance from the Federal Reserve System and did not feel that it interfered seriously with their business. Also, there were other investment alternatives which were still open to the banks

Robben W. Fleming is professor of law and chancellor, Madison Campus, University of Wisconsin, and is currently president of the National Academy of Arbitrators.

which might not be open in other situations. Therefore, it would be fair to say that problems were not of the same order as in the wage-price situation.

We then drifted over almost immediately into the question of the wage and price guideposts. Our talk was primarily in terms of the wages. There were no observable converts from the free market theory across to those who believe there is utility in the guide-post approach, or vice versa. Quite obviously, what distinguishes these groups is a difference in view to what the end result will be —the guidepost people feeling that if you followed the free market theory, you would end up with unacceptable levels of unemployment, and the free market people feeling that not only were the guidelines unworkable but that in fact, they were a first step toward more serious controls which they regarded as completely unacceptable.

Incidentally, with respect to the general controls problem which we discussed at greater length after the Friedman-Solow exchange, it would represent the consensus of our group that more stringent federal controls may be imminent, and that we should be concerned about the growth of such controls in our economy.

As to the wage guideposts, there was a clear feeling in our group that these *are not* working effectively and that they *probably will not* work effectively. Although it is hard to produce conclusive evidence that they do or do not work and there remains some feeling that perhaps they have some effect, the consensus in our group was to the contrary.

If there are to be guideposts, there is a clear and strong feeling that there should be provision for discussion and consultation and that one of the difficulties with such rules at the moment is that there has not been an adequate opportunity for discussion. Consultation admittedly carries some problems of its own, and some of our members would ask, "Well, discussion with whom and if you mean only the parties that are immediately involved, aren't you then neglecting the rest of us who are part of the public but who are affected by what's done?"

On the question that was raised in Mr. Solow's talk of whether it is possible to discuss these complex kinds of subjects with a group when the analytical difficulties are great, one thinks of the British and Dutch experience where they have consulted. I would expect that Mr. Phelps Brown would reply to Mr. Solow by saying that it is possible.

Interestingly enough, in our group—although they could not agree upon either the guideline or the free market approach—*both would say the problem of control is serious.* I was never quite certain in my own mind whether they meant that it was serious in the sense that more stringent controls were ahead and were a dangerous thing in our kind of economy, or whether they thought the problem was serious in the inflationary sense. Perhaps one would simply say a little of both.

All of this led us to a discussion of Mr. John Dunlop's alternative. John, being a member of our group and his usual articulate self, pressed on us this alternative. It was discussed at some length. John seems to be saying: You must be realistic, you must recognize that you are not really going to get a free market approach, you must recognize that the present guidepost approach is not really working and that you need a viable alternative of some kind. He suggests the alternative which you read in his paper.

The significant thing about the Dunlop approach, as I view it, is that as he attacks these bottleneck areas which he outlined, he does not exclude a wage and price plan, but he has a much broader approach than this, which would certainly include manpower policies, purchasing power controls which may be within the control of the government, and other relevant avenues of impact on the problem. He would leave the educational function which Mr. Solow spoke of this morning to the labor-management committee which is being reconstituted.

Those who were critical of the Dunlop approach said, "Well, this really isn't anything different. It's a guideline on a little different scale. It really diverts you from the principal problems. In any event, the time is too short to accomplish anything in this manner, and it would use the same weapons which have failed."

Now, if I may, I should like to add a couple of comments of my own. I do not purport to be speaking for the others.

One general observation is that, unlike most of the western European countries, we have not yet really tried an integrated approach to the national incomes problem; i.e., we have tended to *isolate* the various programs rather than bringing them together in the sense of overall economic goals toward which we wish to strive.

Secondly, all of us who had labor dispute experience in World War II or the Korean conflict would say that it makes a great deal of difference whether you are trying to apply voluntary controls in a period of crisis or whether you are trying to apply them in a period when you simply can't convince people that there is a great national crisis on hand. As one looks at the experience of the countries in Western Europe, one sees this same phenomenon. It is much easier to make a set of voluntary controls effective in a period when people can agree that there is crisis.

Finally, this last observation: It does seem to me that John Dunlop made a great contribution to this conference. Whether one agrees with his proposal or not, he did suggest an alternative, and I could not help but be struck, as we talked along, that we all tend to think only of polar possibilities and too little of completely new alternatives. And in this kind of a group, with as much brain power as there is here, we ought to be producing more alternatives. In my own view, polar positions in a democracy seldom are viable and whether one likes it or not, we do arrive at some kind of compromise on these things. My conclusion is that we ought to have produced more alternatives than we discussed.

THEODORE W. SCHULTZ

Report

I shall begin by summarizing the views of the twenty-five members of this conference for whom I report and shall end with my own views.

ON THE FUNCTIONS OF GUIDELINES

Are they educational? Answer: In the area of wages and prices in large part, yes. In the balance of payments area, no.

Are they designed to correct a temporary disequilibrium? Yes in both areas, for example, to hold in check a premature inflation or to make room for a couple of billions of dollars of United States military purchases abroad required because of the war.

Are they a way of postponing basic decisions while waiting for more information? It could be that the excess demand causing inflation is overrated, or that the balance-of-payments problem will go away should factor prices rise more rapidly in Europe than in the United States. There were some who felt it was pure procrastination.

ON THE EFFECTS OF GUIDELINES

In the area of United States balance of payments the following views predominated:

Theodore W. Schultz is Charles L. Hutchinson Distinguished Service Professor in the Department of Economics, University of Chicago, and a past president of the American Economics Association.

1. United States financial intermediaries and business corporations in general have complied.

2. Interest rates abroad have been pushed up as a consequence. (Mr. Denise cited evidence in support of Mr. Meltzer's hypotheses).

3. A clear side-effect in Canada, reported by Smith, has been the demand by Europeans for loans and the Canadian effort to check such loans.

4. United States corporations face additional resentment abroad.

5. Then the question was raised, Why shouldn't United States corporations operating abroad serve our national interest?, Helstein pressed this query sharply. Several different definitions of our national interest were presented.

6. Particular limited aims of the federal reserve guidelines have been achieved and supporting data were cited.

7. But the balance-of-payments problem remains unresolved.

8. An alternative to the Federal Reserve guidelines was proposed, namely to rescind the special tax treatment of foreign investments made by United States firms.

9. The United States dollar is overvalued. With respect to this judgment there was a consensus, except for Sidney Stein's strong dissent.

In the area of wages and prices the views of this group came off about as follows:

1. In collective bargaining on wages the guidelines have been a small factor.

2. Where they have been a factor the weaker groups have suffered, thus causing inequities.

3. But several businessmen disagreed, holding also that the guidelines were a somewhat larger factor than implied in 1. above.

4. There was disagreement on how well they work in the United Kingdom. Phelps Brown took a fairly optimistic view on what they will do rather than what they have done, and Denise argued that they have not done well and the prospects were likewise.

5. The contradictions among government agencies was stressed as it had been last night by the lawyers.

6. It is plausible that guidelines have checked somewhat premature inflation. The evidence on this was cited in Solow's paper. Solow was there to defend his view. The group was inclined to agree that the evidence has plausibility although Smith gave a

number of cogent factors that also could explain the data.

7. Then the question: Is there now substantial excessive demand? It was felt that the right question to ask is: Is it highly probable that during the next twelve months that there will be substantial excess demand? The answer was in the affirmative with three persons holding the view that it is still premature to be so sure.

I shall not attempt to summarize the views of this group on prices and guidelines because no real clarification of issues was achieved. No one was displeased with the guidelines as they were set forth in 1962.

Having been invited not to conceal my own views, let me simply say in closing, that we have been all too troubled either about pin pricks or about doctrinal issues to have clarified the following matters:

1. What have been the *reasons* for the success in prolonging our high level of production?

2. How large a contribution has this success made to drawing underemployed people out of depressed areas and out of agriculture? My view is that it has contributed more than all of the depressed area programs, agricultural programs, and poverty programs together.

3. How much slack in underutilization of resources, expecially so of labor, still remains? I believe that there are still several millions of workers in depressed areas and in agriculture who are underemployed. But more important, is the vast amount of upgrading of the mainstream of industrial workers, who are presently still undergraded as a consequence of the hiring and placing of workers that took place during the long slack period after 1957.

4. Is the shock effect of some excess demand necessarily all bad for the economy? Here, too, we need clarification. It could be that it is an *efficient* treatment for much so-called structural unemployment. Is there a better way of cleaning up our depressed areas and agriculture? The achievements on this score may well be worth the small inflation price of some excess demand.

5. Lastly, we have not considered how we can best check the growth in excess demand, best in the sense that we will not thereby bring about more slack in the still underutilized capacity and again especially so of labor.

GEORGE J. STIGLER

Report

I shall speak very briefly about the views of my group. My own views are slightly more hostile to the contemporary experiments than those I am about to report, but they can be read in "Private Enterprise and Public Intelligence," printed in a Symposium on Business-Government Relations of the American Bankers Association, 1966.

We discussed first, fairly briefly, the foreign policies which attempt to bring about equilibrium in the balance of payments. Unlike Mr. Fleming's group, we did have one man who was an expert in foreign business and the direct controls over investment abroad. It was his consensus that the direct investment controls had been mild and that we have as yet had no real test of either their effects or their enforceability.

I was impressed in reading the conference papers, as I think the group was, that the economists generally—all those, at least, who spoke explicitly on the issue—were opposed to the sort of medley of policies we have invoked to restore equilibrium in the balance of payments and at least three of them—Meltzer, Johnson, and Friedman—came out explicitly for floating foreign exchange rates. It is not at all clear that, stripped of other responsibilities, any of the other economists on the panel would necessarily have been opposed to this position.

I raised in our group the question of what the objections were

George J. Stigler is Charles R. Walgreen Distinguished Service Professor in the Graduate School of Business and Department of Economics, University of Chicago, and a past president of the American Economics Association.

to a move in this direction, and I was interested in how weak the criticisms of flexible exchange rates were. One can raise technical questions such as that business is harder to conduct with uncertain future exchange rates, and that possibly there can be cumulative destabilizing speculation in the foreign exchanges. But it was clear that such objections (which are not very strong) were not the heart of the opposition. From this, I deduce that the opposition to floating exchange rates is not based upon analytically defensible criticisms of how the economy would behave. Rather the opposition rests upon an instinctive and possibly atavistic belief, on the basis of the century-old history of the gold standard, that a fixed price of gold serves to discipline dangerous fiscal and monetary tendencies. Since the oppostion is inarticulate and unrationalized, we are much less likely to overcome it than if it were a formal position.

This incidentally raises a side question. A great deal has been made of the fact that the federal government has educational functions. I am not convinced that the White House is the university of the future. If you ask yourself what the government can contribute to the education of the American people on the possible desirability of flexible foreign exchange rates, it is immediately obvious that Mr. Martin or the Secretary of the Treasury or Mr. Ackley hardly dare begin to discuss extensively the possibility of unpegging the price of gold, for there would be repercussions of the sort that none of us would like. And it is just possible that the main educational task in all economic matters will have to remain outside Washington.

Now, let me turn to the guidelines at home. I asked our experts, "Have the guidelines had any effect?" "Was the effect desirable?" In our discussion, we found it useful to compare the two kinds of industries. There is a set of industries which are largely decentralized. They may be decentralized geographically, as the various branches of the construction industry, or they may be decentralized in a sense of having no large firms, as in the cases of textiles and shoes. Here it was the verdict of a very substantial number of informed people that the interventions had had no influence upon wages at all. One man in fact said that his fondest hope was someday to reach a market so strong that he could get a 3.2 per cent annual increase in wages! It was a general recommendation to this decentralized sector of the economy that it should not answer the phone!

When we turn to the concentrated industries, the second class of industries, the same indecision and uncertainty which was mirrored in the presentation of our distinguished economists this morning was in our group. There were some who believed—if I may paraphrase them—that it makes a difference in negotiations in a concentrated industry such as automobiles or steel if someone says, "Someone up there is watching us." And others said, "No, look at the settlement. In very prominent cases, they have run 4 or 4.7 or some other percentage points of increase per year." On the other hand, we pretty well agreed that there had been a genuine effect in a few commodity prices such as copper.

Apropos of these concentrated industries, my group had a strong affection for what was called tripartite discussion. And tripartite discussion seemed to mean at least three possible things, with support shrinking as we go down the list.

First, it seemed outrageous to many participants that decrees should be issued on high without consultation. This was a violation of the dignity of the participants of the collective bargaining process or the price setting process. They desired notice and a hearing even if they were not necessarily given legislative power. They were opposed to non-papal bulls.

Secondly, there were some who felt—and I think this is a stronger point—that labor and management should participate with the Council in formulating any guidelines. (I think it has been a sort of abbreviation to talk about the Council making up the guidelines. The guidelines have been a product, I take it, of a large number of forces in the administration and some without.) These participants believe that it has been unwise not to bring in systematically the experience, the wishes and the desires and the knowledge of the business community and the labor organizations. Something would also be learned of the detailed problems of application, if such consultations had taken place. Possibly the deliberative process would end up with guidelines that began to return toward the informality of the 1962 version. These guidelines would take fuller cognizance of the fact that blanket rules were the beginning and not the termination of a useful negotiation. The degree of flexibility was even carried by some to the point of believing that it would be possible to have guidelines in some years and no guidelines in other years (a position I personally find wholly implausible).

Third, some people hoped that these tripartite arrangements would reach the level of actual intervention in the course of economic affairs. Apropos of, but perhaps a foot beyond anything that Dunlop said explicitly, there might actually be policies, for example, to increase the number of skilled workers in the construction trades if that be necessary to open up bottlenecks in that area.

I got the feeling, which may be an inaccurate one, that the participants—on the management side and the labor side—would really prefer a regime of nonintervention by the federal government. They felt that that was unattainable and that therefore they were prepared to settle for a strong, orderly process of suasion with indulgence for departures from the public interest which were not too flagrant. They were prepared to settle for a combination of rear guard actions and education. I am very skeptical that this will yield much. I am not going to deny that you can make a silk purse out of a sow's ear, but I find it inconceivable that you can make one out of a committee's deliberations!

I do not wish to violate the anonymity of our deliberations, but I am going to name one person. That perceptive economist, Philip Kurland, raised a theme which rings very loudly to me. This theme is the widespread evidence of the decline of the prestige of Congress. The labor union representatives and the management representatives apparently almost unaminously believed that the best way to deal with these problems in the economic area was by going to the executive branch. That the executive branch has grown mightily relative to the legislative branch hardly seems open to dispute, and it is high time that we re-examine the merits of the shift in power. We all apparently believe that the political compromises and the preferential treatment of special interests are less well handled in Congress, but it may just possibly be that they are merely illuminated in Congress. Again, we emphasize what are surely true attributes of the executive process—its speed and its flexibility. But these are words that you can use in two ways. You may speak of speed or you may speak of haste; you may speak of flexibility or you may speak of caprice.

I find it somewhat instructive that, in our own deliberations, we did not know what the status of the guidelines policy is at the present moment. Fortunately, we are about to hear the man who can tell us.

Appendixes

Appendix A

SELECTED MATERIALS ON WAGE-PRICE GUIDEPOSTS

(handwritten annotation: Compare to what's taken down)

1948   Agreement between General Motors and the UAW-CIO establishing an annual improvement factor tying wages to productivity.

EXCERPTS FROM THE ECONOMIC REPORTS OF THE PRESIDENT AND COUNCIL OF ECONOMIC ADVISERS
1957–66

1957   Statement that proper governmental fiscal and monetary policies must be supported by appropriate private policies to assure a high level of economic activity and a stable dollar.

1958   Statement that price increases should be warranted by increases in costs and that wage increases should not exceed productivity gains.

1959   Restatement of the public interest in settlements of contracts between business and management. Congress asked to make reasonable price stability an explicit goal of federal economic policy.

1960   Statement that the national average of wage increases should not exceed sustainable rates of growth in national productivity and that price reductions warranted by especially rapid productivity gains should be frequent.

1961   Statement focusing on the responsibility of government not to create inflationary pressures through fiscal or monetary policy. The control of unit labor costs is primarily a private responsibility.

1962   Formal statement of guideposts. Price level stability does not rule out flexible relative prices. Government policies must increase, not limit, private freedom. Guideposts "are not concerned primarily with the relation of employers and employees to each other, but rather with their joint relation to the rest of the economy." Productivity is a *guide* rather than a *rule* for appraising wage and price behavior.

1963   Restatement of the 1962 guideposts, with indication they are designed to provide standards for evaluating the normal processes of free private decisions and negotiations and are not to replace them.

1964   Restatement with some modifications. Productivity trend change defined as the five-year moving average of the annual percentage change in output per man-hour in the private economy. Government will strive to reinforce competition and notes that it is "the economy's single largest buyer of goods and services." A freezing of labor and non-labor shares is not intended; and the guideposts call for price reductions in some instances.

1965   Restatement.

1966   Restatement recommending the continuation of 3.2 per cent as "trend productivity" rather than the five-year moving average.

AGREEMENT BETWEEN GENERAL MOTORS CORPORATION AND THE UAW-CIO, MAY 29, 1948

WAGES

(97) The establishment of wage scales for each operation is necessarily a matter for local negotiation and agreement between the Plant Managements and the Shop Committees, on the basis of the local circumstances affecting each operation, giving consideration to the relevant factors of productivity, continuity of employment, the general level of wages in the community, and the wages paid by competitors. . . .

(101) (a) All employees covered by this Agreement shall receive an increase of 11¢ per hour effective May 29, 1948. 3¢ per hour of this increase is to provide for improvement in the standard of living of employees and will be added to the base rate of each wage classification for the term of the Agreement. 8¢ per hour of this increase is for the purpose of providing for the increase which has taken place in the cost of living. It is agreed that only 5¢ of this 8¢ will be subject to reduction so that, if a sufficient decline in the cost of living occurs, employes will immediately enjoy a better standard of living. Such an improvement will be an addition to the 3¢ an hour annual improvement factor underwritten by the Corporation and will make a total of 6¢ to be added to the base rate of each wage classification, as of May 29, 1948. [Pp. 56–58.]

EXCERPTS FROM THE ECONOMIC REPORTS OF THE PRESIDENT AND COUNCIL OF ECONOMIC ADVISERS

JANUARY, 1957

Economic developments in recent years show the basic role that monetary and fiscal restraints must play if the excesses that often accompany prosperity are to be avoided. At the same time, this experience suggests that fiscal and monetary policies must be supported by appropriate private policies to assure both a high level of economic activity and a stable dollar. When production, sales, and employment are high, wage and price increases in important industries create upward pressures on costs and prices generally. To depend exclusively on monetary and fiscal restraints as a means of containing the upward movement of prices would raise serious obstacles to the maintenance of economic growth and stability. In the face of a continuous upward pressure on costs and prices, moderate restraints would not be sufficient; yet stronger restraints would bear with undue severity on sectors of the economy having little if any responsibility for the movement toward a higher cost-price level and would court the risk of being excessively restrictive for the economy generally.

These are not acceptable alternatives to stable and balanced economic growth. The American economy possesses the potentials for expansion and improvement. If these potentials are supported by proper fiscal and monetary policies on the part of Government, and by appropriate private policies, our economy can achieve and maintain high levels of production, employment, and income with stable prices. [P. 44.]

JANUARY, 1958

THE CHALLENGE TO ECONOMIC POLICIES

A realistic appraisal of our economic prospects, though it warrants confidence, also requires that we acknowledge an unfavorable feature of recent economic developments. In 1957, our gross national product rose 5 per cent, but four-fifths of this increase was accounted for by rising prices.

There are critical questions here for business and labor, as well as for Government. Business managements must recognize that price increases that are unwarranted by costs, or that attempt to recapture investment outlays too quickly, not only lower the buying power of the dollar, but also may be self-defeating by causing a restriction of markets, lower output, and a narrowing of the return on capital investment. The leadership of labor must recognize that wage increases that go beyond over-all productivity gains are inconsistent with stable prices, and that the resumption of economic growth can be slowed by wage increases that involve either higher prices or a further narrowing of the margin between prices and costs. Government, for its part, must use its powers to help keep our economy stable and to encourage sound economic growth with reasonably stable prices.

The resumption and maintenance of economic growth promise greater economic capability for meeting the Nation's needs. If this opportunity is to be fully realized, however, growth must take the form of increases in real output, accompanied by a stable price level. This can be achieved if weight is given to long-run as well as short-run considerations in policies and practices that affect our economic welfare. It can be guaranteed by a public opinion that is alert to the consequences of wrong policies and insists on policies which will yield economic growth without inflation. [P. v.]

Events in 1957 show how important it is for private and public policies and practices to complement each other as we seek to achieve economic growth with reasonable stability of prices. Decisions which give rise to wage increases generally in excess of improvements in productivity, or to price increases that typically go beyond increases in costs, make this task more difficult. If fiscal and credit policies are sufficiently stern to keep the price level from rising, there are risks of economic dislocation, an unnecessarily slow rate of economic growth, and extreme and inequitable pressures on some who are not themselves contributors to the inflation of costs and prices. On the other hand, if economically unwarranted increases in wage rates or prices are validated by credit and fiscal policies, a persistent decline in the value of the dollar results. [Pp. 8–9.]

JANUARY, 1959

Despite recession during the first part of the year, wage rates continued to move upward. The rate of increase was nearly as great as in periods of economic expansion, and higher than the rate at which gains in productivity have been achieved in our economy over extended periods of time. Obviously, if we have only limited success in restraining increases in unit costs during recession, much remains to be done to achieve a basis for holding prices reasonably steady when productive capacity is more fully utilized. To this challenge everyone must respond.

The individual consumer can play an important part by shopping carefully for price and quality. In this way, the American housekeeper can be a powerful force for holding down the cost of living and strengthening the principle that good values and good prices make good business.

Businessmen must redouble their efforts. They must wage a ceaseless war against costs. Production must be on the most economical basis possible. The importance of wide and growing markets must be borne in mind in setting prices. Expanded markets, in themselves, promise economies that help keep costs and prices in check.

Leaders of labor unions, in view of the great power lodged in their hands, have a particularly critical role to play. Their economic actions must reflect awareness that stability of prices is an essential condition of sustainable economic growth and that the only road to greater material well-being for the Nation lies in the fullest possible realization of our productivity potential. This requires not only that our resources be fully employed, but that arbitrary restraints on their most effective utilization be removed. We can realize more from our economy only to the extent that we produce more.

It is not the function of Government in our society to establish the terms of contracts between labor and management; yet it must be recognized that the public has a vital interest in these agreements. Increases in money wages and other compensation not justified by the productivity performance of the economy are inevitably inflationary. They impose severe hardships on those whose incomes are not enlarged. They jeopardize the capacity of the economy to create jobs for the expanding labor force. They endanger present jobs by limiting markets at home and impairing our capacity to compete in markets abroad. In short, they are, in the end, self-defeating.

Self-discipline and restraint are essential if agreements consistent with a reasonable stability of prices are to be reached within the framework of the free competitive institutions on which we rely heavily for the improvement of our material welfare. If the desired results cannot be achieved under our arrangements for determining wages and prices, the alternatives are either inflation, which would damage our economy and work hardships on millions of Americans, or controls, which are alien to our traditional way of life and which would be an obstacle to the Nation's economic growth and improvement. [Pp. 5–6.]

ADDITIONAL GOVERNMENTAL ACTIONS TO MAINTAIN
PRICE STABILITY

Adherence to the financial plan presented in the 1960 budget and the pursuit of appropriate monetary, credit, and debt management policies would help attain rising production and employment at stable prices. Governmental actions in other areas can also help to maintain price stability as our economy expands.

First, the Congress is requested to amend the Employment Act of 1946 to make reasonable price stability an explicit goal of Federal economic policy, coordinate with the goals of maximum production, employment, and purchasing power now specified in that Act. Such an amendment would strengthen Government's hand in restraining inflationary forces and would help build a public opinion favorable to the adoption and vigorous application of needed measures. This amendment would make it clear that Government is as determined to direct its policies toward maintenance of price stability as it is to employ them in combating economic contraction.

Second, a Cabinet Committee on Price Stability for Economic Growth is being established to follow governmental and private activities affecting costs, prices, and economic growth; initiate studies by Government or by groups of private citizens of price stability in relation to economic growth; seek ways to enhance productivity in the American economy and to build a better public understanding of the need for reasonable price stability in a free society and of the conditions necessary to achieve this objective.

Third, a Committee on Government Activities Affecting Prices and Costs is being established, to follow the operation of all relevant Federal programs, including those involving procurement, construction, stockpiling, and commodity price support, and to make recommendations to the appropriate departments or agencies or to the President for the administration of these programs in line with the objective of reasonable price stability.

Fourth, questions concerning the level and movement of consumer prices, changes in wage rates and earnings, and changes in productivity have assumed such significance in our economy as to require more and better statistics concerning them. Accordingly, the Bureau of the Budget has been requested to accelerate programs for enlargement and improvement of public information on prices, wages and related costs, and productivity. [Pp. 52–53.]

January, 1960

ROLES OF INDIVIDUALS AND PRIVATE GROUPS

Since the vast majority of economic decisions in a free society are made by private individuals and groups, the rate at which national output grows and the character of that output are determined chiefly by private attitudes and actions. . . .

In their key role as consumers, individuals can contribute to the Nation's economic strength by spending wisely, just as government, acting as their agent, can promote growth by prudence in its spending. . . .

Individuals and corporate groups, in their roles as business leaders, can help strengthen the economy by the use they make of the resources under their control. . . .

Equally, leaders of labor have an opportunity as well as a responsibility to help realize more fully the Nation's economic potential. They can contribute significantly in this direction by fostering arrangements favorable to higher labor productivity.

And leaders of business and labor have a joint responsibility for facilitating economic growth through the conduct and results of collective bargaining. This responsibility is especially great in industries that are basic to the Nation's defenses and economic health. . . . Labor-management disputes in basic industries should be settled promptly, preferably without recourse to strikes, and certainly without extended interruptions of production that cause widespread dislocation and unemployment and threaten to paralyze our entire economy. They should be settled also on terms that are fair to the public at large as well as to the parties directly involved.

Labor-management negotiations in all industries offer opportunities to help promote sound growth by avoiding settlements that contribute to inflation. Settlements should not be such as to cause the national average of wage rate increases to exceed sustainable rates of improvement in national productivity. A national wage pattern that fails to meet this criterion would put an upward pressure on the price level. Hourly rates of pay and related labor benefits can, of course, be increased without jeopardizing price stability. Indeed, such increases are the major means in our free economy by which labor shares in the fruits of industrial progress. But improvements in compensation rates must, on the average, remain within the limits of general productivity gains if reasonable stability of prices is to be achieved and maintained. Furthermore, price reductions warranted by especially rapid productivity gains must be a normal and frequent feature of our economy. Without such reductions we shall not be able to keep the price level as a whole from advancing. . . .

However, we must go further in establishing a broad public understanding of the relationships of productivity and rewards to costs and prices. It would be a grave mistake to believe that we can successfully substitute legislation or controls for such understanding. Indeed, the complex relationships involved cannot be fixed by law, and attempts to determine them by restrictive governmental action would jeopardize our freedoms and other conditions essential to sound economic growth.

Our system of free institutions and shared responsibility has served us well in achieving economic growth and improvement. From our past experience, we are confident that our changing and increasing needs in the future can be met within this flexible system, which gains strength from the incentive it provides for individuals, from the scope it affords for individual initiative and action, and from the assurance it gives that government remains responsive to the will of the people. [Pp. 7–8.]

JANUARY, 1961

MAINTENANCE OF PRICE STABILITY

In administering fiscal and monetary affairs, the Federal Government makes a signal contribution to growth to the extent that it strengthens confidence in the stability of prices. The threat or experience of inflation tends to undermine thrift, even apart from the inequities inflicted and the hazards raised to sustainable growth of production. A steady and ample flow of savings and a growing volume of productive investment have been crucial to the development of our economy and will be needed more than ever in the years ahead if greatly increased numbers of workers are to be supplied with adequate tools and equipment.

Among Government efforts to maintain a reasonably stable price level, special importance must be assigned to the noninflationary conduct of Federal budgetary and fiscal affairs. Rising Government expenditures can put a direct upward pressure on costs and prices —especially when employment is already high—either because of their very magnitude or because they may concentrate demand on economic sectors in which personnel or supplies are relatively limited. Thus, inflationary pressures can be created throughout the economy, encouraging cost and price increases that do not appear direct traceable to Government action. A significantly large budgetary deficit, too, can impair the effectiveness of an anti-inflationary monetary and credit policy. Furthermore, the example set by Government in the conduct of budgetary and fiscal matters influences public attitudes and the psychology of the marketplace.

The second major Government instrument for controlling inflationary tendencies is monetary policy, for which the independent Federal Reserve System is responsible. Increases in credit, deposits, and currency are required to accommodate the rising volume of payments accompanying higher levels of production and employment, even when prices are generally stable. But these increases must be moderated so that they do not directly or indirectly contribute to the erosion of purchasing power.

The specific goals of monetary policy in particular situations and the best means for achieving them must be determined on the basis of long experience and a deep understanding of economic and financial developments at home and abroad. Experts may well differ on paramount short-term objectives, methods, and timing, especially since a wide variety of national interests have to be taken into account; but there should be no difference of opinion as to the unworkability of a policy of forcing interest rates to artificially low levels and keeping them there. Such a policy would be self-defeating, leading eventually to unbridled inflation or to a network of direct controls of wages, prices, and the use of credit.

Another factor bearing on the maintenance of price stability for sound economic growth is the control of unit production costs —a responsibility that in our free society rests primarily with private individuals and groups. An important aspect of cost control is the achievement and maintenance of a proper relationship between wage and productivity changes in the economy as a whole. In general, if average increases in wages and salaries are inconsistent, over the long run, with average improvements in productivity,

prices may be expected to trend upward. Wage settlements negotiated by management and labor should not preclude price reductions in parts of the economy where productivity rises especially
rapidly. High wages provide a dependable source of increased economic demand only to the extent that they are justified by productivity performance. In the last analysis, the only way to assure
that, for the economy as a whole, maximum employment and
maximum employment and maximum production also mean maximum purchasing power is to keep wage improvements generally
within the range of productivity advance.

The prolonged shutdown of the steel industry in the latter half
of 1959 emphasizes another important implication of labor-management negotiations. Failure to achieve prompt, as well as reasonable and realistic, settlements of outstanding differences can lead to
imbalances in production rates and inventories. These imbalances,
and the attendant uncertainties and disappointments of expectations, can have a harmful effect on economic stability and on the
general level of employment. It is important for labor and management to conduct their negotiations and settle their differences in
a responsible manner and thus avoid inviting new Government
controls and new limitations on their initiative.

The maintenance of price stability is significantly affected also
by Government price and income support policies for agriculture.
In this area, policies that would raise consumer food prices and
tend to increase production costs through compensating wage
adjustments must be avoided. [Pp. 58–59.]

JANUARY, 1962

PRICE BEHAVIOR IN A FREE AND
GROWING ECONOMY

THE OBJECTIVES

Price behavior embraces both changes in the over-all
level of prices throughout the economy and changes in price *structure*—the relation of particular prices to each other. Changes in
either the level or the structure of prices have far-reaching influ-

ences which can affect for better or worse the performance of a free economy. Both aspects of price behavior are closely related to major problems which confront the U.S. economy today. . . .

Large potential gains in national economic welfare are at stake in the course of price developments over the next year or two. Stable prices—together with the many other measures to strengthen our payments position discussed in Chapter 3—will move us toward equilibrium in our international payments. This, in turn, will remove a possible impediment to the vigorous pursuit of full employment. . . .

Price level stability does not, of course, require stability of all prices. On the contrary, the structure of relative prices constitutes the central nervous system of a decentralized economy. Changing relative prices are the signals and stimuli which foster the efficiency and guide the growth of such an economy. . . .

In the context of current economic policy goals, flexible relative prices play an important role in encouraging maximum production and shaping the pattern of growth. As the economy approaches full utilization of productive resources, premature and stubborn bottlenecks may arise in some sectors while labor and capital are underutilized elsewhere. This danger is lessened if productive resources are sufficiently mobile to shift promptly into the sectors of the economy which are coming under pressure. Flexible price and wage relationships are not in themselves sufficient to assure that capital and labor will flow from relatively declining to relatively expanding sectors. But flexible price and wage relationships can smooth the process, both by signaling the directions in which resource movements should occur, and by providing incentives to encourage such shifts. Prices must fall as well as rise, however, if changing relative prices are to play their role in guiding resource movements without forcing a steady rise in the over-all level of prices. [Pp. 167–69.]

This was the first of the four postwar recoveries in which wholesale industrial prices fell during the first 10 months of recovery.

Recent wage changes have been consistent with these price developments. As indicated earlier, annual wage increases in manufacturing have been declining for several years. The index of wage and salary costs per unit of output in manufacturing changed little from the cyclical peak in July 1957 to the peak in May 1960; by contrast, there were substantial peak-to-peak increases from 1948 to 1953 and from 1953 to 1957.

Such encouragement as may be derived from these recent price and wage trends must be tempered by the realization that they do not provide full protection for fixed-income recipients, and relate mainly to a period characterized by excess unemployment and productive capacity. The U.S. economy last experienced full employment in the first half of 1957; the recovery of 1958–60 stopped well short of full employment. While some significance can be attached to the fact that adjusted hourly earnings in manufacturing increased slightly less in 1959, a year of recovery, than in 1958, a cyclical trough year, and from the further fact that wholesale industrial prices fell during the 1961 recovery, the behavior of wages and prices in a period of sustained slack is an insufficient basis for inferences about price-wage behavior when the economy is moving up toward full employment. . . .

Developments in the steel industry in 1961 were propitious for the continuation of price stability. Steel prices at the end of the year were slightly below the level of the end of 1958. This was a striking shift in trend for an industry in which prices had risen at the average rate of 5.8 per cent a year from 1940 to 1958.

In early 1960, the steel industry, after a long strike, reached a wage settlement with the Steelworkers Union which provided for an estimated 3.7 per cent annual increase in employment cost per worker. Though still somewhat above the over-all trend rate of productivity increase, this was a considerably smaller settlement than the 1956 contract, the cost of which was estimated at 8 per cent a year.

Under the 1960 contract, a wage increase was scheduled to take effect on October 1, 1961. Confronted on one side with increasing foreign competition, stronger rivalry with substitutes, and intra-industry price shading, and on the other with an increase in wage rates, steel companies were reported in the press to be weighing the desirability of an October 1 price increase. In this setting, the President on September 6 addressed a letter to the heads of the 12 largest steel companies. Urging them to preserve price stability, the President stressed the damaging impact of a steel price increase on the balance of payments. "Steel is a bellwether," he said, "as well as a major element in industrial costs. A rise in steel prices would force price increases in many industries and invite price increases in others."

The President said:

> In emphasizing the vital importance of steel prices to the strength of our economy, I do not wish to minimize the urgency of preventing inflationary movements in steel wages. I recognize, too, that the steel industry, by absorbing increases in employment costs since 1958, has demonstrated a will to halt the price-wage spiral in steel. If the industry were now to forego a price increase, it would enter collective bargaining negotiations next spring with a record of three and a half years of price stability. It would clearly then be the turn of the labor representatives to limit wage demands to a level consistent with continued price stability. The moral position of the steel industry next spring—and its claim to the support of public opinion—will be strengthened by the exercise of price restraint now.

A week later, the President addressed a letter to the President of the United Steelworkers of America. Referring to the forthcoming collective bargaining negotiations, the President urged "a labor settlement within the limits of advances in productivity and price stability." The President expressed his confidence that "we can rely upon the leadership and members of the Steelworkers Union to act responsibly in the wage negotiations next year in the interests of all of the American people." . . .

POLICIES AFFECTING PRICE BEHAVIOR

THE SETTING

The over-all stability of prices should be achieved in a manner consistent with the flexible response of individual prices and wage rates to changes in cost and demand within an environment of dynamic competition. Thus, government policies to promote price stability must work to maintain and increase the freedom of the private economy, not to limit it. In peacetime, attempts to stabilize prices through the imposition of direct wage and price controls or through interference with the rights of employees to organize and bargain collectively are unacceptable. Also unacceptable are policies which pursue price stability without regard for the effects on employment, production, and purchasing power. Prices might be stabilized in an underemployed economy; but to accept heavy unemployment and persistent slack as the necessary cost of price stability is to undermine the vitality and flexibility of the economy and to reduce American strength. . . .

GUIDEPOSTS FOR NONINFLATIONARY WAGE AND PRICE BEHAVIOR

There are important segments of the economy where firms are large or employees well-organized, or both. In these sectors, private parties may exercise considerable discretion over the terms of wage bargains and price decisions. Thus, at least in the short run, there is considerable room for the exercise of private power and a parallel need for the assumption of private responsibility.

Individual wage and price decisions assume national importance when they involve large numbers of workers and large amounts of output directly, or when they are regarded by large segments of the economy as setting a pattern. Because such decisions affect the progress of the whole economy, there is legitimate reason for public interest in their content and consequences. An informed public, aware of the significance of major wage bargains and price decisions, and equipped to judge for itself their compatibility with the national interest, can help to create an atmosphere in which the parties to such decisions will exercise their powers responsibly.

How is the public to judge whether a particular wage-price decision is in the national interest? No simple test exists, and it is not possible to set out systematically all of the many considerations which bear on such a judgment. However, since the question is of prime importance to the strength and progress of the American economy, it deserves widespread public discussion and clarification of the issues. What follows is intended as a contribution to such a discussion.

Mandatory controls in peacetime over the outcomes of wage negotiations and over individual price decisions are neither desirable in the American tradition nor practical in a diffuse and decentralized continental economy. Free collective bargaining is the vehicle for the achievement of contractual agreements on wages, fringes, and working conditions, as well as on the "web of rules" by which a large segment of industry governs the performance of work and the distribution of rewards. Similarly, final price decisions lie—and should continue to lie—in the hands of individual firms. It is, however, both desirable and practical that discretionary decisions on wages and prices recognize the national interest in the results. The guideposts suggested here as aids to public understanding are not concerned primarily with the relation of employers and employees to each other, but rather with their joint relation to the rest of the economy.

Wages, prices, and productivity. If all prices remain stable, all hourly labor costs may increase as fast as economy-wide productivity without, for that reason alone, changing the relative share of labor and nonlabor incomes in total output. At the same time, each kind of income increases steadily in absolute amount. If hourly labor costs increase at a slower rate than productivity, the share of nonlabor incomes will grow or prices will fall, or both. Conversely, if hourly labor costs increase more rapidly than productivity, the share of labor incomes in the total product will increase or prices will rise, or both. It is this relationship among long-run economy-wide productivity, wages, and prices which makes the rate of productivity change an important benchmark for noninflationary wage and price behavior.

Productivity is a *guide* rather than a *rule* for appraising wage and price behavior for several reasons. First, there are a number of problems involved in measuring productivity change, and a number of alternative measures are available. Second, there is nothing immutable in fact or in justice about the distribution of the total product between labor and nonlabor incomes. Third, the pattern of wages and prices among industries is and should be responsive to forces other than changes in productivity.

Alternative measures of productivity. If the rate of growth of productivity over time is to serve as a useful benchmark for wage and price behavior, there must be some meeting of minds about the appropriate methods of measuring the trend rate of increase in productivity, both for industry as a whole and for individual industries. This is a large and complex subject and there is much still to be learned. The most that can be done at present is to give some indication of orders of magnitude, and of the range within which most plausible measures are likely to fall (Table 26).

There are a number of conceptual problems in connection with productivity measurement which can give rise to differences in estimates of its rate of growth. Three important conceptual problems are the following:

(1) Over what time interval should productivity trends be measured? Very short intervals may give excessive weight to business-cycle movements in productivity, which are not the relevant standards for wage behavior. The erratic nature of year-to-year changes in productivity is shown in Chart 14. Very long intervals may hide significant breaks in trends; indeed in the United States—and in other countries as well—productivity appears to have risen more rapidly since the end of the second World War than before. It would be wholly inappropriate for wage behavior in the 1960's to be governed by events long in the past. On the other hand, productivity in the total private economy appears to have advanced less rapidly in the second half of the postwar period than in the first.

(2) Even for periods of intermediate length, it is desirable to segregate the trend movements in productivity from those that reflect business-cycle forces. Where the basic statistical materials are available, this problem can be handled by an analytical separation of trend effects and the effects of changes in the rate of capacity utilization.

(3) Even apart from such difficulties, there often exist alternative statistical measures of output and labor input. The alternatives may differ conceptually or may simply be derived from different statistical sources. A difficult problem of choice may emerge, unless the alternative measures happen to give similar results.

Selected measures of the rate of growth of productivity in different sectors of the economy for different time periods are shown in Table 26. Several measures are given because none of the single figures is clearly superior for all purposes.

The share of labor income. The proportions in which labor and nonlabor incomes share the product of industry have not been immutable throughout American history, nor can they be expected to stand forever where they are today. It is desirable that labor and management should bargain explicitly about the distribution of the income of particular firms or industries. It is, however, undesirable that they should bargain implicitly about the general price level. Excessive wage settlements which are paid for through price increases in major industries put direct pressure on the general price level and produce spillover and imitative effects throughout the economy. Such settlements may fail to redistribute income within the industry involved; rather they redistribute income between that industry and other segments of the economy through the mechanism of inflation.

Prices and wages in individual industries. What are the guideposts which may be used in judging whether a particular price or wage decision may be inflationary? The desired objective is a stable price level, within which particular prices rise, fall, or remain stable in response to economic pressures. Hence, price stability within any particular industry is not necessarily a correct guide to price and wage decisions in that industry. It is possible, however, to describe in broad outline a set of guides which, if followed, would preserve over-all price stability while still allowing sufficient flexibility to accommodate objectives of efficiency and equity. These are not arbitrary guides. They describe—briefly and no doubt incompletely—how prices and wage rates would behave in a smoothly functioning competitive economy operating near full employment. Nor do they constitute a mechanical formula for determining whether a particular price or wage decision is inflationary. They will serve their purpose if they suggest to the interested public a useful way of approaching the appraisal of such a decision.

If, as a point of departure, we assume no change in the relative shares of labor and nonlabor incomes in a particular industry, then a general guide may be advanced for noninflationary wage behavior, and another for noninflationary price behavior. Both guides, as will be seen, are only first approximations.

The general guide for noninflationary wage behavior is that the rate of increase in wage rates (including fringe benefits) in each industry be equal to the trend rate of over-all productivity increase. General acceptance of this guide would maintain stability of labor cost per unit of output for the economy as a whole—though not of course for individual industries.

The general guide for noninflationary price behavior calls for price reduction if the industry's rate of productivity increase exceeds the over-all rate—for this would mean declining unit labor costs; it calls for an appropriate increase in price if the opposite relationship prevails; and it calls for stable prices if the two rates of productivity increase are equal.

These are advanced as general guideposts. To reconcile them with objectives of equity and efficiency, specific modifications must be made to adapt them to the circumstances of particular industries. If all of these modifications are made, each in the specific circumstances to which it applies, they are consistent with stability of the general price level. Public judgments about the effects on the price level of particular wage or price decisions should take into account the modifications as well as the general guides. The most important modifications are the following:

(1) Wage rate increases would exceed the general guide rate in an industry which would otherwise be unable to attract sufficient labor; or in which wage rates are exceptionally low compared with the range of wages earned elsewhere by similar labor, because the bargaining position of workers has been weak in particular local labor markets.

(2) Wage rate increases would fall short of the general guide rate in an industry which could not provide jobs for its entire labor force even in times of generally full employment; or in which wage rates are exceptionally high compared with the range of wages earned elsewhere by similar labor, because the bargaining position of workers has been especially strong.

(3) Prices would rise more rapidly, or fall more slowly, than indicated by the general guide rate in an industry in which the level of profits was insufficient to attract the capital required to finance a needed expansion in capacity; or in which costs other than labor costs had risen.

(4) Prices would rise more slowly, or fall more rapidly, than indicated by the general guide in an industry in which the relation of productive capacity to full employment demand shows the desirability of an outflow of capital from the industry; or in which costs other than labor costs have fallen; or in which excessive market power has resulted in rates of profit substantially higher than those earned elsewhere on investments of comparable risk.

It is a measure of the difficulty of the problem that even these complex guideposts leave out of account several important considerations. Although output per man-hour rises mainly in response to improvements in the quantity and quality of capital goods with which employees are equipped, employees are often able to improve their performance by means within their own control. It is obviously in the public interest that incentives be preserved which would reward employees for such efforts.

Also, in connection with the use of measures of over-all productivity gain as benchmarks for wage increases, it must be borne in mind that average hourly labor costs often change through the process of up- or down-grading, shifts between wage and salaried employment, and other forces. Such changes may either add to or subtract from the increment which is available for wage increases under the over-all productivity guide.

Finally, it must be reiterated that collective bargaining within an industry over the division of the proceeds between labor and non-labor income is not necessarily disruptive of over-all price stability. The relative shares can change within the bounds of noninflationary price behavior. But when a disagreement between management and labor is resolved by passing the bill to the rest of the economy, the bill is paid in depreciated currency to the ultimate advantage of no one.

It is no accident that productivity is the central guidepost for wage settlements. Ultimately, it is rising output per man hour which must yield the ingredients of a rising standard of living. Growth in productivity makes it possible for real wages and real profits to rise side by side.

Rising productivity is the foundation of the country's leadership of the free world, enabling it to earn in world competition the means to discharge its commitments overseas. Rapid advance of productivity is the key to stability of the price level as money incomes rise, to fundamental improvement in the balance of international payments, and to growth in the Nation's capacity to meet the challenges of the 1960's at home and abroad. That is why policy to accelerate economic growth stresses investments in science and technology, plant and equipment, education and training—the basic sources of future gains in productivity. [Pp. 180–90.]

January, 1963

WAGE AND PRICE "GUIDEPOSTS"

To aid public understanding, the 1962 Economic Report concluded (Pp. 185–90) with a set of "guideposts for noninflationary wage and price behavior." These guideposts were designed to provide standards for evaluating those price and wage decisions where the public has an interest in their content and consequences. They cannot, and should not, replace the normal processes of free private decisions and negotiations.

As the margin of unemployed labor and idle capital narrows, and as markets for goods and services become tighter, the guideposts will gain in importance. They are restated here in the belief that an enlightened public understanding of the nature and causes of inflation would be an additional force minimizing any inflationary threats in the years ahead.

The guideposts themselves involve *general* guides for noninflationary wage and price behavior, subject, in each case, to a number of important and specific *qualifications* required by the objectives of equity and efficiency.

The general guide for wages is that "the rate of increase in wage rates (including fringe benefits) in each industry be equal to the trend rate of over-all productivity increase." Under these conditions the gain from increases in productivity throughout the economy would be shared between wage and nonwage incomes by allowing each to grow at the same percentage rate. Each sector of economic life would share in the gains of advancing productivity. The qualifications call for faster increases in wage rates in an industry that (2) would otherwise be unable to attract sufficient labor to meet demands for its products, or (b) currently pays wage rates exceptionally low compared with those earned elsewhere by labor of similar ability. Symmetrically, increases in wage rates would fall short of the general guide rate in an industry that (a) could not provide employment for its entire labor force even in generally prosperous times; or (b) currently pays wage rates exceptionally high compared with those earned elsewhere by labor of similar ability.

The general guide for prices is that prices should fall in an industry whose rate of productivity increase exceeds the over-all rate, rise in the opposite case, and remain stable if the two rates of productivity increase are equal. The qualifications call for a faster price increase or slower price decrease in an industry in which (a) the level of profits is insufficient to attract the capital required to meet expansion of demand, or (b) costs other than labor costs have risen. On the other hand, increases in price would be slower or decreases faster than indicated by the general guide in an industry in which (a) productive capacity exceeding full-employment demand shows an outflow of capital to be desirable, or (b) costs other than labor costs have fallen, or (c) excessive market power has resulted in rates of profit substantially higher than those earned elsewhere on investments of comparable risk. [Pp. 85–86.]

JANUARY, 1964

THE PRICE-WAGE SITUATION AND THE PROSPECTS

The impressive noninflationary record of this expansion thus far —the stability of wholesale prices and the slow upward movement of over-all consumer prices—has been reviewed in Chapter 1 and is portrayed in Chart 11. At the same time, as Tables 20 and 21 show, the price stability has not been "paid for" either by a failure of wages to keep up with the trend change in productivity in the economy as a whole or by a corporate profits squeeze. (In the tables, "trend change in productivity" for any given year is defined as the 5-year moving average of the annual percentage changes in the Bureau of Labor Statistics index of output per man-hour in the total private economy. These estimates use labor input data collected primarily by establishments.) While money wages have not risen as fast as in some earlier expansions, the gain in purchasing power has been eroded very little by price increases. And while over-all profits have continued to rise, this has been achieved without substantial price increases. In terms of the balance among wages, prices, and profits, the economy is in good position, as it enters 1964, to avoid inflationary price and wage decisions.

The price stability of 1961–63 has resulted in part from persistent slack in the economy. But another major factor has been the responsible action of most union and business leaders in making noninflationary wage and price decisions. Although shifting patterns of demand and supply are the major factors ruling prices, wages, and output in our market economy, there is considerable room for discretionary decision making in most major industries. In the past, wage and other cost increases, together with price decisions based on fixed markups or target-profit policies, have combined to push up prices. And price increases often have led to wage increases.

The postwar record, shown in Tables 20 and 21, indicates how the complex interaction of wage increases to catch up with prices, and price increases to preserve profit ratios, worked in ratchet fashion. The net result has been that prices have risen roughly in proportion to the difference between increases in labor compensation per man-hour and national trend productivity gains. In particular, the experience of the years 1956–58 shows that sharp price advances can occur in periods of increasing unused capacity and rising unemployment. The data do not establish causality. But clearly the collective bargaining power of unions and the market power of large firms can interact to inject an inflationary bias into our price-wage performance. [Pp. 112–14.]

ANTI-INFLATIONARY POLICIES FOR HIGH EMPLOYMENT

It is the business of responsible government to try to achieve the best possible balance among such major economic objectives as full employment, economic growth, reasonable price stability, and the promotion of economic freedom and opportunity. The importance of price stability as compared with the other goals is sometimes minimized. But there are compelling reasons why we can ill afford to neglect prices. . . .

GOVERNMENT ACTIONS

For its part, the Government will be striving energetically to reinforce one of the most significant comparative advantages that the American economy has over nearly all other industrialized nations—namely, a tradition and an institutional structure that nurture vigorous internal competition. . . .

Finally, as the economy's single largest buyer of goods and services, the Federal Government will redouble its efforts in 1964 to get full value for each dollar it spends.

PRIVATE DECISIONS AND THE PRICE-WAGE GUIDEPOSTS

Government policies can only provide an environment conducive to responsible private price and wage decision making. By choice, our Government can advise, inform, and bring to bear the pressure of public opinion—but it cannot direct.

With so much at stake, however, the Government's opportunity to advise and inform the public is one it must seize. In the Kennedy Administration, general advice as to the pattern of private price-wage decision making that would take account of the public's interest in avoiding market-power inflation was first formally set forth in the Economic Report of January 1962. The "guideposts" therein described—and repeated in the 1963 Report—offered standards by which union and business leaders themselves—along with the general public—could appraise particular wage and price decisions. They are restated here.

The guideposts contain two key propositions. The first—the general guideposts for wages—says that, in a particular firm or industry, the appropriate noninflationary standard for annual percentage increases in total employee compensation per man-hour (not just in straight-time hourly rates) is the annual increase in *national trend* output per man-hour. The standard is not the productivity trend in the particular firm or industry in question. Nor is it the particular year's productivity change, which can be influenced by short-run transitory factors.

The general guidepost for prices specifies that when an industry's trend productivity is growing less rapidly than the national trend, prices can appropriately rise enough to accommodate the labor cost increases indicated by the general wage guidepost. Similarly, in an industry whose trend productivity is growing more rapidly than the national average, product prices should be lowered enough to distribute to the industry's customers the labor-cost savings it would make under the general wage guidepost.

It should be emphasized that the general price guidepost does not counsel against price changes per se in a particular firm or industry. On the contrary, it contemplates changes in specific prices —downward in industries with high rates of productivity gain, as well as upward in industries with lower-than-average productivity gains.

Adherence to these general guideposts not only would make for over-all price stability but would be generally consistent with the tendencies of competitive labor and product markets. The principles established by the guideposts do not imply that the entire gains from productivity improvement should go either to labor or to capital. Rather, they suggest a proportionate sharing of average national productivity gains among labor, capital, and the other related factors of production throughout the economy.

The general guideposts can cover the vast majority of wage and price decisions, but cannot provide for all of the adjustments the economy requires, especially over an extended period. Hence, the guideposts, as originally expounded in 1962, appropriately included a set of exceptions that reflected certain considerations of equity and resource allocation. . . .

These modifications of the general guideposts still apply, but it must be emphasized that they are intended to apply to only a relatively few cases. Particularly at a time when our national capabilities for responsible price and wage making may undergo a more serious test than in recent years, the most constructive private policy in the great majority of situations would be to arrive at price decisions and wage bargains consistent with the general guideposts.

Two other comments on the guideposts seem appropriate this year. First, it is not the purpose of these advisory policies permanently to freeze the labor and nonlabor shares of total industrial income, as would a rigorous, unrelieved application of the general guideposts. The 1962 Report noted that "The proportions in which labor and nonlabor income shares the product of industry have not been immutable throughout history . . ." It went on to point out that bargaining over the shares is consistent with the guideposts if it is conducted "within the bounds of noninflationary price behavior." Specifically, this means that it is consistent with the guideposts for wage and profit shares to be bid up or down in a particular industry *so long as price behavior in that industry remains consistent with the general price guidepost indicated above.*

Second, it is appropriate to focus special attention this year on *price reductions.* The guideposts call for reductions in those industries whose trend productivity gains exceed the national trend. It is fair to say that large industrial enterprises thus far have not widely heeded this advice. And yet, as noted earlier, there will be ample room for such price reductions in 1964. If they are not forthcoming, over-all price stability will be rendered more difficult, since price increases are likely in industries that are progressing at a less-than-average rate. Moreover, in industries whose trend of productivity rises faster than the national average, if wages conform more nearly to national than to industry productivity trends (as the guideposts would have them do), failure to follow the general price guide will cause profits to pile up. Such profits become highly visible to the public and constitute a lure for strongly intensified wage demands.

Such circumstances pose a most unattractive dilemma from the viewpoint of the public interest. On the one hand, extra increases in wages or fringe benefits might tend to spread to other industries, creating a general cost-push from the wage side. On the other hand, there is no justification, on either economic or equity grounds, for distributing above-average gains in productivity exclusively through the profits channel. The real way out of this dilemma is for the firms involved to remove its cause by reducing prices. [Pp. 116–20.]

JANUARY, 1965

WAGES, PRICES, AND PRODUCTIVITY

Sustained economic expansion during the past four years was accompanied by a healthy balance among wages, prices, and productivity. Wholesale prices in 1964 averaged no higher than in 1960; consumer prices rose 1.2 per cent a year; the growth in productivity was fairly steady, averaging 3.5 per cent annually for the private economy; and wage gains kept up with, but did not outdistance, the trend in productivity. As a result, unit labor costs showed no general increase over the four-year period; income shares were free of distortions arising from inflation; and restrictive policies to curb an inflationary spiral were unnecessary. . . .

COMPARISON WITH PREVIOUS EXPANSIONS

The course of wages, prices, productivity, and unit labor costs for both total manufacturing and the total private economy in the years since the prerecession year of 1960 is compared in Chart 7 with movements in the two "peak-to-peak" periods—1953–57 and 1957–60. The upward surge of wages, unit labor costs, and prices in the final two years of the 1953–57 period and the steady climb of costs and prices during 1957–60 are in clear contrast to the stability of the past four years. (In measuring price movements for the total private economy and for manufacturing, the "implicit deflators" prepared for calculations of "real" GNP were used. These deflators do not move identically with the wholesale price index, but they are consistent with the output and compensation data that are used.)

The moderate gain of about 3.6 per cent a year in hourly compensation in the total private sector during the present expansion compares with an advance averaging 3.9 per cent a year in 1957–60 and 4.5 per cent in 1953–57.

The rise in output per man-hour from 1960 to 1964 was larger and more evenly sustained than in the previous two periods considered. Gains in output per man-hour in the private sector in 1960–64 averaged 3.5 per cent a year, compared with 2.5 in 1953–57 and 2.7 in 1957–60.

Strong gains in output and productivity typically take place during the recovery from a recession; they stimulate investment and extra hiring by business in anticipation of further gains in output. After the recoveries of 1955 and 1958, expected gains were not realized, the advance of productivity was retarded, unit labor costs were increased, and profits were squeezed. Especially in 1955–57, this helped to upset the balance among costs, prices, and income shares, and aggravated the wage-price spiral.

The better record of productivity performance during the past four years is in large measure the result of a sustained expansion of output that has kept operating rates moving upward. Total private output rose at an average annual rate of 4.1 per cent a year from 1960 to 1964, or about 1½ times the average rate of about 2.7 per cent during the two earlier periods considered. The difference in manufacturing is even more striking, with output gains averaging 4.8 per cent a year since 1960, compared with about 1¼ per cent a year in the two earlier periods.

The steady gains in productivity and the moderate wage increases have held unit labor costs practically unchanged in the total private economy during the past four years and have resulted in a slight net reduction in manufacturing labor costs. Similarly, the implicit price deflators have risen very little, as Chart 7 makes clear. . . .

Despite occasional exceptions—as in automobiles and construction—the general pattern of recent wage and price changes has closely approximated the Government's wage-price guideposts.

To be sure, the guideposts have not been completely effective either in simulating all warranted price reductions, or in preventing some individual wage and price increases that are not in accord

CHART 7

Compensation, Productivity, Unit Labor Costs, and Prices in Three Postwar Periods

PREVIOUS PEAK YEAR = 100[1]

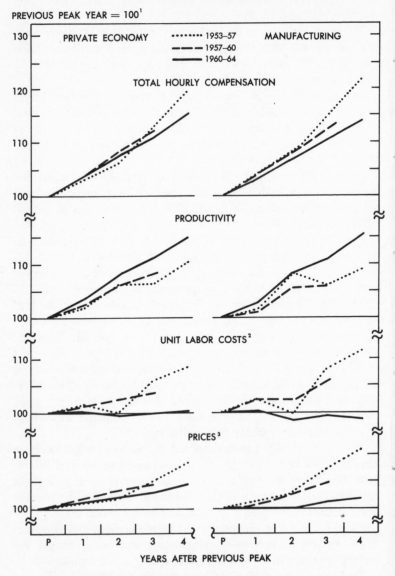

YEARS AFTER PREVIOUS PEAK

[1] PREVIOUS PEAK YEARS WERE 1953, 1957, AND 1960.

[2] RATIO OF TOTAL HOURLY COMPENSATION (FOR EMPLOYEE MAN-HOURS) TO PRO-
DUCTIVITY (FOR ALL MAN-HOURS).

[3] IMPLICIT DEFLATORS FOR THE TOTAL PRIVATE AND MANUFACTURING SECTORS OF
GROSS NATIONAL PRODUCT.

SOURCES: DEPARTMENT OF LABOR AND COUNCIL OF ECONOMIC ADVISERS.

with their criteria. Nevertheless, the very fact that representatives of both labor and management have often explicitly indicated their compliance with, or tried to justify any deviations from, the guidepost standards suggests that these standards have had a useful influence.

In addition to any direct influence that they may have had on the wage and price policies of unions and managements, the guideposts have helped to create a new climate of opinion. Many groups in our society now have a better understanding of the relationships between costs and prices. There is increasing realization that it is appropriate—indeed necessary—to consider whether a proposed course of action, if followed by others in similar circumstances, would be consistent with over-all stability. Decision makers in unions and managements are increasingly aware both of the fact that their decisions affect the public interest and of the fact that the public is interested in their decisions. [Pp. 54–59.]

WAGES, COSTS, AND PRICES

Maintaining essential price stability in 1965 must be a national objective of high priority. The record of price stability in recent years has made possible a substantial improvement in our ability to compete in world markets. This record has also contributed to a balanced advance and has kept fiscal and monetary policies free to be expansionary. Furthermore, price stability has promoted equity by preserving the purchasing power of people with fixed incomes and liquid assets. . . .

Because flexible and competitive market forces are not alone in affecting prices and wages, a modern economy needs new policies to reconcile the objectives of full employment and stable prices.

In one way or another virtually every advanced country has devised policies aimed at this reconciliation. Several nations have pursued such policies for many years. In December 1964, the United Kingdom launched a major new venture aimed at the cost problems which have contributed so much to her economic difficulties: leaders of business and labor signed a declaration of intent to pursue price, wage, production, and employment policies that will result in over-all price stability and an improved competitive position.

Because of differences among nations in political and economic systems, each country must find a solution appropriate to its own institutions. The U.S. economy is larger than the others and, as a result, many of our industries, including heavy industries requiring large scales of operation, are more competitive than in Western Europe or Japan. Major discretionary market power is found less frequently here, but it is found in important industries which have a wide and pervasive influence on prices and wages elsewhere through emulation and direct cost-push.

PRICE-WAGE GUIDEPOSTS

To deal with the problem of reconciliation—achieving noninflationary price and wage behavior under prosperous conditions—the Council's Annual Report in 1962 advanced the guideposts which were endorsed by President Kennedy and have been firmly restated by President Johnson. . . .

The guideposts are not meant to preclude the possibility of a change in distribution of income between labor and capital in industry. Where one side or the other is able to increase its share of industry income, but not at the expense of the public, the national interest need not be involved. However, it should be kept in mind that in most concentrated industries the division of income between labor and capital remained essentially unchanged all through the wage-price spirals of the 1950's. The repeated attempts to alter income shares proved self-defeating: neither side gained, and both lost through higher prices, weaker markets, reduced profits, and lower employment.

Table 12 illustrates the postwar experience with prices, wages, and productivity in the United States. Recent changes in employee compensation have conformed to productivity gains much more closely than in the 1950's, and price increases have been much more modest.

The guideposts offer a standard for responsible business, labor, and Government leadership in an environment of informed public opinion. They are an attempt to operate our economy as it is—without controls, without wholesale fragmentation of our large, successful enterprises—and to maintain stable prices while using our resources, our capital, and our labor to' their full potential. They are in the tradition of America, asking those to whom the society has entrusted economic power to exercise it in ways consistent with the national interest.

TABLE 12.

Changes in Productivity, Wages, and Prices in the
Private Economy Since 1947

Year	Productivity[1]	Trend productivity[1]	Total compensation per man-hour	Implicit GNP deflator	Wholesale	Consumer
				Prices		
1948	3.6	...	8.6	6.8	8.3	7.7
1949	2.8	..	2.5	−0.8	−5.0	−1.0
1950	7.1	..	5.7	1.2	4.0	1.0
1951	2.5	..	9.3	7.9	11.4	8.0
1952	2.2	3.7	5.9	1.6	−2.8	2.2
1953	4.0	3.7	5.8	0.6	−1.4	0.8
1954	1.8	3.5	3.3	0.8	0.2	0.4
1955	4.4	3.0	2.9	0.9	0.3	−0.3
1956	0.2	2.5	6.1	3.1	3.2	1.5
1957	3.5	2.8	5.9	3.5	2.9	3.5
1958	2.4	2.5	3.6	1.7	1.4	2.8
1959	3.6	2.8	4.6	1.6	0.2	0.8
1960	2.0	2.3	3.6	1.2	0.1	1.6
1961	3.4	3.0	3.6	1.0	−0.4	1.1
1962	4.5	3.2	4.0	0.7	0.3	1.2
1963	2.9	3.3	3.1	1.2	−0.3	1.2
1964	3.1	3.2	3.8	1.4	0.2	1.3

Large corporations and labor unions can—and generally do—use their power to play a constructive role in our economy. At the same time they must be accountable for their actions to public opinion, and must recognize that the public will ask "Why?"
    —when a union insists on a wage settlement that, if universally applied, would mar the price record of the economy;
    —when a firm or industry agrees willingly to a wage settlement above the guideposts which it then translates into higher prices for its products;

—when a firm or industry with extraordinary productivity gains
fails to share the benefits with consumers in the form of lower
prices;
—when a firm or industry with average productivity gains
chooses to raise its prices. [Pp. 107–10.]

January, 1966

Prospects for Cost-Price Stability

As the economy enters its sixth year of uninterrupted
expansion and its third successive year of high growth, the gap
between potential and actual production is fast disappearing.
Unemployment is near 4 per cent, and operating rates in many
industries are moving close to preferred rates. The past 5 years
have demonstrated that the economy can operate free of recurrent
recession. Now the United States is entering a period that will
test whether sustained full utilization of our human and physical
resources is possible without the injustice, dislocation, and decline
in competitive position that accompany inflation. . . .

Productivity gains are larger and more extended. Private attitudes in key wage and price decisions are considerably more
responsible. New competition from abroad reinforces keen domestic
competition for markets, and new policies of active manpower
development are permitting the fuller use of our human resources.
[P. 63.]

Labor Cost Trends

Labor costs per unit of output are an important determinant of
over-all cost and price changes. In the postwar period, their widely
varying movements have frequently been associated with similar
changes in the price level (Chart 10).

Labor costs per unit of output reflect both hourly compensation
and output per man-hour or productivity. Increases in compensation raise unit labor costs; increases in productivity lower it.
Whether labor costs per unit of output rise during the particular
period depends on the relative balance between increase of compensation and of productivity. . . .

CHART 10

Changes in Compensation, Prices, and Productivity in the Private Economy

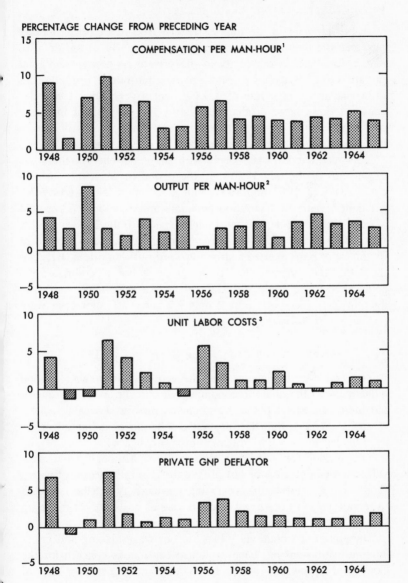

PERCENTAGE CHANGE FROM PRECEDING YEAR

COMPENSATION PER MAN-HOUR[1]

OUTPUT PER MAN-HOUR[2]

UNIT LABOR COSTS[3]

PRIVATE GNP DEFLATOR

[1] TOTAL COMPENSATION DIVIDED BY ALL PERSONS MAN-HOURS WORKED.

[2] PRIVATE GNP DIVIDED BY ALL PERSONS MAN-HOURS WORKED.

[3] COMPENSATION PER MAN-HOUR DIVIDED BY OUTPUT PER MAN-HOUR.

SOURCES: DEPARTMENT OF LABOR, DEPARTMENT OF COMMERCE, AND COUNCIL OF ECONOMIC ADVISERS.

PRODUCTIVITY AND UNIT LABOR COSTS

A key element in the impressive U.S. record of price stability has been the high rate of productivity advance. Based on tentative figures for 1965, productivity in the private economy (real total private GNP divided by total private man-hours worked) has grown at an average rate of 3.6 per cent a year since 1960. Because of these large productivity gains, average annual increases of 4.2 per cent in compensation per man-hour have raised average unit labor costs in the private economy by only 0.6 per cent a year.

This record contrasts sharply with the experience in the short expansions of the mid-1950's. In the period between the business cycle peaks of 1953 and 1957, unit labor costs increased by 2.1 per cent a year; compensation per man-hour rose by 4.6 per cent a year while output per man-hour advanced only 2.4 per cent a year. In 1956 and 1957, an average annual increase of 4.5 per cent in unit labor costs exerted a strong upward push on prices. Between the 1957 and 1960 cyclical peaks, average hourly compensation gains were more moderate—4.2 per cent a year—but since productivity was rising at a rate of only 2.7 per cent, labor costs were pushed up by 1.4 per cent a year. [Pp. 76–79.]

OUTLOOK FOR COST-PRICE STABILITY IN 1966

The above review shows that the economy is making a good adjustment to the altered economic environment. With the unemployment rate at 4.1 per cent and clearly moving downward, there is strong evidence that the substantial inflation of industrial prices experienced in the mid-1950's is not recurring.

The outlook for unit labor costs is good. Although a few individual settlements may be out of line, the general advance of wages should not accelerate this year, and productivity can be expected to remain close to the trend rate. So long as costs do not move up substantially, price changes will remain limited. . . .

The apparent "inflationary bias" in our wage-making and price-making institutions has been of almost continuous concern for the Council of Economic Advisers for many years. Appeals for responsibility and moderation—for taking the public interest into account in wage and price decisions—have had a perennial place in successive Economic Reports. In its Annual Report of January 1962, the Council for the first time attempted to provide private decision-makers with rather more specific standards for judging whether their decisions were responsible and took adequate account of the public interest. These standards or "guideposts" were also designed to permit the public to reach its own conclusions concerning the degree of responsibility exercised by leaders of business and labor.

INCREASING IMPORTANCE OF THE GUIDEPOSTS

In the years since 1962, the guideposts have gained increasing significance. The slow and difficult progress in restoring equilibrium in our international balance of payments has underlined the necessity that American goods retain or improve their competitive position in export markets and in our own market. Our goal of balance of payments equilibrium in 1966 and thereafter will permit no retreat from cost-price stability.

During the recent years of still excessive unemployment and idle capacity, strong competition for jobs and markets reinforced a growing sense of responsibility on the part of labor and management. The fuller use of resources achieved last year and the excellent prospects for 1966 may reduce that reinforcement. We now confront the task of reconciling full employment with stable prices.

The record reviewed in previous sections of this chapter makes it clear that the overwhelming majority of private wage and price decisions in recent years has been consistent with the guideposts, whatever the extent to which the guideposts may have consciously entered into the decisions reached. It is clear, however, that in many instances the guideposts have consciously affected these decisions. On numerous occasions, Government officials have specifically reminded unions or managements of the guidepost standards —either publicly or privately, either generally or with reference to specific situations. Several of the more important of these situations have attracted considerable public attention.

In January 1965, the President requested the Council of Economic Advisers to prepare an analysis of steel prices, following certain increases in such prices and at a time when important wage negotiations were pending. The Report, made public in early May, analyzed the position of the industry and the factors affecting it. It showed that wage and price decisions consistent with the guideposts would be in the interest of both labor and management and of the Nation. Later, the Government helped the two parties to reach a peaceful settlement in the steel wage negotiations. A damaging strike was avoided, and a settlement was achieved within the wage guideposts. According to the best estimates of its cost available to the Government, the settlement averaged 3.2 per cent a year, computed over the full 39-month period.

Following the labor settlement, prices on tin plate were raised in October; this was accompanied by a price reduction on a new black plate, which is expected to substitute increasingly for tin plate in many uses. At the year's end, the Bethlehem Steel Company announced a $5 a ton increase on structural steel and pilings. The Council pointed out that such an increase was not justified under the guideposts. In January, the U.S. Steel Corporation announced a smaller increase, accompanying it with price reductions on other steel products.

In October, the Council prepared a guidepost analysis of price increases initiated by producers of primary aluminum; the companies later rescinded these increases.

Also in October, the President, by threatening a veto, persuaded the Congress to enact a pay increase for civil service and postal employees of the Federal Government which was within the guideposts.

These actions and many others clearly reaffirmed the Administration's strong commitment to the guideposts as an essential pillar for price stability. . . .

EXCEPTIONS TO THE GENERAL GUIDEPOSTS

Some exceptions to the general guideposts are necessary to promote economic objectives. Wage increases above the general guideposts may be desirable

—where wage rates are inadequate for an industry to attract its share of the labor force necessary to meet the demands for its products;

—where wages are particularly low—that is, near the bottom of the economy's wage scales; or

—where changes in work rules create large gains in productivity and substantial human costs requiring special adjustment of compensation.

Because the industries in which unions possess strong market power are largely high-wage industries in which job opportunities are relatively very attractive, the first two of these exceptions are rarely applicable.

On the price side, increases in price above the general guidepost standard may occasionally be appropriate

   —to reflect increases in unit material costs, to the extent that such increases are not offset by decreases in other costs and significantly impair gross profit margins on the relevant range of products, or

   —to correct an inability to attract needed capital.

The large firms to which guideposts are primarily addressed typically have ready access to sources of capital; moreover, the profits of virtually every industry have risen sharply and are at record levels as a byproduct of the general prosperity in the economy. The second exception is thus not widely applicable in the present environment.

SHORT-RUN AND TREND ELEMENTS IN PRODUCTIVITY
AND THE GENERAL WAGE GUIDEPOSTS

In the original discussion of the guideposts in the Council's Annual Report of 1962, it was pointed out that, "it is desirable to segregate the trend movements in productivity from those that reflect business-cycle forces." During the last 5 years, the economy has been closing a substantial gap between actual and potential production. This has augmented the yearly productivity gain beyond the long-term sustainable trend. Now that the economy has little gap remaining to close, the trend of productivity gains will be determined only by capital investment, an improving labor force, and technological progress. The temporarily high productivity gains that come from utilizing equipment and manpower more efficiently through higher operating rates are largely behind us.

To assure future stability of unit labor costs, wages should increase no faster than the sustainable trend of productivity.

The original formulation of the guideposts did not specify any particular trend productivity figure, but rather listed various historical averages, covering different time spans and various segments of the economy. Since the economy was just recovering from the second of two recessions in a very short interval, it was difficult to identify the trend productivity rate from the immediately preceding experience. This difficulty was compounded by speculation that the trend rate might be accelerating as a result of faster technological change, particularly the spread of automation.

In the Report of 1964, no single figure for trend productivity was specified, but in a related table the now well-known 3.2 per cent appeared as the latest figure in a column labelled "Trend productivity." The figures in that column were described as the "annual average percentage change in output per man-hour during the latest 5 years." A 5-year period was chosen because, at that time, it was sufficiently long to include both the extraordinarily high productivity gains of a year of recovery (1962) and the extraordinarily low productivity gains of a year of recession (1960). Under the conditions of 1964, a 5-year average gave a good approximation of the trend productivity, because, in effect, it averaged out the ups and downs of cyclical productivity swings. These same conditions prevailed in 1964, and the 3.2 per cent figure appeared for that year in a similar table in the 1965 Report. Subsequent revisions of GNP data would have made the 5-year average 3.4 per cent in both 1964 and 1965.

Now that the economy is at the end of its fifth year of uninterrupted expansion, a 5-year average no longer gives a reasonable approximation of the true productivity trend. The last recession year drops out of the average, yet the unsustainable productivity gains of a year of recovery and 4 years of improving utilization are retained. If use of the 5-year average were continued this year and in coming years, the figure yielded by the 5-year moving average would rise at this time to 3.6 per cent and would undoubtedly fall substantially thereafter.

An analysis of recent productivity movements was presented earlier in this chapter. It is clear from this analysis that 3.6 per cent would not be an accurate measure of the true trend of productivity. Rather, it appears that the long-term trend, independent of cyclical swings, is slightly over 3 per cent.

For 1966, the Council specifically recommends that the general guidepost for wages of 3.2 per cent a year be continued. We make this recommendation in the light of the following additional considerations:

(1) With the economy approaching full employment and the crucial test of our ability to reconcile our employment and our cost-price goals at hand, it would be inappropriate to raise the guidepost.

(2) The actual productivity gain that can be expected over the next few years is not likely to be above the trend value.

(3) The 3.2 per cent rate has been consistent with the approxi-

mate stability of industrial wholesale prices which has strengthened our competitive position in the world. Now is not the time to abandon that standard.

(4) On January 1, employer payroll taxes to finance social security and Medicare rose substantially, raising labor costs per hour by an average of two-thirds of a per cent. These taxes are not included in the definition of employee compensation for purposes of the guideposts, since the rates and the benefits are determined by law rather than by collective bargaining. Nonetheless, recognition has to be taken of the extraordinary increase in these taxes at this time, which will both raise unit labor costs and yield future benefits to employees.

GUIDEPOST POLICY ON PRICES

The guideposts must continue to aim at complete stability of average domestic prices. While individual prices will rise from time to time, others must fall if upward pressure on the general price level is to be avoided. To achieve that goal in a fully employed economy will require that unions refrain from insistence on irresponsible wage settlements and an even greater willingness by management to take the public interest fully into account in its pricing decisions. Every management with some market power must ask itself: Is a price increase justified by increases in costs? Or is it an attempt to take advantage of prosperity to widen profit margins? Those companies that incur rising costs for materials or purchased services must see if these cannot be absorbed from lowered costs elsewhere in their operations. And those companies with exceptionally favorable productivity gains must consider whether this is the time to seek to keep the gains in the form of still higher profits, or whether to share them with consumers through lower prices. Unions which are in a favorable bargaining situation must remember that wage increases that force employers to raise prices will be paid for by the workers in other industries.

Both unions and managements should reflect on the fact that if their actions create an inflationary spiral, the most likely outcome will be restrictive fiscal and monetary policies which will aim to stop further price increases but will in the process also reduce output, cut back profits, and reduce employment. [Pp. 87–93]

Appendix B

SELECTED MATERIALS ON GUIDELINES FOR BANK CREDITS AND INVESTMENT ABROAD

Excerpts from the Annual Report of the Council of Economic Advisers accompanying the Economic Report of the President, 1966
The selective measures to contain private capital outflow are reviewed together with the programs for financial institutions.

U.S. DIRECT INVESTMENTS ABROAD

The March, 1965, Statement of the Secretary of Commerce
An appeal to American industry—a voluntary program. An average improvement in balance of payments terms of 15–20 per cent over the 1964 results is indicated as a target.

The December, 1965, Statement of the Secretary of Commerce
A renewed appeal to industry expanding the geographic coverage and increasing the number of cooperating companies. The new target limits direct investment during the two-year period 1965–66 combined to 90 per cent of the amount during the three-year period 1962–64. It is also asked that investment in Canada be moderated.

CREDIT RESTRAINT PROGRAM FOR FINANCIAL INSTITUTIONS

The March, 1964, Statement to the Federal Reserve Board on the Voluntary Credit Restraint Program for Financial Institutions

The December, 1965, Statement to the Federal Reserve Board on the Voluntary Program for Financial Institutions

EXCERPTS FROM THE ANNUAL REPORT OF THE COUNCIL OF ECONOMIC ADVISERS ACCOMPANYING THE ECONOMIC REPORT OF THE PRESIDENT

JANUARY, 1966

U.S. BALANCE OF PAYMENTS

The U.S. balance of payments moved significantly closer to equilibrium in 1965. In considerable part, this reflected the effects of the President's program announced in February. The improvement was primarily manifested in a substantially reduced outflow of private capital, which more than offset a drop in the trade surplus. . . .

CHART 12   U.S. Balance of International Payments

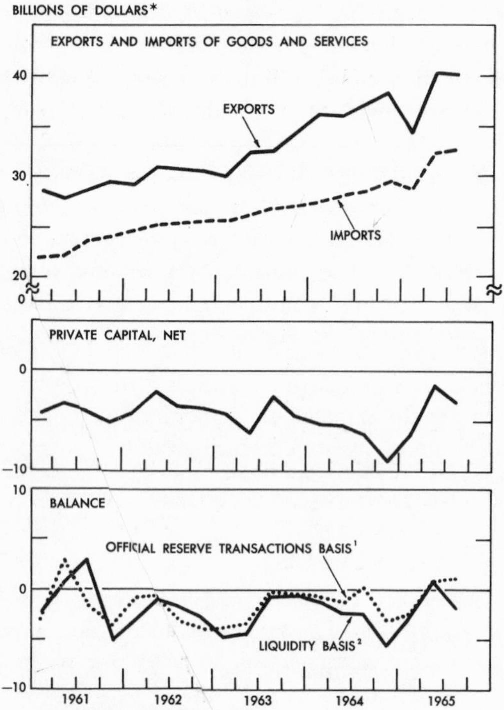

BILLIONS OF DOLLARS*

* SEASONALLY ADJUSTED ANNUAL RATES.

[1] EQUALS CHANGES IN LIQUID AND NONLIQUID LIABILITIES TO FOREIGN OFFICIAL HOLDERS AND CHANGES IN OFFICIAL RESERVE ASSETS CONSISTING OF GOLD, CONVERTIBLE CURRENCIES, AND THE U.S. GOLD TRANCHE POSITION IN THE IMF.

[2] EQUALS CHANGES IN LIQUID LIABILITIES TO FOREIGN OFFICIAL HOLDERS, OTHER FOREIGN HOLDERS, AND CHANGES IN OFFICIAL RESERVE ASSETS CONSISTING OF GOLD, CONVERTIBLE CURRENCIES, AND THE U.S. GOLD TRANCHE POSITION IN THE IMF.

SOURCE: DEPARTMENT OF COMMERCE.

GROWTH OF PRIVATE CAPITAL OUTFLOWS

The outflow of U.S. private capital rose from $3.9 billion in 1960 to $6.5 billion in 1964. Through this outflow, the United States was acquiring a large volume of foreign assets and adding rapidly to its net international ownership position as well as to its future receipts of interest, dividends, and remitted profits. But the assets acquired through this investment were largely illiquid, and were obtained by parting with liquid assets that added to both private and official claims against us. The U.S. reserve position declined continually.

The growth of U.S. private capital outflow is not difficult to explain. As market integration has progressed and as individuals and businesses have become increasingly familiar with international financial operations, there has been a natural tendency for capital to become more mobile, and more responsive to market forces.

U.S. corporations have shown an increasing interest in business operations overseas and have been sending a rising flow of funds abroad to build and equip new plants and distribution facilities. The extremely rapid growth of incomes, particularly in Europe, Canada, and Japan, has greatly expanded consumer demand, especially for manufactured goods. Wage rates generally are lower abroad, and when American management and technology are exported the productivity of foreign labor is frequently brought close to the U.S. level, making American enterprises in other countries often extremely profitable. The virtual disappearance of internal tariffs in the EEC and EFTA, while external tariffs are retained, has created a large and expanding market which can be readily served by large-scale production in Europe. Of course, direct investment abroad is also made for the purpose of developing or expanding sources of raw materials, often for use in the firm's operations in the United States or elsewhere.

With few exceptions, U.S. money and capital markets are much better developed and freer from restrictions than those abroad, and this attracts foreign borrowers. In part because of this better organization, interest rates and flotation costs are considerably lower in this country. Consequently, there is a tendency for foreigners seeking capital to look to U.S. markets and for interest-sensitive funds to move abroad in search of higher returns.

Long-standing interest rate differentials, and the growing mobility of capital, were important factors in the spurt of long-term portfolio lending that occurred in 1962 and 1963. New foreign security issues in the U.S. market doubled from 1961 to 1962, and the acceleration continued in early 1963. This growth was arrested by the introduction in mid-1963 of the Interest Equalization Tax (IET), which raised the effective interest rate for most foreign borrowing here. Meanwhile, other capital flows began to accelerate, offsetting much or all of the gains from the IET. Bank loans rose sharply, from $1.5 billion in 1963 to $2.5 billion in 1964. Direct U.S. investment abroad also accelerated in 1963 and 1964.

THE FEBRUARY 1965 PROGRAM

At the beginning of 1965, it was evident that the rapid rise in capital outflows was creating growing problems for the U.S. balance of payments. Accordingly, the program announced by the President on February 10 applied the IET to most bank loans with a duration of a year or more to borrowers in developed countries, asked for a 2-year extension of the IET, and attempted in other ways to stem the outflow of private capital through the voluntary cooperation of American business.

U.S. banks and other financial institutions were asked to observe appropriate "guidelines" with respect to their foreign operations in 1965. Banks were asked by the Federal Reserve System to limit the increase in their claims on foreigners in 1965 to 5 per cent of the value of their outstanding foreign credits as of December 31, 1964. Top priority was to be assigned to *bona fide* export credits, and second priority to credits to less developed countries. A related program was applied to credits and investments abroad by nonbank financial institutions.

Under the part of the program administered by the Department of Commerce, about 500 large non-financial corporations were asked to make a maximum effort to expand the net balance of (a) their exports of goods and services plus (b) their repatriation of earnings from the developed countries less (c) their capital outflows to such countries. They were also asked to bring liquid funds back to the United States.

Although considerable skepticism was initially expressed—particularly abroad—regarding the effectiveness of a voluntary pro-

gram, it is now clear that the response was excellent. The net outflow of U.S. private capital declined from $6.5 billion in 1964 (and
an annual rate of $8.9 billion in the fourth quarter) to an annual
rate of $3.6 billion in the first three quarters of 1965. Short-term
capital—both bank and nonbank—accounted for a great part of
this dramatic shift: the movement of such funds changed from a
net outflow of $2.1 billion in 1964 to a net inflow at an annual rate
of $1.0 billion in the first three quarters of 1965. The success of
the voluntary program in shifting the movement of short-term
funds was reinforced by the intensified demand for funds in the
domestic market, as a result both of sharply rising activity and some
tightening of monetary policy.

The U.S. payments deficit in 1965 was adversely affected by
certain unusual transactions of the United Kingdom. As a part of
the U.K. program to protect the pound, the British authorities converted certain holdings of U.S. securities. Together with the defer-
ment of payments on intergovernmental debts, these transactions
reduced U.S. net receipts by well over $½ billion, on both the offi-
cial settlements and the liquidity basis.

Despite good over-all results of the payments program, the volume of U.S. direct investment outflows were at a record high in
1965. In the first three quarters, they reached an annual rate of
$3.4 billion, compared with a 1964 total of $2.4 billion. However,
they declined substantially during the course of 1965. Since such
outflows are usually planned long in advance, and businesses were
not asked to interrupt projects already underway, a lag in the
response to the February program was expected. Nevertheless,
there was disquieting evidence that plans for direct investment in
1966 remained at a high level. With the sharp reversal in the trend
of bank lending abroad, direct investment became the primary area
of concern.

PROGRAM FOR 1966

By the autumn of 1965, it was clear that the February program
had been successful and that a substantial improvement in the balance of payments had been achieved Nevertheless, even further
improvement was necessary if payments equilibrium was to be
attained. Consequently, decisions were announced in December to
reinforce and renew the existing programs for 1966. Further

attention was placed on encouraging U.S. exports, on promoting foreign tourism and foreign investment in the United States, and on minimizing the effect on the balance of payments of Government transactions. But the principal focus of the supplementary steps had to be on the further containment of direct investment outflows.

Consequently, new guidelines for direct investment were developed for nonfinancial corporations. Each of about 900 individual corporations was asked to hold its combined 1965 and 1966 direct investment outflows (plus earnings retained abroad) in specified advanced countries and mineral exporting nations to no more than 90 per cent of the total of these items in the years 1962–64. This will permit an increase of about 35 per cent in the average annual outflow of direct investments in 1965–66 over the average annual rate in the 1962–64 base period. A joint target was set for the years 1965 and 1966 in order not to penalize firms which had cut back in 1965, and in order to seek greater restraint by those which had invested more heavily last year. Direct investment in 1966 under the program would be lower than in 1965, though it would remain high relative to outflows of earlier years.

Financial institutions were given guidelines for 1966 that permitted about the same outflow as had been suggested for 1965. The guidelines provided for nonbank institutions were somewhat more detailed than those for 1965. New arrangements with the Canadian authorities were announced on the understanding that continued exemption from the IET would not threaten the goals of the U.S. program.

Efforts to reduce even further the impact of Government activities on the balance of payments will continue in 1966. Net overseas defense expenditures have been quite successfully reduced since 1960. Unfortunately, expanding defense needs will prevent further reduction in 1966. The bulk of Government aid will continue either to be given "in kind," with no dollar flows, or tied to procurement in the United States. . . .

CONCLUSION

Over the longer run, the policies required to assure equilibrium in the U.S. balance of payments will be influenced by many factors, including—among others—the growth rates of our major trading partners throughout the world, the extent to which European nations learn to rely actively on fiscal as well as monetary policy as a means of adjusting over-all demand, the development of capital markets in Europe, changes in the indispensable foreign exchange costs of national security, our rate of technological innovation, our record of productivity growth and price stability, and the progress of improvements in international financial machinery.

If our current account surplus continues to expand, a renewed growth of capital outflows could be compatible with over-all payments equilibrium. For the present, however, the volume of capital outflows likely to occur in the absence of any measures to moderate them would clearly be inconsistent with equilibrium in our external payments. Given that private capital outflows must be contained, the selective measures currently in use seem, for the present, an essential component of our policy. Compared with reliance solely on restrictive general monetary measures that might conceivably hold down capital flows to the same extent, the selective credit techniques have the obvious advantage of allowing monetary policy to respond to the needs for domestic credit, as well as to affect the 5-10 per cent of total credit that flows abroad.

The selective approach is consistent with an appropriate composition of the private capital outflow. The exemptions in the IET and the priorities established in the voluntary programs protect the access of less developed countries to U.S. capital. The Federal Reserve program, moreover, gives priority to export financing, which could be squeezed under a highly restrictive monetary policy. By increasing the cost of borrowing in the United States, the IET contains its own escape valve: countries in urgent need of new U.S. capital issues are still free to enter our markets; the less urgent needs are screened out. The guideline approach of the voluntary programs tends to permit the business firms and banks themselves to select the most attractive investment opportunities; the investments foregone would yield a smaller return than the average for all new U.S. foreign investments.

The voluntary program continues to permit growth in both the ownership of U.S. productive facilities abroad and of the U.S. loans outstanding abroad. But it keeps that growth within the bounds permitted by the U.S. current surplus and the cost of essential defense and aid. The voluntary program remains the foundation of improvement in the U.S. balance of payments this year. [Pp. 160–69.]

THE MARCH, 1965, STATEMENT OF THE SECRETARY OF COMMERCE ON THE VOLUNTARY RESTRAINT PROGRAM FOR U.S. DIRECT INVESTMENT ABROAD

MARCH 12, 1965

The President has asked me to handle the voluntary cooperation program with American industry which is a key part of our overall effort to improve our Nation's balance of payments situation. Since the success of this program depends entirely on full cooperation and help from the heads of the U.S. corporations doing a significant amount of business internationally, I am writing to you to enlist your personal support.

As you can see from the enclosed press release, the Advisory Committee for this industry program, chaired by Mr. Albert L. Nickerson, Chairman of the Board of Socony Mobil Oil Company, is composed of outstanding leaders from the business community who have been active in direct overseas investments and international trade. That Advisory Committee met with me on February 26, and strongly urged that our program be set up on as informal and personal a basis as possible, with a minimum of formal reporting requirements and other "red tape." All members of the Advisory Committee have given me their judgment that the leaders of American industry will respond quickly and favorably to that kind of approach and that, as a result of such leaders taking personal responsibility for this effort, our voluntary program will produce significant reductions in the balance of payments deficit. The Advisory Committee is particularly in favor of a flexible approach that enables each company head to work out his own program based on the operating facts of his own business, rather than limit the means of meeting each company's objective by having the government prescribe some formula of general application.

That advice makes sense to me, and the form of the program that we had been planning has been modified along the lines suggested.

Consequently, I ask for your help specifically as follows:

1. Please set up for your company a balance of payments "ledger" for the year 1964 which shows the selected debits and credits. I enclose a summary work sheet to indicate the needed figures, and some instructions to help your technical people in preparing it for you.

2. After looking at your 1964 results—and we realize in most cases a significant favorable balance will be shown—please consider how that 1964 result can be improved for the years 1965 and 1966. We have been thinking in terms of an average improvement in balance of payments terms, in 1965 of 15–20 per cent over the 1964 results. We realize, however, that any such target will be inappropriate for many corporations—either on the low or high side—but the important thing is to make an extraordinary effort. Therefore, we have concluded that only you are in a position to set up a reasonable but meaningful objective for your own company, in light of your operating facts and problems. The nine suggestions listed on the enclosed press release do not exhaust the list of possibilities that you and your associates can put together in devising an approach meeting the national purpose, yet tailored to your particular circumstances. In short, I am asking you to establish, *and then let me know,* your best *personal* estimate of how much of an improvement in terms of net dollars you think your company can make overall in 1965, compared with 1964 by taking all feasible steps to help the Nation deal with this serious problem.

3. It would also be helpful for us to have a few of your summary figures for the year 1964 showing credit and debit items separately. The work sheet referred to in paragraph 1 would be appropriate for your 1964 report and should be returned to us. It may also be helpful in calculating your 1965 target. We understand that for many firms or industries, such as petroleum operations or contract construction, there may be a need to include in their "ledger" other information on foreign transactions in order to show a realistic balance of payments performance. In such situations, we would welcome any supplementary figures you wish to supply, and will take them into consideration in reviewing your results.

4. Because of the unique opportunity to shift short-term assets

and make an early improvement in the balance of payments I would also like to have your figures at the end of 1963 and 1964 for short-term assets held abroad either directly or through U.S. banking or other financial institutions. In addition, we would like to have figures on such assets held in developed countries by your subsidiaries and branches.

5. I would like to receive your first set of figures by April 15, if this is possible, and I hope it is.

6. Thereafter, I am asking you to send me quarterly reports through the years 1965 and 1966 showing the data in paragraphs 2, 3 and 4 above and revisions, if any, in your overall goal for the year. You should also give your personal evaluation of points or problems you consider to be of particular significance.

7. While prior notification regarding substantial new investments or expansions abroad, including information indicating how they would be financed, would be helpful, we have decided against a formalized program asking for such information. It is our hope that the overall estimates and reports that I am requesting will prove to be adequate, and that the results will be clear enough to obviate the need for prior notification of new investments. We, of course, expect that care will be taken to minimize the balance of payments effects of large investments and either we, or the appropriate Federal Reserve officials when their program is involved, would be glad to discuss such situations should you so desire.

8. We shall be very glad to talk on the telephone or meet with you to discuss this or any other aspect of this voluntary program of interest or concern to you as it moves along.

Your company's report and estimates will be treated by us as strictly "Confidential" and shown only to those few government officials who are working with us directly in this program. We do plan to put together a periodic summary of the reports in aggregate terms for consideration with the Advisory Committee and for reports to the President, the Cabinet, and the public.

There are a few special problems which I would like to call to your particular attention.

First, we regard the national objective of increasing the contribution by private enterprise to growth in less developed countries of such importance that we do not wish this program to inhibit the flow of these investments.

Second, while relatively rapid progress in repatriating short-term financial funds invested abroad, wherever appropriate, would be helpful, we request that this be done with caution in the case of balances in countries subject to balance of payments problems. We are naturally concerned not to cause difficulties on the exchanges and it would be desirable for companies with large balances to consider consulting with the appropriate Federal Reserve Bank on this problem.

Third, we do not anticipate cutbacks in Canadian direct investments, but firms should take particular care to assure that short-term funds put at the disposal of your subsidiaries in Canada serve only to meet operating needs in Canada. Opportunities should be explored for obtaining at least a portion of working capital requirements from the Canadian market. In this process, we hope that short-term investments in Canada by parents or subsidiaries clearly in excess of working requirements will not be increased. No doubt opportunitites will arise to reduce these balances, particularly those denominated in U.S. dollars, but this should be done only in a gradual and orderly way.

I am sure you are aware of the vital importance of improving the U.S. balance of payments position. Such improvement is essential to international monetary stability, to this Nation's economy, and to continued business progress. The capability of this nation to manage its international fiscal affairs is being carefully watched around the World.

President Johnson is confident, as am I, that you will cooperate with us in this extremely important program of serious concern to you and to our country. We urgently need your help.

Sincerely yours,

John T. Connor

THE DECEMBER, 1965, STATEMENT OF THE SECRETARY OF COMMERCE ON THE VOLUNTARY RESTRAINT PROGRAM FOR U.S. DIRECT INVESTMENT ABROAD

TEXT OF SECRETARY CONNOR'S LETTER TO CHIEF EXECUTIVES OF

COMPANIES PARTICIPATING IN THE VOLUNTARY PROGRAM
TO IMPROVE THE U.S. BALANCE OF PAYMENTS

DECEMBER 8, 1965

The President has again called upon American industry to make an extra effort during 1966 to help reduce further the deficit in our balance of payments. At his direction, I am again writing to you personally to ask your assistance.

The voluntary program in which you and other corporate executives have cooperated has been a major factor behind the substantial improvement in our balance of payments during 1965. The evidence clearly indicates that the program is working well. However, because it is necessary to continue our efforts to bring our balance of payments into equilibrium, the voluntary program must be strengthened.

In making our program more effective, it will remain *voluntary*. The President is convinced that the voluntary approach adopted this year was the correct way to proceed, and it will continue during 1966.

In summary, I am asking each chief executive:

—To maximize his company's over-all contribution to the balance of payments in 1966 through a variety of means.

—To moderate the outflow of funds from the United States for direct investment in developed countries.

—For the two years 1965 and 1966 combined to keep the total of such investment within 90 per cent of the amount for the three years 1962–1964. We will be glad to discuss any special problems that this formula may raise.

—To provide us with statistics for recent years, and projections for 1966, relating to selected foreign transactions. Quarterly reports during 1966 are also requested.

—To give with each quarterly report the personal appraisal of the chief executive as to how his company is progressing toward its over-all target for 1966.

—To name an alternate, familiar with company policy, who would be available for periodic consultation.

In the year ahead, we will continue the basic strategy followed in 1965 under which each chief executive is asked to maximize his company's contribution to the balance of payments through measures such as export expansion, repatriation of income from abroad, repatriation of short-term foreign financial assets, and the maximum use of funds obtained abroad for investment purposes. The result of these efforts should be a considerable over-all improvement by American industry as a whole compared with 1965.

In addition, we must ask each company to make a special effort to temper the outflow of funds from the United States for direct investment abroad. To help achieve this objective, we are recommending a separate target for direct investment for business corporations as a group. The basic aim is not to restrain expenditures by U.S. companies on plant facilities abroad. Rather it is to minimize the impact of the outflow of funds on the United States balance of payments.

We are also suggesting to individual companies a separate formula for direct investment which will enable them to fix their own direct investment targets in a meaningful way and yet permit companies to continue their business abroad in an orderly fashion.

We are modifying the geographic coverage of the program, but it will still apply primarily to developed countries. We still wish to encourage American private enterprise to help raise standards of living in the developing countries of the free world.

To assist us in the administration and appraisal of the program through the year ahead, we are making some improvements in the voluntary reporting system adopted for 1965.

The revised worksheet and some instructions to aid your technical people in its preparation will be sent to you in the very near future. In the meantime, I can describe the principal features of the general program for 1966.

It is estimated that the business community may improve its net contribution to the balance of payments by $1.3 billion in 1965 compared with 1964. During 1966, we are hopeful that this over-all improvement can be raised to $3.4 billion—if the business community is successful in restraining direct investment, maximizing export shipments, repatriating income and foreign financial assets— along with other measures. I am asking you and other corporate executives to review the situation of your company and determine your own best estimate of the over-all improvement which you think is possible during 1966 compared with 1965.

I am recommending the following target to American industry

in planning its direct investment for 1966: Direct investment during the two-year period 1965–66 combined should be limited to 90 per cent of the amount during the three-year period 1962–64. For this purpose, direct investment is defined to include the net outflow of funds from the United States plus the undistributed profits of affiliates abroad. For industry as a whole this target would permit an annual average rate of direct investment during the two years 1965 and 1966 combined approximately 35 per cent above the annual average during the 1962–64 base period. This rate of increase should result in a level of direct investment outflow of about $2.4 billion in 1966—roughly the same as in 1964, following an expected substantial rise in 1965 compared with the previous year. The expected result can also be expressed as a projected increase of more than $1.3 billion in the surplus of total direct investment income over direct investment outflow in 1966 compared with the level anticipated in 1965.

I am also recommending that each company head use the above formula in estimating his own target for direct investment during 1966. In calculating the target, companies should use the same base period of 1962–64. In defining direct investment, they should add together the net outflow from the United States and the undistributed profits of their affiliates. (This is the same definition used in Line "D" of the 1965 worksheet). They should make the same calculations for 1965–66. For the latter two years combined, direct investment as defined should not exceed 90 per cent of such outflow during the three-year base period. In suggesting this formula, I realize fully that it will catch individual companies in different circumstances. For some it would undoubtedly place a severe strain on their ability to carry out projects abroad already in the advanced stages of planning or actual construction. For others, it may result in a target considerably in excess of what the companies would actually need to fulfill their plans, and we hope they would use only the minimum amount necessary. But in all of these cases, we are fully prepared—and would want—to discuss particular situations with individual companies.

The over-all industry improvement target of $3.4 billion in 1966 would include the balance of payments savings expected through the restraint on direct investment. For the individual company, the estimated improvement for the next year should also include the savings on direct investment outflow which corporate executives think they can make during 1966.

The target as formulated for direct investment has several advantages. In the first place, the three-year base period allows companies to account for direct investment activities in a way which reduces the influence of numerous aberrations which might occur in a single year, and it puts individual companies on a more equal footing. Secondly, by combining direct investment flows for 1965 and 1966, there is greater flexibility allowed companies who have been the most cooperative under the 1965 voluntary program. Those companies which have repatriated a substantial share of their earnings and have minimized capital outflow this year will have considerable headroom in 1966. Those companies whose situations did not permit them to make a similar contribution in 1965 would be called upon to make a correspondingly greater effort next year. Thus, the two-year planning period seems to be desirable from the point of view of equity. Moreover, the target essentially permits companies on the average to invest in two years up to 90 per cent of the amount they invested during the previous three years. Thus, it allows an average annual rate of investment during the two years 35 per cent higher than the average for the three years 1962–64.

The geographical coverage of the program in 1966 will again apply principally to developed countries. However, the list of developed countries will be expanded. The new list will be the same as that prepared for the application of the Interest Equalization Tax. The targets will apply to direct investment in countries defined as developed for the 1965 program together with Canada, Abu-Dhabi, Bahrain, Indonesia, Iran, Iraq, Libya, Qatar, Kuwait-Saudi Arabia Neutral Zone, and Saudi Arabia.

We are asking for moderation on direct investment in Canada during 1966. This was not the case in 1965. However, this year we did ask companies to expand exports to Canada and to repatriate income and short-term financial assets held with Canadian institutions. We are repeating this request for 1966. In view of the large prospective increase in direct investment in Canada by American firms next year, we think it is desirable to ask for moderation on the outflow of direct investment funds to that country along with other developed areas. At the same time, we realize that U.S. companies, partly because we did not ask for restraint in 1965, have underway firm investment commitments in Canada (for example those incurred under the U.S.-Canadian automotive parts agreement) which they will find it necessary to carry out. But it is our impression that companies will have ample opportunity within the direct investment target to fulfill these commitments, and we are certain they would want to give them the highest priority.

The other countries included in the expanded geographic coverage of the program possess large reserves of internationally traded natural resources in which U.S. direct investment is substantial. We think it is reasonable and equitable to include the substantial flows of investment funds to these countries in the base and target for balance of payments improvement during 1966.

This year between 500 and 600 companies cooperating in the program are submitting quarterly reports on their progress. In 1966 we are asking an additional 400-odd companies to do the same. We are particularly interested in expanding the list of companies to include more firms with direct investments abroad, although the individual amounts involved may not be large. Initially, I am asking each company to report if it had direct investments abroad of $2 million or more at the end of 1964 (and if it is not currently reporting under the voluntary program). At the same time, however, it is vital that *all* American industry participate in the effort to improve the balance of payments—although we are not asking every company to give us periodic reports.

During this year we have found the statistical information submitted by companies each quarter to be helpful in administering the program. However, we have also found that the lack of somewhat more detailed information has made it difficult for us to appraise the progress of the program and to chart the contributions which the cooperating companies are making compared with developments in the balance of payments as a whole. For this reason, we have adopted several improvements in the reporting system. The specific types of information requested will be detailed in the revised worksheet and the instructions which will accompany it.

We will repeat this year's request for a quarterly report on the amount of short-term financial assets held abroad by the parent company and by its foreign affiliates. This year we requested that parent companies reduce these assets at least to the level outstanding at the end of 1963. Many companies have responded, and a large number have cut their holdings even below the 1963 level. We are hopeful that other companies will make the reduction as soon as possible, consistent with the maintenance of orderly conditions in money markets abroad, and that others will not rebuild previously reduced holdings. I also asked companies in 1965 to economize on holdings of short-term assets by their foreign affiliates. I hope they will continue this effort in 1966.

During the year ahead, we will want to work closely with individual companies in the management of the voluntary program. During 1965, I have communicated periodically on an informal basis with the chief executives of the cooperating companies. I plan to continue this procedure in 1966. However, experience this year has also demonstrated that the management of the program would have been facilitated by an additional level of communication. I am now recommending that such a level of contact be established and maintained during 1966. Consequently, I am asking you and other principal officers of each company to name an alternate who is familiar with company policy and yet who may be somewhat more available for periodic discussions of the company's progress. Commerce Department officials who are assisting me in the management of the program would maintain liaison with your designee in those matters not requiring your personal attention.

I am requesting that the chief executive of each company continue to review the worksheets reported each quarter to the Department of Commerce. It would be helpful if you could give me each quarter your *personal* appraisal of the extent to which your company is making progress toward achieving its over-all target forecast for 1966. I am also requesting company officials to enclose with their quarterly statistical report a commentary on their company's experience during the quarter from the point of view of the main items reported in the worksheet.

In making the revisions in the voluntary program for 1966, I have worked closely with the leaders of American business—particularly with the Balance of Payments Advisory Committee of the Department of Commerce. In administering the program in 1966 —as in 1965—I will continue to benefit from the advice and counsel of this distinguished group of American businessmen. As you will recall, this Committee is chaired by Mr. Albert L. Nickerson,

Chairman of the Board, Socony Mobil Oil Company. The other members are: Carter L. Burgess, Chairman of the Board, American Machine and Foundry Company; George S. Moore, President, First National City Bank; Elisha Gray II, Chairman, Whirlpool Corporation; Sidney J. Weinberg, General Partner, Goldman, Sachs and Company; Carl J. Gilbert, Chairman, The Gillette Company; Stuart T. Saunders, Chairman, Pennsylvania Railroad Company; J. Ward Keener, President, B. F. Goodrich Company; and Fred J. Borch, President, General Electric Company.

These members of our Advisory Committee have approved the revisions in the voluntary program for 1966. They join me in asking the continued support of the business community in our efforts to improve the balance of payments.

This year I have also benefited from the advice and counsel of many other leaders of American industry; I am certain they will continue to volunteer such guidance in the year ahead and it will be welcomed.

Finally, I am personally confident that the leaders of American business fully understand the seriousness of the foreign situation which we face. Furthermore, the increased military effort in Viet Nam will put further pressure on our balance of payments. To help compensate for the added drain, we have found it necessary to strengthen the voluntary program for 1966.

But I am confident that the business community appreciates the urgency of the task to reduce further the deficit in our balance of payments. I also have no doubt whatsoever that they will cooperate on a voluntary basis in our extraordinary effort to achieve this vital national goal.

Sincerely yours,

John T. Connor

THE MARCH, 1965, STATEMENT TO THE FEDERAL RESERVE BOARD ON THE VOLUNTARY CREDIT RESTRAINT PROGRAM FOR FINANCIAL INSTITUTIONS

BALANCE OF PAYMENTS PROGRAM

GUIDELINES

FOR BANKS AND NONBANK FINANCIAL INSTITUTIONS

On February 10, 1965 the President sent to the Congress a message on the U.S. balance of payments in which he presented a program aimed at achieving quickly a substantial improvement in our balance of payments position. This program is of major importance since the balance of payments deficit is a serious national problem.

A major responsibility in carrying out the President's program was placed on the Federal Reserve System and on the banking and financial community. The System has already taken the first measures in carrying out the program.

On the day the President delivered his message, the Federal Reserve Banks issued a circular soliciting the cooperation of the commercial banks and outlining specific steps to be taken by the banks.[1] On February 18, in Washington, Chairman Martin and Governor Robertson, who is coordinating the System's activities in this matter, discussed the request in detail with representatives of the banking and financial community, following a meeting of these representatives with the President.

The Board of Governors has now issued guidelines to be followed by banks and by nonbank financial institutions in their foreign lending activities. The guidelines for each group are printed below.

GUIDELINES FOR BANKS

The following guidelines, designed for use in implementing President Johnson's program for the voluntary curtailment of foreign credit by banks, will be in effect until modified or supplemented. However, they may be changed from time to time in the

---

[1] The President's program and the statement issued by the Federal Reserve Banks were published in the BULLETIN for February 1965, pp. 256–57.

light of new circumstances and in the light of the experience gained as the program goes forward. The guidelines should be helpful to individual banks as they play their own particular part in the achievement of the President's over-all balance of payments program, and each bank should feel free at any time to discuss its problems with the Federal Reserve Bank of its district.

It is clear that banks, in undertaking a voluntary role in the program, are being called upon to make sacrifices. In restraining the growth of their loans to foreigners they will be foregoing some of the gains that would otherwise have accrued to them. But, if a voluntary program is to be effective, decisions on future specific loan transactions must be made primarily with an eye to the national interest rather than profits. The achievement of the President's goal will be in the long-term interest not only of the nation, but also of the individual institutions which are now being called upon to forego immediate advantage or gain.

(1) ESTABLISH A TARGET BASE FOR AN INDIVIDUAL BANK

The objective of the program is that outstanding bank credit to nonresidents of the United States not rise above the amount outstanding at the end of 1964 by more than 5 per cent, subject to the conditions set forth in guideline (3).

The following steps are involved in calculating the base, and the amount of credit outstanding on any particular date, for an individual bank:

1. Take outstanding claims of U.S. banking offices on foreigners as of December 31, 1964, as required to be reported on Treasury Department foreign exchange forms B-2 and B-3. Contingent accounts, such as unused balances of letters of credit and commitments to lend, are excluded from the base. (For further information, reference is made to the instructions printed on forms B-2 and B-3.)

2. Subtract from this amount any claims for account of customers included on the forms, as well as any participations in individual loans arranged by the Export-Import Bank or made with Export-Import Bank guarantees.

3. Add any claims not reportable on forms B-2 and B-3, such as long-term foreign securities and permanent capital invested in foreign branches and subsidiaries.

4. Compensating balances, or any other claim on the lending bank of the debtor or of any other person by arrangement or understanding with the debtor, should not be deducted from loans or other claims on foreigners for purposes of determining the base.

5. It is expected that a simplified form for making the above calculations, and for making monthly reports on foreign credits, will be furnished to the banks within a short time.

Banks that are exempted from reporting on the Treasury forms because their foreign credits are below the minimum reporting requirement are nevertheless included in the program.

(2) PARTICIPATIONS IN EXPORT-IMPORT BANK LOANS AND LOANS GUARANTEED BY THE EXPORT-IMPORT BANK

Participations in individual export loans arranged by the Export-Import Bank, loans with Export-Import Bank guarantees or insurance, and holdings of "Export-Import Portfolio Fund" participations are excluded from the 5 per cent target.

The role of the Export-Import Bank within the framework of the President's program will be coordinated by the National Advisory Council for International Monetary and Financial Problems.

(3) BANKS IN EXCESS OF 5 PER CENT TARGET

It is clearly recognized that some banks may currently be above the 5 per cent target because of loans made prior to February 11, 1965, or may subsequently be brought above the target as a result of (a) binding commitments entered into before February 11, or (b) the extension of bona fide export credits, or (c) the extension of credits at the specific request of an agency of the U.S. Government. A bank in such circumstances would not be considered to be acting in a manner inconsistent with the program; however, it should reduce its claims on foreigners to 105 per cent of the base as quickly as possible. Even in the most extreme case, this reduction should be accomplished within the next 12 months.

Such a bank will be invited periodically to discuss with the Federal Reserve Bank of its district the steps it has taken and proposes to take to bring about the reduction of its claims on foreigners consistent with these guidelines.

Banks with bona fide commitments are clearly not being asked to refuse to honor such commitments, even if honoring them involves a temporary excess of lending above the target. However, banks would be expected to seize every opportunity to withdraw or reduce commitments, including credit lines, that are not of a firm nature, and to ensure that drawings under credit lines are kept to normal levels and usage. At time of renewal, all credit lines should be reviewed in light of their consistency with the voluntary foreign credit restraint program. Proposed extensions or renewals of existing bona fide commitments should be reviewed in the same manner.

(4) LOAN PRIORITIES

Within the 5 per cent guideline, absolute priority should be given to bona fide export credits. Credits that substitute for cash sales or for sales customarily financed out of nonbank or foreign funds are not entitled to priority.

With respect to nonexport credits, banks should give the highest priority to loans to less developed countries and should avoid restrictive policies that would place an undue burden on countries such as Canada and Japan, which are heavily dependent on U.S. financing, and on the United Kingdom, which is suffering from balance of payments difficulties.

Given the probability of some expansion of the end-of-1964 volume of loans for financing exports and the priorities established for the less developed countries, as well as the need to avoid restrictive practices with regard to Canada, Japan, and Britain, it is expected that nonexport credit to the other advanced countries will be cut back to the extent needed to achieve the goal of the President's program.

Without attempting to specify all types of loans that will need to be restricted, it is obvious that credits to developed countries that can be cut back with benefit to our balance of payments and with the least adverse side-effects include: credits to finance third-country trade; credits to finance local-currency expenditures outside the United States; credits to finance fixed or working capital needs; and all other nonexport credits to developed countries that do not suffer from balance of payments difficulties.

(5) BANK SALES OF FOREIGN ASSETS TO U.S. RESIDENTS

In general, banks should not expand their lending abroad by selling to U.S. residents (including U.S. banks) claims on foreigners existing as of the base date and replacing such assets with other loans to foreigners. Sales to U.S. residents of foreign securities owned on the base date, which would be free of the interest equalization tax, or of loan participations, could assist an individual bank to stay within the 5 per cent target, but would clearly not benefit the U.S. payments position. Therefore, in the event of any such sales the bank's base should be reduced by an amount equivalent thereto.

(6) BANKS WITH NO FOREIGN LOANS OUTSTANDING ON
    DECEMBER 31, 1964

In general, banks with no previous foreign lending experience would be expected not to make foreign loans during 1965. However, bona fide export loans to foreigners may be made in reasonable amounts, provided this financing does not represent a shift from previous U.S. or foreign sources of financing. Banks making foreign loans for the first time should take precautions to ensure that their activities do not become a means through which credit is extended to foreign borrowers who have been denied credit by established lenders cooperating in the voluntary program.

(7) BANKS WHOSE PREVIOUS FOREIGN BUSINESS HAS
    CONSISTED ALMOST ENTIRELY OF EXPORT FINANCING

The few banks falling in this category would ordinarily be expected to keep within the 5 per cent ceiling. Since they would have no maturing nonexport loans to provide funds for additional export credits and would therefore need to rely upon nonrenewal of maturing export loans, reasonable amounts in excess of the target from time to time would not be considered in conflict with the program. But every effort should be made by such banks to keep their lending within the ceiling. They should take care to ensure that export loans do not represent a shift from previous U.S. or foreign sources of financing.

(8) TRUST DEPARTMENTS

Managing officers of trust departments should be made familiar with the voluntary restraint effort. They should bear the purpose of that program in mind by making any acquisitions of foreign obligations for trust accounts. For example, they should not exercise their authority under any trust account to acquire foreign obligations which, in the absence of the restraint program, would have been acquired by the bank for its own account. Pension funds, including those administered by banks, will be furnished separate guidelines, as part of the program to restrain foreign credits of nonbank financial institutions.

(9) FINANCIAL TRANSACTIONS FOR CUSTOMERS

While banks must, of course, follow instructions given to them by their customers, it is expected that, in buying foreign investments for customers, they will be guided by the principles inherent in the President's balance of payments program. They should not encourage customers to place liquid funds outside the United States. Banks should not place with customers foreign obligations which, in the absence of the restraint program, they would have acquired or held for their own account.

(10) FOREIGN BRANCHES

It is assumed, of course, that U.S. banks having branches, as well as subsidiaries and affiliates, in foreign countries will not utilize them to avoid the foreign credit restraint program for U.S. banks.

Foreign branches have independent sources of funds in the countries in which they are located and from third countries, in many cases through the attraction of Euro-dollar deposits. The balance of payments program is not designed to hamper the lending activities of the foreign branches insofar as the funds utilized are derived from foreign sources and do not add to the dollar outflow. Concern arises only in those cases where the resources are derived (directly or indirectly) from the United States.

Total claims of the head office on overseas branches, including permanent capital invested in, as well as balances due from, branches, represent bank credit to nonresidents for purposes of the program.

(11) PROBLEMS OF EDGE ACT CORPORATIONS

Edge Act and Agreement Corporations are included in the voluntary credit restraint effort. The foreign loans and investments of such a corporation may be combined with those of the parent bank for the purposes of the program, or separate targets may be set for the parent bank and the subsidiary.

An Edge Act Corporation that has not yet undertaken any significant volume of loans and investments may take as a base, alone and not in combination with its parent, its paid-in capital and surplus, up to $2.5 million, even though an equivalent amount of foreign loans and investments had not yet been made as of December 31, 1964.

(12) U.S. BRANCHES AND AGENCIES OF FOREIGN BANKS

Branches and agencies of foreign banks located in the United States are requested to comply with the principles of the program of credit restraint applicable to domestic banks.

(13) SUBSTITUTION OF EXPORT CREDIT FOR CREDIT
        FOR OTHER PURPOSES

Banks should be on the alert to avoid granting credit to domestic customers if the result would be to aid the latter in making foreign loans or investments inconsistent with the program. Even export credit to foreigners, if it supplants credit previously obtained from foreign sources and thus frees the foreign funds for other uses, may be detrimental to the U.S. payments position.

This is obviously a difficult area and one in which there is considerable room for possible damaging substitution of domestic for foreign financing, and for substitution of export credits to foreigners for other credits to foreigners. In general, success will depend on the ability of banks to identify loans that are inconsistent with the program and on the application of the Department of Commerce program with respect to foreign credit and investment by nonfinancial firms.

(14) MANAGEMENT OF A BANK'S LIQUID FUNDS

Banks that have placed their own funds abroad for short-term investment purposes, including U.S. dollar deposits outside the United States or the acquisition of non-U.S. money market paper, should refrain from increasing such deposits and investments and should, in a reasonable and orderly manner, seek to reduce them. Since such funds are ordinarily placed outside the United States solely to provide a slightly higher rate of return, they are strong candidates for reduction under the program.

This guideline applies equally to deposits and investments payable in foreign currencies and to those payable in U.S. dollars.

This guideline does not call for a reduction in necessary working balances held with foreign correspondents, although such balances are also considered claims on nonresidents for the purposes of the program.

TENTATIVE GUIDELINES NONBANK FINANCIAL INSTITUTIONS

(1) DEPOSITS AND MONEY-MARKET INSTRUMENTS

Holdings of liquid funds abroad should be limited to the 1964 year-end total, and the longer-term objective is to reduce such investments in a gradual and orderly manner to the December 31, 1963, level. Included in this category of liquid investments are dollar-denominated deposits held in foreign banks and foreign branches of U.S. banks; short-term securities of foreign governments and their instrumentalities; foreign commercial paper, finance company credits and bankers' acceptances; and all other negotiable instruments maturing in 1 year or less. Foreign bank deposits denominated in local currencies may be maintained to the extent needed to support ordinary business operations in that country.

(2) FOREIGN CREDITS WITH ORIGINAL MATURITIES OF 5 YEARS OR LESS

Holdings of investments other than those listed above, and written to have final maturities in 5 years or less, should not be increased by more than 5 per cent during calendar 1965. Included in this category are securities, mortgage and other loans, and credits of all other types. The 5 per cent growth ceiling is to be measured against the total of all such holdings at the end of 1964, without regard to type of instrument or country of origin. Priority should be given to credits that directly finance U.S. exports, however, and special care should be taken to avoid the extension of credit to borrowers who would have been accommodated by commerical banks in the absence of the voluntary restraint program.

(3) FOREIGN CREDITS WITH ORIGINAL MATURITIES OVER 5 YEARS

In the area of long-term financing, there would seem to be no present need for a guideline under the voluntary restraint program. Developments in the long-term credit area will be followed closely, however, so that we may be alert to excessive foreign financing demands if they should materialize. The issues of industrialized countries are subject to the interest equalization tax, and have been very small in volume since that tax became effective. Borrowing by the less developed countries has been relatively light also, and in any event should not be substantially restricted in view of our national policy encouraging productive investment in these countries. In the case of Canada and Japan, separate agreements will serve to limit aggregate financing in United States capital markets.

(4) DIRECT INVESTMENT IN FOREIGN BRANCHES AND SUBSIDIARIES

Some types of financial institutions may conduct operations abroad through foreign offices, branches, and subsidiaries. In such cases, institutions are urged to limit their additional investment in these operations to the fullest extent practicable during 1965. Particular care should be taken to restrict any increase in net loans and advances outstanding to foreign branches and subsidiaries; ordinarily, expansion in such credit during 1965 should be held within 5 per cent.

In the case of insurance carriers doing business abroad, these guidelines are not applicable to holdings of foreign investments in amounts up to 110 per cent of foreign policy reserves.

THE DECEMBER, 1965, STATEMENT TO THE FEDERAL RESERVE BOARD ON THE VOLUNTARY CREDIT RESTRAINT PROGRAM FOR FINANCIAL INSTITUTIONS

DECEMBER 3, 1965

THE 1966 VOLUNTARY CREDIT RESTRAINT PROGRAM FOR FINANCIAL INSTITUTIONS

PREFACE

Since inception of the voluntary foreign credit restraint effort, immediately following announcement by the President of his balance of payments program in February 1965, commercial banks and other financial institutions have contributed substantially to the improvement in the nation's payments position. This has been accomplished by the high degree of cooperation and statesmanship exhibited by the financial community in restraining the growth of (and in some instances reducing) claims on foreigners in accordance with guidelines issued by the Board of Governors of the Federal Reserve System.

Although considerable progress has been made and although the voluntary restraint program is temporary in nature, perseverance by financial institutions in the program through 1966 is necessary to attain the goal of equilibrium in the nation's balance of payments and represents the appropriate response to the President's message of February 10, 1965, in which he issued a personal "call on American businessmen and bankers to enter a constructive partnership with their Government to protect and strengthen the position of the dollar in the world today."

The main feature of the guidelines for 1965 has been a percentage limitation on increases in foreign credits from the base date of December 31, 1964. In general, each bank was requested to restrict its foreign credits outstanding to an amount not in excess of 105 per cent of the amount outstanding at the end of 1964, and each nonbank financial institution was requested to operate within a framework roughly similar to that suggested for banks.

For the year 1966 the guidelines for both banks and nonbank

financial institutions have been revised to suggest limitations on expansion of foreign credits which are comparable to the limitations suggested for 1965. These will permit some further expansion in such credits, and provide for variations to remove certain inequities inherent in the 1965 program.

Notwithstanding the fact that the banking system as a whole is presently well below the suggested target for 1965, this additional expansion has been allowed for two reasons: (1) it is believed that banks will continue to cooperate with the spirit as well as the letter of the program and will utilize the expansion suggested only to the extent needed to meet priority credit requirements; and (2) it is intended to make certain that export financing is available in adequate amounts, and that the *bona fide* credit needs of less developed countries will continue to be met.

Continued restraint on the increase in foreign credits is the basic objective of the bank program for 1966. Generally speaking, commercial banks are requested to restrain any expansion in foreign credits to such an extent that the amount outstanding at year-end will not exceed 109 per cent of the amount outstanding on December 31, 1964. Further, in order to spread throughout the year any outflow necessary to meet priority credit requirements, it is requested that the amount outstanding not exceed 106 per cent of the 1964 base during the first quarter, 107 per cent during the second, and 108 per cent during the third quarter. Special consideration for banks with small bases will add one per cent or less to the total, bringing the potential amount outstanding at the end of 1966 for the banking system as a whole to about 110 per cent of the 1964 base as compared with the 105 per cent target for 1965.

The guidelines for 1966 for nonbank financial institutions have been revised to reflect provisions broadly comparable with those of the bank guidelines. Investments of liquid funds abroad are to be held to minimum practicable levels and ordinarily should not be permitted to exceed the reduced September 30, 1965, total. Investments in credits maturing in 10 years or less and in foreign branches and financial subsidiaries are subject to the same ceiling as suggested for the banks. Long-term investments in developed countries other than Canada and Japan are subject to a ceiling of 105 per cent of the September 30, 1965, amounts during 1966; this base was selected because retroactive use of a 1964 year-end base might have been inequitable for some institutions.

As in 1965, financial institutions are requested to give priority to export credits and credits to less developed countries. In instances where the special base and ceiling calculations for banks with small bases result in a ceiling in excess of 109 per cent, it is requested that the amount in excess of 109 per cent of a bank's base be used exclusively for such priority credits. The leeway for additional foreign credits provided by the 1966 guidelines plus the funds available from repayments on outstanding credits will provide larger resources than last year to finance an expanded volume of exports and to satisfy credit requirements of less developed countries.

Participants

Benjamin Aaron, Professor of Law, University of California, Los Angeles

Gardner Ackley, Chairman, Council of Economic Advisers, Washington, D.C.

Robert Z. Aliber, Associate Professor of International Economics and Finance, Graduate School of Business, University of Chicago

Ernest T. Baughman, Vice President and Director of Research, Federal Reserve Bank of Chicago

Irving Beller, Economist, Research Department, AFL-CIO, Washington, D.C.

Joseph L. Block, Chairman, Inland Steel Company, Chicago

Joseph J. Botica, Member of the Executive Board, International Association of Bridge, Structural and Ornamental Iron Workers (AFL-CIO), Chicago

Robert E. Brooker, President, Montgomery Ward, Chicago

Harold E. Brooks, Vice President, Armour and Company, Chicago

Arthur W. Brown, Manager, Employee Relations Department, Standard Oil Company (New Jersey), New York

Douglass V. Brown, Alfred P. Sloan Professor of Industrial Management, Massachusetts Institute of Technology, Cambridge

E. H. Phelps Brown, Professor of Economics, The London School of Economics and Political Science

Yale Brozen, Professor of Business Economics, Graduate School of Business, University of Chicago

William Clark, Financial Editor, *Chicago Tribune*

Dwight M. Cochran, President, Kern County Land Company, San Francisco

Fairfax M. Cone, Chairman of the Executive Committee, Foote, Cone & Belding, Chicago

Louis Couillard, Vice Chairman, Economic Council of Canada, Ottawa

Edwin L. Dale, Jr., *The New York Times,* Washington Bureau, Washington, D.C.

D. D. Danielson, Director of Research, United Brotherhood of Carpenters and Joiners of America (AFL-CIO), Washington, D.C.

Peter E. de Janosi, Program Associate, Program in Economic Development and Administration, The Ford Foundation, New York

Harold Demsetz, Associate Professor of Business Economics, Graduate School of Business, University of Chicago

Malcolm Denise, Vice President (Labor Relations), Ford Motor Company, Dearborn, Michigan

John J. Deutsch, Chairman, Economic Council of Canada, Ottawa

John T. Dunlop, David A. Wells Professor of Political Economy and Chairman of the Department of Economics, Harvard University, Cambridge

Walter D. Fackler, Associate Dean, Graduate School of Business, University of Chicago

Robben W. Fleming, Chancellor, University of Wisconsin, Madison

Milton Friedman, Paul Snowden Russell Distinguished Service Professor of Economics, Department of Economics, University of Chicago

Howard G. Gamser, Member, National Mediation Board, Washington, D.C.

W. H. Krome George, Vice President in Charge of Finance, Aluminum Company of America, Pittsburgh

Pat Greathouse, Vice President, International Union, United Automobile, Aerospace and Agricultural Implement Workers of America (AFL-CIO), Detroit

Carl M. Halvorson, Carl M. Halvorson, Inc., Portland, Oregon

Mary Hamilton, University of Chicago

R. V. Hansberger, President, Boise Cascade Corporation, Boise, Idaho

Arnold C. Harberger, Professor of Economics and Chairman, Department of Economics, University of Chicago

Madison Haythe, Economist, Morgan Stanley & Co., New York

Ralph Helstein, President, United Packinghouse, Food and Allied Workers (AFL-CIO), Chicago

Albert Herling, American Bakery and Confectionery Workers' International Union (AFL-CIO), Washington, D.C.

Merritt Hill, Chairman of the Board, J. I. Case Company, Racine, Wisconsin

Wayne L. Horvitz, Vice President of Industrial Relations, Matson Navigation Company, San Francisco

Jacques Houssiaux, Professor of Economics, Center for International Affairs, Harvard University, Cambridge

Robert S. Ingersoll, Chairman, Borg-Warner Corporation, Chicago

D. Gale Johnson, Dean, Division of Social Sciences, University of Chicago

Harry G. Johnson, Professor of Economics, University of Chicago

David M. Kennedy, Chairman of the Board, Continental Illinois National Bank and Trust Company of Chicago

Theodore W. Kheel, Battle, Fowler, Stokes & Kheel, New York

Philip B. Kurland, Professor of Law, University of Chicago

R. Heath Larry, Administrative Vice President and Assistant to Chairman, United States Steel Corporation, New York

Edward H. Levi, Provost, University of Chicago

Sid A. Levy, Associate Editor, Kiplinger Letters, Washington, D.C.

Frederick R. Livingston, Kaye, Scholer, Fierman, Hays & Handler, New York

James H. Lorie, Professor of Business Administration, Director of the Center for Research in Security Prices, Graduate School of Business, University of Chicago

Sherman J. Maisel, Member of the Board, Board of Governors of the Federal Reserve System, Washington, D.C.

Joseph F. Maloney, General Organizer, International Association of Bridge, Structural and Ornamental Iron Workers (AFL-CIO), Washington, D.C.

John E. Mara, General President, Secretary-Treasurer, Boot and Shoe Workers' Union, Boston

Allan H. Meltzer, Professor of Economics, Graduate School of Industrial Administration, Carnegie Institute of Technology, Pittsburgh

Bernard D. Meltzer, Professor of Law, University of Chicago

J. Wade Miller, Jr., Vice President of Personnel and Organization, The B. F. Goodrich Company, Akron, Ohio

David Meiselman, Office of the Controller of the Currency, United States Treasury, Washington, D.C.

Charles A. Myers, Professor of Industrial Relations, Massachusetts Institute of Technology, Cambridge

Phil C. Neal, Dean, The Law School, University of Chicago

Hubert Nexon, Vice President, Commonwealth Edison Company, Chicago

R. I. Nowell, Vice President and Economist, The Equitable Life Assurance Society of the United States, New York

Leif H. Olsen, Senior Vice President and Economist, First National City Bank, New York

Herbert V. Prochnow, President, The First National Bank of Chicago

S. Frank Raftery, General President, Brotherhood of Painters, Decorators, and Paperhangers of America (AFL-CIO), Washington, D.C.

Abraham H. Raskin, *The New York Times*

Melvin W. Reder, Professor of Economics, Stanford University, Stanford, California

Albert Rees, Professor of Economics, University of Chicago

William J. Reilly, Manager, Labor Relations Department, International Harvester Company, Chicago

Richard Richardson, Bureau of the Budget, Washington, D.C.

Arthur M. Ross, Commissioner, Bureau of Labor Statistics, Washington, D.C.

Theodore W. Schultz, Charles L. Hutchinson Distinguished Service Professor of Economics, University of Chicago

Harvey H. Segal, *The Washington Post,* Washington, D.C.

John Sheahen, Professor of Economics, Williams College, Williamstown, Massachusetts

George P. Schultz, Dean, Graduate School of Business, University of Chicago

William E. Simkin, Director, Federal Mediation and Conciliation Service, Washington, D.C.

Arthur J. R. Smith, Director, Economic Council of Canada, Ottawa

Robert Solomon, Board of Governors of the Federal Reserve System, Washington, D.C.

Robert M. Solow, Professor of Economics, Massachusetts Institute of Technology, Cambridge

Beryl W. Sprinkel, Vice President and Economist, Harris Trust and Savings Bank, Chicago

Herbert Stein, Fellow, Center for Advanced Study in the Behavioral Sciences and Director of Research, Committee for Economic Development, Stanford, California

Sydney Stein, Jr., Stein, Roe & Farnham, Chicago

George J. Stigler, Charles R. Walgreen Distinguished Service Professor of American Institutions, Graduate School of Business, University of Chicago

Lloyd Ulman, Director, Institute of Industrial Relations, University of California, Berkeley

Saul Wallen, Arbitrator and Mediator of Labor Disputes, Boston

John H. Wills, Senior Vice President, The Northern Trust Company, Chicago

Theodore O. Yntema, Professorial Lecturer in Business Policy, Graduate School of Business, University of Chicago